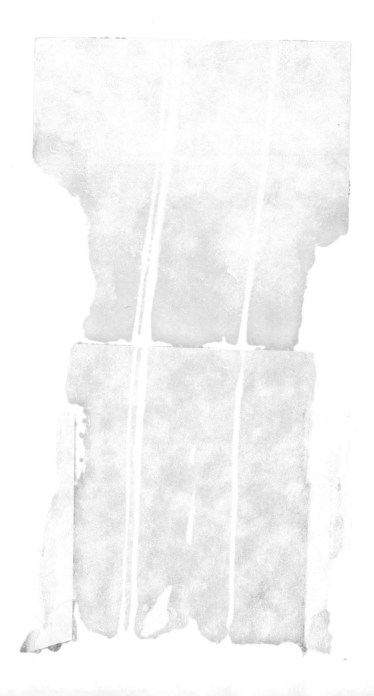

STARTING OVER

Help for Young Widows
and Widowers

STARTING OVER

Help for Young Widows and Widowers

Adele Rice Nudel

Dodd, Mead & Company
New York

Copyright © 1986 by Adele Rice Nudel

No part of this book may be reproduced in any form
without permission in writing from the publisher.
Published by Dodd, Mead & Company, Inc.
79 Madison Avenue, New York, N.Y. 10016
Distributed in Canada by
McClelland and Stewart Limited, Toronto
Manufactured in the United States of America

Designed by Erich Hobbing

First Edition

Library of Congress Cataloging-in-Publication Data

Nudel, Adele Rice.
  Starting over.

  Bibliography: p.
  Includes index.
  1. Widows—Life skills guides. 2. Widowers—Life
skills guides. I. Title. II. Title: Young widows and
widowers.
HQ1058.N83   1986   646.7'0880654   85-20709
ISBN 0-396-08726-4

To my loving family,
David, Lisa, and Marc

Contents

Acknowledgments

Without the rich and varied contacts I had with so many younger widows and widowers, it would have been difficult to write this book. I think of just a few who were in my widowed persons support groups: Vivian, Katherine, Sandy, Debra, and Shirley; Jay, Richard, Manny, Raymond, and Curtis. The others, you know who you are.

Elaine A. Briggs-Cox shared her feelings as a woman who was widowed at the age of thirty-six. We have not yet met. We have spoken on the phone, and Elaine has sent me her thoughts on paper. I have her letters beside me now, as I type on my blue wooden table, and they have been invaluable in their insights.

Nancy Goldblatt, M.S.W., provided me with much information on bereaved teenagers; children who lost a parent to death; adolescents who had participated in teenage support groups.

Good people shared important papers and books: Victor Miller, Rebecca Alban Puharich, Marilyn Schloss, and Frances Kasinof. Victor is on the staff of the National Academy of Sciences; Rebecca has worked with Elizabeth Kubler-Ross; Marilyn was the previous director of Sinai Hospital's Widowed Persons Service; and Frances is a career specialist who works with different populations, including widowed persons.

It was Joe Rhodes, my agent, who immediately saw the need for this book and gave it much personal attention. It was Susan Moldow, my former editor at Avon, who generously led me to my present editor at Dodd, Mead, Cynthia Vartan. Cynthia, caring and perceptive, was very supportive with her skillful editing and respect for what I was attempting to do.

I worked in the field of aging for twelve years before working with older *and* younger clients in the area of widowhood, and it was the older widows and widowers in senior centers who gave me a basis of comparison when this book began brewing in my mind.

Other persons who were supportive: my sister, Toby Rice Drews (also an author), who shared many hours with me, as we discussed the craft of writing; Michael Baer, who helped shape the book before it was written, with his fine editorial eye, which is as good as his painter's eye; Leonard Rothstein, who helped me reshape my work life; and David Nudel, who was always there.

Introduction

Loss of a husband or wife leads to grief, and the yearning to retrieve what has been lost. This book deals with the loss of *younger* women and men. As a specialist in the field of bereavement, I haven't heard enough professional clinicians differentiate between the needs of younger and older widows and widowers. I haven't seen enough support groups especially for the widowed person who is twenty-five, thirty, or forty-five. There are few books available for the younger widowed person that explain the dynamics of grieving and show the bereaved person how to cope. Perhaps this is because social workers, psychologists, and psychiatrists are like the rest of the population—threatened by death in a younger person. "If it can happen to him, it can happen to me." We're afraid to deal with threatening topics. We turn away.

But, as director of the Widowed Persons Service at Sinai Hospital in Baltimore, I have found that the younger person *is* different. Academic journals and papers confirm this: articles and reports state that younger bereaved spouses have more sleep disturbances, and that they experience more somatic problems (particularly gastrointestinal diseases and disorders). Researchers tell us that younger men and women who have lost spouses to death suffer a higher incidence of psychiatric problems.

At first, I mixed younger widows and widowers with older bereaved persons in the support groups for newly widowed persons at the hospital. The most apparent difference was in their problems. The younger widowed person felt helpless, attempting to deal with the grief of a small child. Some women mourned the fact that they were married such a short time, they didn't get around to starting a family before the death. Others were left with infants; they grieved that their children would never know their fathers. I met women and men who had been left with teenagers who were in a stormy adolescence at the time they lost a parent.

Income problems loomed large. Women were too young for social security widow's benefits and many were too "old" to be hired. (Ageism hits even women in their late thirties and early forties.) Men were often left with huge medical bills from a wife's terminal illness, with no resources to pay; medical insurance covered little, and, being younger, they hadn't had the years behind them to build up financial equity. Quality childcare, for a widowed parent who is working, costs much money. I spoke to men who were victims of an economically depressed society—they were out of work or facing a layoff, now left with children and no wife who could go out to work. Loneliness was always a monumental problem. Unlike older widowed persons, the bereaved spouse who is younger rarely knows other widowed persons the same age.

Strong feelings emerged from their profound loss and their problems. Anger. Depression. Guilt. Helplessness. Hopelessness. Acute anxiety.

That's when I realized that special support groups for younger widowed persons were needed. In 1983, I organized the first Younger Widows Group. I took it out of the hospital. I wanted these women to meet, weekly, in a warm supportive environment, in a living room instead of an impersonal hospital conference room. I chose a caring, perceptive group leader. Alice Hoffman had also been widowed. She had taken care of a terminally ill husband, and, after he died, she had to work through the same feelings as every widow sitting in her living room. Three years after his death, she had finished her grief work—or at least she was in the last stage, recovery. She was reinvesting herself in new persons. Now she was dating. She had taken her first vacation by herself, she had rented a condo on a Florida beach, and it was there, watching the sunsets, that she healed. "I could feel myself healing, as though I had gone through a very long sickness," she says. Alice was a role model for each of the young widows in her groups. They needed a role model more than a therapist: they needed to see success.

Because many men find it hard to join groups—they're taught not to openly share painful feelings—I utilized a peer-counseling service for the widowers, where I matched younger men who had just been widowed with younger widowers who had been alone longer. The telephone was their main link. Perhaps not seeing each other's faces made it easier for those newly widowed men to talk.

Dr. Leonard Woolf's contributions were invaluable. A widower, a volunteer with the Widowed Persons Service, and then later a group leader, facilitating our new support group for men, he acted as a friend and mentor. These men knew they could always call Len in times of crisis. When he moderated a panel for a meeting in the hospital auditorium, "Is It Different for Widowers?" the feedback was awesome. One of the panelists broke down and cried when he talked about the grief of his teenage son, and you could feel the tense, hushed empathy from the audience. After the presentation, people spontaneously came up to the microphone to tell *their* stories. It had the feeling of a revival meeting. I knew, then, that the vast silence around the plight of the younger widower must be broken.

I began to give educational workshops for younger widows and widowers outside of my professional job. I had given workshops for a number of years on many topics for many kinds of people, but now I wanted to offer help to widowed persons mainly in their twenties, thirties, and early forties. I was becoming a specialist without having made a conscious decision to become one.

This book comes from deep caring and the privilege of talking to countless younger widows and widowers. Occasionally, I see one of them long after we've worked together, and I see the difference in the way they feel and act, now that they're finally recovering from the trauma of the loss. I feel then as many teachers must feel when they run across an adult they taught as a child who's now doing very well, thank you. It's a *very* nice feeling.

1. How Are You Different?

Widowed persons in their twenties, thirties, and early forties *are* different. Their life situation is different than bereaved persons over forty-five. Their changed lives are also different than those of their married peers: now that they're widowed, there is so much unfinished business that will never be finished. Their friends will go on to build houses and see children born. They won't. Their families will celebrate the birthdays of husbands and wives. They won't. The feeling of isolation is keen for the younger widowed person. The aloneness is worse when friends and family distance themselves, and this often happens. Some of these important people in their lives don't allow themselves to think about the differences because they're frightened; they want to block out the death, they don't want to believe a younger person can die. The young survivor reminds them. Their presence, as survivors, is a testimonial to other people's vulnerabilities: if it can happen to younger people, it can happen to me. If they don't think about it, they don't have to be reminded of their own or their spouse's mortality. Some of them render the bereaved person invisible. One way of doing this is not to call, or not to say, "Come to dinner." Another way is not to talk about the death.

Here's Lisa:

"When I'm with my friends, they talk about their babies and husbands and what they all do together as a family. Don't they realize life has drastically changed for me?"

I told Lisa, who will now never have children with Jim, that her friends are pushing the death away because it terrifies them. If Jim died, their husbands could die. After all, he was only twenty-nine, a healthy man who suddenly developed a blood clot and died within a day. They just cannot deal with it, so silence and denial.

Here's Marvin:

"I visit my folks and they never let me talk about Hillary. They shush me when I try. 'Don't talk about it, don't talk about it, you'll only upset yourself,' they say. What's wrong with them? It's as though she never existed!"

His family doesn't know what to say, so they say nothing and want their son to be quiet. Death in the young is an obscenity and one doesn't know how to deal with obscenities. Besides, Marvin's parents are frail and elderly (he was the product of a late marriage). They know their own lives are playing out, and their daughter-in-law's death makes them especially afraid. If a woman can die at the age of thirty, *they* could drop dead tomorrow.

Drastically changed lives. Unfinished business. Isolation. Conditions that are compounded by strong feelings: Anger. Hurt. Helplessness. Hopelessness.

A woman looks around and sees her friends' husbands, men in their twenties and thirties, and they are active and healthy. She bitterly remembers how her husband died jogging at the age of twenty-eight. A man looks into the face of his eleven-year-old, and he grieves for her because she'll never see her mother again.

Differences From Older Widowed Persons

Older widowed persons are also hurt and angry, but they have the comfort of support. Many of their friends are widowed (the average age of widowhood for women is fifty-six). They've lived long enough to know that life is finite. Sickness and death is part of their vocabulary, they've seen so much of it. The obituary page is as much a part of their breakfast as their morning coffee. Parents have died, some siblings may no longer be alive, a grown child may have died, and they are witnessing the deaths of some close friends.

The seventy-year-old widowed person's world has already shrunk because of the death of special people, but the younger person expected her or his world to continue—and it didn't. Of course there's rage.

How else is the younger survivor different? There are often children who are small, or teenagers. This is frightening. The parent, now alone, asks: "Can I make it by myself?" Older persons have completed their child-rearing years long before the death. They don't have to question themselves anxiously: "Will I be able to deal with my child's grief as well as my own?"

Older persons learn from their peers. They take long looks at friends who are also widowed and measure how *they're* doing: have they adjusted to being alone and how did they achieve this? Younger widows and widowers have no role models.

None of their friends are widowed. They have no mentors or success stories. They're on their own.

Older people have memories . . . many. With thirty or forty years of marriage behind them, they remember the first home they bought, the graduation of a child from high school, their first trip abroad, a child's wedding. Younger survivors are bitter: there wasn't enough time to accumulate memories.

A young widow turned to a woman who was choosing a

gift for her husband; it was his fiftieth birthday. The younger woman said, "I'll never know what my husband would have looked like at the age of fifty!" The older woman's hand faltered on the shirt. She didn't know what to say. She said nothing. Usually she knew what to say.

Older persons are often in better financial shape than the younger bereaved person. They've had decades to save and invest.

Many older persons are retired at the time of a spouse's death. They have leisure time to golf, shop, and lunch with other widowed persons. They lead full social lives. Younger widows are frequently stuck alone in their homes with preschoolers, and this means no adult voices throughout the twenty-four-hour day; no meaningful conversation that goes beyond, "Honey, don't dribble your cereal." There is no longer a husband coming home at suppertime to provide adult companionship.

Sex may or may not be important to the older widow and widower. But a twenty-four-year-old widower misses it sorely. A thirty-five-year-old widow was at the peak of her sexual interest when her husband died.

Older women and men have had years of living experience where they've developed coping strategies for loss. They've dealt with the empty nest. They've lost friends who have died, or have gone into nursing homes. Some friends have moved far away, to warmer climates, and they've lost touch. Chronic health problems are common after the age of fifty, so they've had to deal with the loss of perfect health. They've certainly lost their youth, a hard thing to lose in our culture where being older means negative things. If they've been forced to retire through mandatory retirement, they've lost the role of worker. They have lost mobility if they can no longer drive or if their arthritis means they can't travel as they used to, or even climb three flights of steps. Those who must take money from grown children feel a strong loss of valued independence.

Any or all of these losses are profound, but they do provide lessons in coping. (Some older persons have lost a second spouse to death.) Most younger widows and widowers report that death is their first real loss in life.

There are other differences.

Parents can become overprotective after the death. Phone calls twice a day to the younger woman: "Are you all right?" Unsolicited advice: sell the house, stop crying, don't sell the house, go to work, don't go to work, be with people, stay home with the children, stop crying. Some well-meaning parents pressure the younger widow to move back home. It can be tempting. No more money worries, built-in baby-sitters, and someone always there to keep her company. But then she faces the inevitable questions: "Will I regress to being a child again?", and "Will they feel they have a right to tell me how to live?" She wonders, "Will I ever move out, once I move in?" And there's a nagging question, "If I start dating later, what will my dates think—a grown woman living with her parents?!"

Differences From Divorced Persons

There are also the differences between the younger widowed person and the divorced person. One woman was passionate: "I went to this singles discussion group and it was mostly separated and divorced singles. Well! The *bitterness*. I couldn't handle that, let me tell you. There's so much bitterness after a divorce, I can't get over it. Me, I had a good marriage. I'm going through a lot of bad feelings these days, but I remember my husband with love. All those people did was complain. The men kept saying how their ex-wives try to take them for every cent and the women complain about how their ex-husbands take the kids to expensive restaurants during visitation and *they* have to play the heavy disciplinarian during the week. I felt like I was in a different planet, I have nothing in common with them.''

A forty-two-year-old widower said reflectively, ''I'm just not comfortable dating divorced women. Every divorced woman I've gotten involved with seems to have a vindictive husband lurking in the background. The men either try to turn the children against me, or they insist she keep the kids that weekend after they've agreed they would take them so we could get away. Forget it, who needs it.''

A tiny woman with a heart-shaped face that looked poignantly young said, ''Divorced people just don't seem to grieve the way we do. Especially if they were the ones to leave the marriage. They can't know what I'm feeling.''

Divorced persons, if they want to be part of a social community, have access to the well-known Parents Without Partners. P.W.P. does invite widowed persons to join, but it mainly attracts separated and divorced persons. No social group equivalent in size exists just for widowed persons.

The Need to See the Difference

There are twelve million widows in the United States, and one out of four is under the age of forty-five. That's three million widows who are in their late teens, twenties, thirties, and early forties. An army!

There are two million widowers in this country. Half are under the age of forty-five.

Approximately 237,000 men are widowed every year. Around 506,000 women are widowed annually. Many of these persons are young.

So no matter how threatening young death is to relatives

and friends and society, no one can push the issue away. It isn't fair or just.

It isn't fair to the children, either. They need a great deal of help with their grieving.

All bereaved children grieve, even the ones who run off to play twenty minutes after they've sobbed in pain. (Running off to play is their self-protective way of denying the death.)

For a child whose parent has died, grieving is not the same as it is for a child of divorce. A young woman told me, "I dread the first couple of weeks of school every fall, because my child comes home and reports her teacher has asked what everyone's daddy does for a living—we live in a conservative town where the daddies, not the mommies, have the important careers, and where the teachers still ask that question. The kids whose parents are divorced can answer like the other children, but my child comes home and throws up. She can't handle saying, 'My father is dead.' "

Differences Between Younger Widows and Younger Widowers

Are there differences in the way younger widows and younger widowers react? A study completed at Johns Hopkins University documents that there are. The researchers found that the first task of bereavement, where the bereaved person has to believe the death, is the same for both sexes. The second task, where the pain and distress have to be worked through, differs in the length of time it takes, and the intensity of the distress. Many men often have a harder time than women. The man who led a traditional married life, a role-defined life, depended on his wife for many basic things: cooking, homemaking, hostessing, and even shopping for his clothes. She was the main caretaker of the children. She was the partner who initiated any social engagements. She was his health monitor, making his dental and doctor's appointments. *He now has to learn to do all of this by himself.* It's a very difficult and slow process, and he resists learning because he feels so bad. He may grab sandwiches for supper and forget to call the dentist. He may drink too much. He may become withdrawn. But the factor that causes the most stress is that he no longer has his wife as his closest friend. Women, in our culture, use other women for intimate friendships, where they share problems and concerns. Men do not use other men. A man may have been gregarious before he was married; he may have been president of his fraternity or active in his lodge, but he rarely confided in other men.

After marriage, he found himself opening up with his wife. This was the one person with whom he could share his vulnerabilities. Now, suddenly alone, this man has no one to turn to who can take his wife's place. As before, he talks to other men about real estate and baseball and politics, but that is not enough. The void may provide somatic symptoms and depression.

Expressiveness is very important to good grieving and he has no one with whom he can express his sadness, anxiety, longings, and anger.

An advantage for men is that they have more access to dating and mating. (Statistically, there are more women out there.) That doesn't mean he will feel less isolated; he can be just as impersonal with these women as he is with his male friends. He can stick to "safe" topics.

I also think it's different for men and women when it comes to parenting. It's harder for widowers, if their wives were the main source of nurturing for the children. It is overwhelming to have to learn quickly how to kiss bruises away, comfort crying babies, and find out where chubby dresses are sold, at the same time you're learning how to cook and help with homework.

Perhaps this new and monumental task of child rearing is the reason more men than women "farm out" their children after the death. (Farming out means leaving the kids with strangers or relatives.)

You're Very Special

Differences. There are many of them. As a younger widow or widower, you are unique. You need all the solutions to your problems and all the emotional support you can get.

This is what this book is all about, being a younger person who has been widowed and what to do about it. How to grieve. How to cope. And, finally, how to build a second life.

2. The Facts About Grieving

I listened to Margie tell me about her vacation—it was the first trip she had taken alone since her husband's death. Her face was animated. Her hands were flying as she described hang gliding. Her eyes crinkled as she laughed. I said, "You're laughing a lot!" With an amused smile, she said, "Should I feel guilty?" And then more seriously, "I would have at one time, you know. I felt terribly guilty when I'd forget Ralph's death for just a few minutes. I felt guilty if I had a good time for an evening." Putting her feet up on my hassock, she added, "And that wasn't too long ago, you know."

I know. Margie had been in one of my workshops for younger widows. She was in bad shape those first months. No, even longer. I asked, "How are you feeling now?" She gazed at the ceiling, thinking. "Like I'm getting it together, finally," she said. She added, "I laugh more now, as you said. I have many more good days, even though I dive occasionally. Let's see. I had a super time on my vacation, and at this time last year I never could have gone away alone, I would have fallen apart. I'm sleeping better. My appetite has picked up. My stomach isn't giving me as much trouble as before. What else? Oh! I can look at a photograph of Ralph now." She said, "Remember how I couldn't stand the pain of looking at his pictures? But," she warned me, "don't be surprised if I fall apart in three weeks. That's the anniversary of his death, remember?'' I nodded. A shadow flickered across her face.

"Listen," I said, "be sure you spend that day with people you love. And make your plans ahead of time, don't wait until the last minute. You want to be sure they're available."

Grimly, she nodded. A thirty-three-year-old redhead with high cheekbones and a sprinkling of freckles, whose life had fallen apart when her husband had unexpectedly died. A woman who had married at the age of thirty, expecting life to be happily-ever-after because she was a successful stockbroker and he was a physician. They worked hard; they were in bursting good health; they loved each other and knew they deserved the good life. They had been in the midst of drawing up plans for their first house. They were talking about having a baby. Who would have thought that Ralph would suffer a massive coronary and die?

Typical of many younger widows, Margie had grown up in comfortable middle-class circumstances. She had gone to good schools and chosen a career that offered financial security and upward mobility. She had leisure time and the money to go with it, so she could collect paintings and enjoy extensive traveling. After she married, she contributed hours of volunteer work, helping disadvantaged youths. She and her husband flew to Vail every winter to ski. They belonged to a tennis club. They never missed an opening night—they were avid theatergoers. These multiple activities and roles had later helped Margie in working through a major task of her grief, reinvesting herself in a life without Ralph.

At one point, we compared her life as a widow with her mother's life. When Margie's father died (her mother had also been in her thirties), her mother rarely left the house during the first year. Never having worked outside the home, with her roles limited to wife, mother, homemaker, and hostess, she felt invisible, a woman of no importance. Deeply depressed, she drifted through the house, keeping the blinds drawn all day, never taking off her blue robe, chain-smoking. Now her life consists of luncheons with friends and compulsive shopping, getting her hair done, and calling Margie every day. "What a waste," Margie said.

I reminded her that her mother is a product of her times, as we all are: that, today, younger women are usually in the work force (over 50 percent of the women in our country are working outside their homes), and this helps during grieving. Work provides a social experience, a place where you're expected every day and where people interact with you. Margie's mother never worked after she was married. And isn't it true, I asked Margie, that your mother never went to college? (Times during the Depression were tough. In many families, the boy was groomed for college instead of the girl, and this is what happened to Margie's mother.) You had many advantages, I told Margie. You went to private schools and then you went to a very good college. You took art history courses, and studied literature. Your background gave you a base on which to later enjoy museums and plays, books and films. You're now diverting yourself, during your grief, by going to art shows and continuing to attend the theater. Your mother, I said, followed a commercial track in high school and then she got married. After her marriage she was so busy in her caretaking role that she never took the time to develop herself. She doesn't have your diversions. Today, she's a woman who lacks self-confidence and passions. Her earlier life had been limited because of not having enough money and her married life was spent caring for others, I continued. She *is* a product of her times. We agreed that many mid-life women, despite the limitations of their backgrounds, broke through those limitations and started businesses or returned to school after their children were older. They brought the experience and compassion of

12

having known hard times to the fields of teaching, nursing, and social work. But it hasn't been easy for them, because many never had a chance to take science or math in high school. They were afraid to go to college, afraid they couldn't learn. Margie's mother had been married during the early 1950s, a decade of "togetherness," when women were expected to stay home while their husbands, back from World War II, getting late starts, were beginning college and careers and businesses. Their husbands' careers came first. Many, like Margie's mother, did *not* break out of their caretaking roles and build new lives in their mid-life years.

Margie's world had always been larger than her mother's. At the age of fourteen, her mother was helping her parents in the grocery store after school. At the age of fourteen, Margie was taking ballet and piano lessons after school. All of this gave her a foundation for building a second life after her widowhood.

There are many Margies. Younger women who have lost their husbands to death, and who can draw on advanced degrees and careers for starting over and can pull out of their acute grief, momentarily, by enjoying the interests and passions their good educations have given them.

It is different for younger widows, as we look at them from this historical perspective.

The deep grieving is the same as their mother's grief after the death. But recovery, or adapting to a life without their husband, is easier. There are more inner and outer resources. (It isn't easy, just easier.)

Margie is in the last stage of her grief; she's addressing the third task of her bereavement, reorganizing her life. She has some bad days, but recovery isn't a straight upward line on a graph. It's zigzag. As we talked that afternoon after her hang gliding trip, she said she couldn't actually put her finger on the time she began to feel better, the process had been so slow. We remembered, together, the first months after Ralph's death. Those months, filled with disbelief, were months when she felt like she was watching a movie—it couldn't be happening to her. She'd hear a car pull up in the driveway and for a split second she'd *know* it was Ralph. The telephone would ring—Ralph! Once, she told me, she was sure she saw him at a swimming pool, sitting in a chaise across from her. Paranormal phenomena is typical after the death of a loved one. Most people experience it and they never tell anyone, they're afraid they're going crazy—they "see" and "hear" their husbands or wives. They "sense" their presence. Ride with it when it occurs, I had advised Margie when she was going through this. It's a sign of your yearning. I had told her about a woman who felt comforted when she felt her husband's presence. "I felt his arm around my shoulder one night," she said, "and it was like he was actually standing next to me. I was so grateful for that wonderful experience."

When Margie realized her loss was final, when it hit her in the gut, she felt rage. Anger at the doctors who couldn't save him. Anger at friends who still had husbands. Anger at God. Anger at Ralph, who had abandoned her.

"Then I felt guilty because I was angry at him, and I felt guilty because I talked him into our putting off having a baby. Then when I finally agreed, I felt guilty because I didn't want to take a year off after the baby was born and Ralph wanted me to. And because I worked so hard at the office, I didn't always make time for him. I felt guilty about everything. I felt guilty about surviving!"

That's when the rage and guilt turned into depression. She couldn't sleep. She'd awaken every morning around three, toss and turn and doze lightly until it was time to get up for work. She was exhausted as she rushed through her shower, grabbed a cup of coffee, and raced to find a taxi. "But you learned to compensate, remember?" I said. "You

14

learned to take a catnap after work, before supper." "I was a basket case," she said. "No more than any other widowed person," I replied. Those first two years, after the death, were filled with distress. She needed to "run." She couldn't stay home nights or weekends, and then when she'd get where she was going, she couldn't stay there, either. What she was really doing was attempting to run from her grief. We remembered her problem concentrating. She had trouble on the job. She couldn't remember where she had put certain papers; she couldn't remember what she had done that morning and what she had to do that afternoon. Lists became crucial to her work life. She kept lists of what had to be done, and what she already had done. She constantly cried, and without warning. She felt apathy, as though nothing mattered anymore. She remembered irritable feelings and being overwhelmed by everything.

After a couple of years, Margie decided she couldn't stand the loneliness. "Moving from my co-op into a collective household really helped," she said. She had found two women who lived in a large apartment and needed an extra person to share space and expenses. These were women who enjoyed the same lifestyle as Margie, who made handsome incomes, and who were her age. She packed her bags, sold some of her furniture, and never looked back. That's another plus if one is younger—you don't feel as rooted; physical change is easier. And many younger women haven't swallowed the myth that women cannot share a kitchen; they shared kitchens with roommates before their marriages. Some of their best friends are former roommates.

In her new living situation, Margie had companionship; women with whom to spend Sundays, holidays, and vacations; women with whom to talk. One of them, a woman who runs a modern dance company, introduced Margie to the world of dance.

15

It isn't only younger women who are flexible enough to make these living-arrangement changes after widowhood, many younger men are doing it, too. Some younger widowers also live collectively. Sometimes men and women share old houses, large apartments, and new split-levels. The advantages of mixed-sex sharing are many for men: surrogate mothers for their small children, prepared meals if they've never learned how to cook (with the assumption they will learn), nurturing from the women in the house, and sometimes the possibility of a new relationship. And especially, they now have the feeling they are again part of a whole family.

Margie and I must have spent several hours together that afternoon. We remembered other signals of her bereavement distress: her eerie sense of waiting for something to happen while she felt so lost, her inability to plan activities for herself (a new experience for a woman who had been so independent), and her feeling that life and time had been suspended.

Her yearning.

We talked a lot about her yearning, or what some people call pining. She yearned for the life she had with her husband. She yearned for Ralph. She said, "I felt compelled to retrieve what I had lost." And, of course, she couldn't.

Now that Margie has moved to the last part of her grieving time, reorganization of her life, she is finally beginning to focus on the present instead of always dwelling on the painful past. She has started to date. It felt awkward at first, and she had to stop herself from comparing these men with her husband. Sometimes she'd be sitting at a table with a man and she'd be overcome with the feeling, "What in God's name am I doing here?" But she wants to get married again because she had such a good marriage. She liked being married. She wonders what it will be like, the next time. "It would have to be someone who loves and accepts me no matter how I look or how I act," she said. "I had that with Ralph." She is afraid that she won't find someone for years; that when she does finally meet someone, she'll be too old for childbearing. That worries her. It gives her a sense of urgency, and she doesn't like the feeling. Would she marry someone with children? She brushed my question away. She couldn't think about that, it was too early.

The consideration of remarriage is sometimes a difference between younger and older widows. For younger women who are in good health and expect many years ahead of them, remarriage is often a goal. Most of their friends are married, or expecting to eventually marry (or remarry). Their sexual needs are keen. They're lonely. They want a father for their children. Older widows may be in poor health and not have the physical energy for the demands of marriage. They may not want to share their changing bodies— they're self-conscious about sagging skin and bulges. Many older women are afraid to share money and property; they're insecure about their future. ("Who will take care of me if my health becomes bad? I *need* my money.") Others widowed for some time are no longer used to sharing time and space and privacy; they don't want to begin cooking and cleaning for another person; they're used to making their own decisions. Some women who took care of terminally ill husbands emphatically say, "I'm too old and tired to go through that again!" And of the few men who are their age, many of them are looking for women with money, or younger women.

Younger men, too, are more apt to want remarriage than older widowers. For one thing, the older man expects to leave his estate to his grown children. He'd feel guilty if he didn't, and he finds his lady-friend is aghast at this attitude:

she expects him to share with her if they marry. Many plans for remarriage have broken off at the attorney's office, during the writing of prenuptial agreements. This usually isn't an issue with the widower in his twenties or thirties.

Younger widowers also want mothers for their children. They want a sexual partner, whereas some older widowers suffer from impotence and feel marriage will put demands on them they can't meet.

But back to Margie. She still doesn't have it all together, but she now remembers her husband with poignancy instead of sharp pain. She *is* making it. As you will.

One of the first systematic accounts of bereavement was done in 1944. Dr. Erich Lindemann, a psychiatrist, studied 101 bereaved persons who had relatives die in the fire in Boston's Coconut Grove nightclub. His work was a milestone. However, he claimed that it is possible to settle uncomplicated grief in four to six weeks. Today, decades later, we know better. Bereavement specialists now realize it takes *at least* three years to complete the process of grieving.

So try not to be impatient with yourself.

Friends and relatives don't usually know much about death and dying and grieving. They may expect more of you than is realistic. They may say "Stop crying already!" or "Pull yourself together, you're going to make yourself sick!" If you have the emotional strength, say to them, "I know you care about me, but grieving takes a long time. I'll have to do it my way. Please don't push."

I think getting through grief is harder for women and men who have a tremendous need to be strong and to be thought of as strong by others. You know people like that, you may be one of them. If you are, allow your self-image to shift from "strong" to "human." (What's wrong, you thought you weren't human?) You'll then give yourself permission to express the full range of emotions during this bad time, and that's what will allow you *good grief.*

Each stage of your grief must be experienced to a peak of intensity before you can finish that stage and go on. You won't be so afraid to feel those bad feelings if you tell yourself, "The worst that can happen is that I'll feel bad."

And your bad feelings are an appropriate reaction to your profound loss. This means all the crazy ways you're feeling and acting is appropriate. If you're no longer sure of who you are, and you feel confused and without a sense of identity, that is appropriate: you have lost a part of yourself.

Freud coined the phrase "grief work." He called it work because it takes a great deal of hard work and energy to get through grief. But you already know this. You know how exhausted you feel.

How quickly you recover depends on many things: how much good support you get from friends and family, how much you're able to openly express all of your feelings, the state of your physical health, your income, and how much caretaking you're doing while you are in grief. (Some younger widowed persons are taking care of teenage children *and* aged parents.) It also depends on how you've coped with past losses, how many present losses you are experiencing along with the death, and how afraid you are of future losses.

Gilda is the daughter of concentration camp survivors. She was scarred by their lives. They passed along their feeling that life is precarious and that one is always in danger. When her young husband died, Gilda again felt the intense renewal of the frightened feelings she had grown up with—of being in danger. It took Gilda longer to recover from her husband's death because of her acute anxiety.

*   *   *

Joe is a recent widower. A few months after his thirty-five-year-old wife died, he lost his job. A year after that, he suffered the death of his mother. I expect it will take him longer to recover from his wife's death because he's using up so much energy attempting to deal with his multiple losses.

Doreen's husband died last year. Their three-year-old daughter has leukemia. Doreen lives a life of fear—will her child live or die? Her grief over her husband's death will probably take longer to complete because of her fear of the future.

This is what's meant by past, present, and future fears and losses, and how they affect grieving.

There is no set way to grieve. There is no formula, or strict timetable. It depends on your life and your personality.

Guilt is part of grief. Morris went through a lot of guilt feelings after his forty-two-year-old wife died of cancer. I asked him, "So you're sure you could have saved her if you would have changed her doctor? Are you God? Are you absolutely sure that you, as a mere human being, could have saved her?" That helped, but a few months later, when he was looking at some photographs of his wife that were taken before she got sick, he fell apart again. He was comparing the photographs with the ravaged face he remembered before her death. "Morris," I said, "ask yourself, 'Am I God?'" He grinned sheepishly. "What are you smiling about?" I asked. "Of course I'm not God," he said. "Well, then," I said, "how can you be so sure you could have saved her?" He needed to hear that simple truth again. And if you feel guilty, ask yourself: "In which ways did I help? How did I show my love and concern?"

Anger is taboo in our society. We grow up learning never to show anger. Our parents commanded, "Smile!" Our mothers chided, "You're so pretty when you smile. Why such a long face? You look angry." Our fathers scolded, "Don't walk around with a scowl." Many of us smile when we're crying inside, and we smile at people we don't like. We smile when we're angry. But anger is a legitimate part of grief. If you don't express it, it might turn into depression or show itself in physical symptoms of illness.

Are you afraid you'll lose control if you show anger? *You will not lose control if you show anger at the time you feel it.*

I advised a widower to buy a punching bag and bang away when he was furious. It really worked.

Bang firm pillows when you're angry. (Not soft ones, you'll feel like you're hitting mush.) Close the doors and windows and yell out your anger. Countless widows and widowers yell at the photographs of their dead spouses, "How could you leave me like that?"

There are special kinds of death that mean special grieving. Suicide. Homicide. If your husband or wife completed suicide, I grieve with you. You're no doubt plagued with anger and guilt. You also feel rejection and shame. Anger because your spouse *deliberately* abandoned you. (At least you feel this way.) Guilt because you're angry. Guilt because deep inside of yourself you wonder: was it my fault? Rejection because you've been dealt the most final kind of rejection possible. Shame because suicide is considered shameful. Your neighbors might be shunning you. Your spouse's family might be blaming you. You feel everyone is wondering: whose fault was it? Even religion blames: at least one denomination refuses to allow the suicide to be buried within the cemetery grounds.

Homicide brings its own burdens upon the survivors. After the death, the surviving husband or wife is unwittingly made a victim by the police, who must, as a matter of procedure, consider the spouse a suspect until proven otherwise. (Unless it's obvious, from the start, it's someone else.) Days, and even months, of interrogation play a relentlessly cruel role in the family nightmare. The spouse feels confused and then enraged. Small children in the family are especially confused: why are they taking daddy to the police station? What happened to mommy? There's fingerprinting, a humiliation. The house is overrun by photographers, detectives, and reporters. All of this while the family is in shock. Neighbors and friends are either supportive or they distance themselves, and one cannot anticipate their behavior. Their behavior often changes. Family frequently blames the widowed person. A woman accuses her son-in-law: "You let her go out at night by herself! You killed her!"

Get help if you're a suicide or murder survivor. You need understanding and comfort, and you need it fast. There are survivor groups, where each person in the group has shared the same experience. In the back of this book you will find a directory of self-help and professionally led groups for widowed persons. You can also call your local social service agencies for group referrals.

And then there is the kind of death that affects one exclusive group: the younger woman. With few exceptions, it is the woman under forty-five who is the survivor of a death through war. During a war where feeling is unanimous about the conflict, such as World War II (most persons supported our entry into that war), patriotism runs high and can act as a great support to a war widow. She is a heroine as well as her husband being a hero. During the war in Vietnam, where public feelings were sharply split, war widows often felt ignored and shunned by the public. Bitter feelings emerged from many of these women, who felt their husbands were unjustly scorned and blamed. The resolution of their bereavement grief was particularly complex. (For the women who have husbands listed as "missing in action,"

22

there may be no satisfactory resolution of grief; prolonged or chronic grief is what usually occurs.)

During a terminal illness, researchers have found that anticipatory grieving occurs. The spouse grieves. The dying person grieves. All or some of the stages of grief may be experienced before the death. Bereavement specialists usually feel that anticipatory grieving helps the survivor; that the after-death grieving isn't as harsh and doesn't last as long. In my professional work, I have found this isn't necessarily so. The initial period of disbelief may be shorter, but the grieving process can be as painful.

And an afterthought: persons whose spouses died suddenly and unexpectedly, especially younger bereaved persons, need to tell their story over and over in order to finally believe it. (At a conference on bereavement, I met a psychiatrist whose specialty is marathon weekends where sudden-death survivors repeatedly tell their stories. He says there are dramatic results, where the survivors report a feeling of relief at the end of the weekend.)

If your spouse died unexpectedly, and you're repeating the details of the death over and over, protect yourself by spreading out your support system: find many people who will listen. If one person acts tired of hearing your story, there will be other sympathetic persons. (This is a good reason to join a support group for widowed persons—there are many caring listeners.)

Mourning rituals help you believe the death. The funeral. The memorial service. Burial rites. The period of shiva. The wake. The more structured the ritual, the more real the death seems.

Grieving allows you to take that long and anguished road from spouse to widowed person to woman or man. When you allow yourself to grieve, you are then able to move from one place to another, from one stage of your grieving to the next. You don't become stuck. (We all know someone who's stuck in their grief.) When your grief frightens you, read this chapter again. It will be reassuring.

3. When Does It Get Better?

People expect younger widows and widowers to snap back faster, to be their old selves within a few months, and to pick up their lives and go on. It isn't that way. Grieving takes a long time. Because the death (and the illness, if there was illness preceding the death) was so unexpected, grieving sometimes takes longer than it does with the older widowed person.

The Suddenness and Unexpectedness of the Illness

It's not unusual for an *older* man to suffer a heart attack. We hear often of *older* persons who have cancer. Chronic illness is expected in persons over sixty. It's totally unexpected when it happens to a thirty-, thirty-seven-, or forty-year-old. The unexpectedness of it makes the reality very harsh.

If you nursed your spouse through a terminal illness, it was as if you entered a nightmare world, wasn't it? Older persons talk about aches and pains and sickness and death; you never talked about any of this. It wasn't part of your couple world. You were young. You both expected a long life ahead, with occasional flu attacks, a sore throat here and there, and that's all; a healthy life as all of your friends have.

When it happened, there was shock. And denial. Days when you were sure he'd get better, and other times when you let the reality hit. The doctors didn't lie. They told you the truth, in their own ways. You weren't willing to hear it

25

all the time. You pushed the truth away, especially in the beginning.

It never did become completely real, even when he was lying there, looking so different than before. It seemed like a bad dream.

One widow told me, "Until the end, I refused to believe he'd die. I was sure we could lick it. I was sure *I'd* pull him through."

If your spouse died in a hospice program, you were helped to accept the reality. But it still didn't seem completely real, did it? At least not all the time.

Healthy couples came to see you. It hurt you, that your friends were healthy, that the husbands and wives looked so robust. It hurt, knowing that all of these couples were leading normal active lives and that they had futures.

It might have made you angry.

No matter what illness your spouse had, it was totally unexpected. Who would expect that a *young* healthy person would suddenly get sick and die?

The Unexpectedness of the Accident

Many fatal accidents are suffered by persons in their twenties, thirties, and early forties.

Car crashes. A tree falls on a man. A man goes into his cellar and is electrocuted. A woman crosses the street and is run over. A fire. So many ways to die.

The shock is numbing after you hear the news. Time stands still. Frozen moments. Frozen weeks. It doesn't seem real, nothing does. And you go through the "If Only's."

- "If only I hadn't left him that evening."
- "If only she had stayed home."
- "If only we had gotten the car inspected."

26

- "If only I had been there, maybe I could have saved his life."

Vivid and horrible pictures go through your mind when there's been a fatal accident. You imagine how she felt and looked and acted when she was drowning: did she know she was going to die? You picture him pinned behind the wheel (you were told he was found behind the wheel that way) and you torture yourself: was he conscious, was he in terrible pain?

No healthy couple broods over the possibility of a fatal accident, despite the statistics. When life was going so well, you expected life to go on forever. You didn't imagine an accident . . .

Blame

You don't only blame yourself, you blame the doctors for not saving him. You blame the restaurant owner for not having a guardrail on the parking lot. You blame God for taking him.

You may blame friends for laughing. For having a good time. For *living*.

You're so angry at what happened to you ("Why me?") that you can't contain all that anger, so you blame.

(And in some cases, it *was* someone's fault.)

The blame eats you up. It's a continual anger. You lose patience with people. You lose your temper. You hate it when others are happy.

This is normal. It will pass.

Emptiness

At times you feel empty. Devoid of feeling. Nothing matters. You hear terrible news: you feel "So what?" The worst has happened. Nothing more can make you feel worse.

You're defending yourself against more pain: that's why you feel empty.

This emptiness will also pass. It is part of grieving.

It's a time when you don't care if the house is dirty, or your mother is sick. You don't care about anything.

You don't care if you live or die.

I'm not worried about your thoughts of suicide. Many persons think about suicide after the death of a loved one. I am concerned if you are making plans about how you will kill yourself. Please tell someone you are doing this. Please call your doctor immediately and tell him. If you can't get up enough energy to track down your physician (if he's not in the office), call your local suicide crisis center. It's listed in your phone book. Talk on the phone to one of their counselors. Please do this right away.

If there is no suicide crisis center in your town, call your local hospital and ask to talk to someone in the psychiatry department, a nurse or a physician. Please do it *now*.

People Expect You to Be the Same

A woman told me, "I was always the strong one. *I* was the one everyone came to and told their troubles. I was the Earth Mother, you know? Well, I don't want to hear about anyone else's troubles now! I don't want to take care of anyone or be helpful."

Another woman said, "A friend called me the other night and said, 'A woman I work with just lost her husband and she's about your age, she's also in her early thirties. Could you call her and give her some comfort?' What makes people think I should be the one to reach out and give people comfort? *I* need comfort!"

People's expectations are unrealistic. They don't realize you need a center of calmness and strength in order to reach out and help. You don't have that calmness and strength right now, you're in grief.

They don't understand that you have no energy. All of your energy is being used up in feeling bad. One needs energy in order to help other people.

They don't understand that.

You're preoccupied with your grief, so you are not motivated to help other persons.

Why can't they understand this? Because they haven't gone through what you have.

And you have a right not to want to help. You want to *be* helped. This is your need right now and it's all right.

People Say, "You Look So Well!"

Many widows say, "I'm told I look so well. What do they expect me to do, look terrible, not put on makeup?" A man said, "There's an implication when they tell me I'm looking so well. It's as though they're thinking, 'If he's looking so well he must be feeling much better.' Why do they have to believe I'm feeling better? I'm *not*."

Those people, they want you to feel better: if you feel better they don't have to worry about what to say and how to relate to you.

Some of them have their own recent pain: a stillbirth, or a divorce. They're in too much pain to reach out.

And others think you want to hear that you are looking well.

Your angry reaction also says something: that you want them to accept you as you are; that you want them to be willing to deal with your pain; also, that you want them to be willing to help you with your pain.

It's very hard to accept this truth, but *people give only what they can.* If your friend refuses to acknowledge your deep grief by denying it ("You look good!"), it's because she cannot deal with it.

Remind yourself of this from time to time: it will help you in relating to people. It will relieve the sting when you're told, "Oh, you look wonderful! You must be feeling better."

You Internalize Their Expectations

But many widows and widowers think to themselves, "If they expect me to feel better, why am I not feeling better?" or "If they expect me to be doing better, I *should* be doing better."

Another reason people expect themselves to get over the loss sooner is that the pain is so terrible. They want to be relieved of the pain.

Yet another reason for expecting quick recovery is that you've never had to cope with the loss of a loved one before; *you don't know it takes a very long time.*

When Does It Get Better?

Being younger, you're used to specific time frames: it took twelve years until you graduated from high school; it took four years to get through college; graduate and postgraduate work took a specific amount of time. You knew your pregnancy would be over in nine months. You know your period will take no longer than five days. On the new job, you know you'll be on probation for six months.

You're not used to waiting when there isn't a time frame.

And when you're in such pain, the waiting is harder: you wonder, will it ever get better?

Each day is so hard you don't think you can wait.

"When does it get better?" is a question that is often heard in younger widowed persons support groups. The members ask the group facilitator, and if the group facilitator is perceptive and informed, she will say, "Eventually it gets better. It doesn't happen overnight. It takes a long time. Some days are better. There are setbacks. But it slowly gets better."

And for the members who are persistent—who want more definite answers—she will say, "Grieving takes a long time. It isn't completely over in a year, although you may feel better then. Most people find they have to work hard at feeling better for the two years following the death. By the third year you don't have to work so hard; you feel better all by yourself, even though you have temporary setbacks."

Everyone is different. For persons who always were optimistic about life and their future, it might be a little easier and their grieving might not last as long. Persons who always took charge of their own lives might find it lasts longer, that their grieving is very difficult: they're used to being in control of what happens to them, and now they're completely out of control.

A physician said, "I may be a doctor and know how to deal with death and dying, but I'm like anybody else right now, since my wife died. I'm in lousy shape. All I'm doing these days is crying."

He was asked, "Why do you think it's so hard for you?" He answered, "Because I always was in control of what happened to me. I was a top student, all through medical school. I knew that if I studied, I'd do exceptionally well in my tests. I knew that if I did exceptionally well in medical school, I'd probably get accepted just where I wanted, to do my internship. The same with my residency. I know how to be charming—that sounds like I'm bragging but I'm not—so I knew that when I eventually met the woman I wanted to marry, I'd know how to win her, and I did. I knew, when I went into private practice, that I could afford the house and the trips and the sports car, everything, and I bought what I wanted. I did it. I was in control."

He buried his head in his hands. "And now I'm completely out of control. I couldn't control her illness. I couldn't control her dying or her death. I was and am helpless!"

It *is* harder for persons who are used to being in control.

When does it get better? I wish I could give you a definite answer, but I can't. I can only tell you it does get better.

Prolonged Grieving

Prolonged or chronic grief is when you continue grieving without any lessening of pain, despite the passage of time.

That's when, in the third year of bereavement, every day is as difficult as it was during the first six months of your bereavement.

It's when you are stuck in your grief after your spouse has been dead four years. You feel as depressed as you did the first year.

It has been speculated among bereavement specialists that the inability to work through grief is preferable, to some bereaved persons, to the terrible hopelessness they're sure they will feel if they give up their deceased spouse. (They're terrified by the prospect of hopelessness.)

Persons who suffer from prolonged or chronic grieving refuse to acknowledge a future, even after a couple of years.

Self-blame and guilt feelings don't diminish.

Anger continues, even after three or four years, and it's a steady anger.

Persons who suffer from prolonged or chronic grief need special help. If you suspect you are suffering from prolonged grief, please make an appointment with a professional helper.

Absent Grief

You might know someone who didn't seem to grieve at all.

These are persons who seem to be proud of the fact they got up, dusted themselves off, and got on with life. That they went back to work a week after the death. That they don't dwell on the past. That they never cried. That they began dating a few months after the death. When friends and family refer to their loss, they brush it aside and change the subject. They never refer to their dead spouse. They sometimes remarry very soon.

Persons who do not allow themselves to grieve are protecting themselves from the pain of grief. They are pushing away threatening feelings. It takes energy *not* to grieve. That's why some of these persons are very tense.

Their coping ability is frail. That's why they avoid grieving. They instinctively know they can't cope well.

They're avoiding any expression of their grief, but they are *feeling* grief, at least unconsciously: if it's not conscious, their suffering could show itself in bodily aches and pains or physical illness.

A woman's husband died, and she was talking about dating within a month after the death. She didn't seem to be grieving. In fact, she never talked about the death. (Her in-laws were furious about that!)

She began to date right away. It seemed that all she talked about were clothes and going out and all the fun she was having. She laughed a lot, even though she seemed a little nervous.

Five months after her husband died, she began to have stomach pain. Also, she had trouble with her bowels: first constipation, then diarrhea. It got so bad she went to her internist. A spastic colon, he diagnosed. He works closely with a social worker, and he referred this patient to his colleague. Slowly, the social worker helped her understand she was repressing any expression of her grief, and the repression had caused her spastic colon attacks. She was encouraged to express her feelings of loss within the safety of the social worker's office, where she knew the social worker could help her if her feelings got out of control. Releasing her feelings of anger at the death and then seeing that nothing terrible happened, allowed her to cry at home for the first time. Today, she is allowing herself to express the full range of her grief; the anger, guilt, anxiety, all of the intense feelings. She is still seeing the social worker, and that is appropriate. She needs the safety of someone being there if she trips and temporarily falls. Her spastic colon attacks have subsided. (Her in-laws are glad she's expressing her grief—it was their son. Her parents are confused and angry—she seemed to be doing so well!)

Delayed Grief

Self-protection can be so strong that a person doesn't allow herself to grieve for *years*.

A woman's husband died. She didn't grieve.

Ten years later her father died. She had always been a daddy's girl; she was devastated. Hit hard by depression, she made an appointment with a psychotherapist. He helped her work through her grieving, and in the process, unexpectedly, she began to grieve the death of her husband.

What happened? Her grief over her father's death reactivated repressed feelings about her husband's death. Seeing that she was safe, expressing sorrow over her father's death, she then felt safe finally expressing feelings about her husband's death. It was ten years later, but she did complete her grieving. (And this enabled her to finally remarry; in order to relinquish her deceased husband, she had to complete the grieving process.)

How Do You Picture Yourself?

We all have a self-image: how we picture ourselves. If you saw yourself as a separate individual within your marriage as well as being part of a couple, you'll see yourself as being able to function as an individual after the death, even though it's very difficult. If you saw yourself as an appendage to your spouse, not separate, you may now feel too weak to function without him or her. This can answer the question, "When does it get better?" It may take longer.

Because more women work today than in their mother's day and have built meaningful careers, there are more wives who have a healthy sense of separateness. They have this developed sense of self during their bereavement and it helps.

A woman who was a full-time homemaker may have developed her sense of separateness through fulfilling volunteer work, or strong involvement in organizations. A woman poet told me that she felt her sense of self through her writing.

One woman saw herself as selfish (this was her self-image) and it prolonged her grieving. "I couldn't bear being in the house with him day and night," she said. "He had cancer, and it upset me to look at him, I hated changing his bandages, I hated taking care of him, it upset me so."

She looked down at her hands that were clasped tightly in her lap. "His mother came to help out, and I started avoiding going in his bedroom. I avoided him, I avoided her. I stayed out of the house as much as possible. When he died at home, I was at the movies." If she had gone for professional help while he was dying, she might have learned to use the strengths she does have to help her be with him more often, and she would have learned how to forgive herself for not being with him all the time. But she didn't. And *now* she has the task of forgiving herself. Meanwhile, because of her negative self-image, she is grieving longer than the usual two or three years.

The Quality of Your Marriage

A clinical investigation of sixty-eight widows and widowers conducted by well-known bereavement specialist Colin Murray Parkes showed that recovery happens more within the expected time if the marriage was a good one. Parkes concluded that anger (leftover anger accumulated during the bad marriage) interfered with the grieving.

You might wonder: why would persons who were in a bad marriage grieve at all? Because many bad marriages are ambivalent; hostile feelings are often mixed with affection, and if not with affection, with the animal comfort of having this person always there.

Guilt feelings can follow the death of a bad marriage. This, as well as anger, can interfere with the completion of grieving.

Were You Very Dependent?

Women and men who were excessively dependent on their spouse may take longer to grieve. They feel and act more helpless after the death, and this affects their feelings about being able to work through their grieving in an active way. For instance, the man who was passive and wanted his wife to make all the decisions now has a difficult time making even the smallest decisions by himself. He knows he should get out of the house and be with people because it will help him work through his grieving, but he can't make up his mind to call anyone; one minute he's going to call, the next minute he gives up the idea, his passivity taking over. Or a woman who was a little girl instead of a wife, dependent on her husband for transportation, food shopping, child rearing, and socializing, stays stuck in the child role; she stays stuck in *yearning* the return of her spouse who will again take care of her. (And until she does stop yearning, she won't relinquish her role as "wife"; she will not reinvest herself in any new relationships.)

Conflict Avoiders

Women and men who always tended to avoid conflict and confrontation may take longer grieving. After the death, they need to pretend to themselves that their marriage was perfect; they're prone to use denial as a defense against their pain. Instead of directly acknowledging to themselves that there was some anger in the marriage that wasn't expressed because they *are* conflict avoiders, they're more apt to pretend to themselves that they had the ideal marriage. If they persist in idealizing the relationship, they are not going to allow themselves to acknowledge even the anger that is a legitimate part of normal bereavement where the surviving spouse feels angry at being left completely alone. All that unexpressed and unrecognized anger holds up good grieving.

Good Grieving?

It's a term I like, good grieving. To me, it means allowing oneself the full gamut of feelings during bereavement: rage, some self-pity, guilt feelings, panic, depression, despair, quiet sorrow, loneliness, hysteria (no one talks about that inner hysteria), and apathy.

To get rid of all those feelings, it takes a great deal of time.

You can't be rushed. It feels terrible, going through those feelings, but you can't be rushed and it is necessary to *feel* in order to heal. When you really accept that, you'll no longer need to ask, "When does it get better?" You'll be more able to ride with your own pacing.

4. Coping With
Your Loneliness

Younger widowed persons' friends are married, separated, divorced, or they've never married.

They are not widowed.

A young woman finds she's the only widow on her block.

A young man is the only widower at the dinner party, or he has a beer with a friend he hasn't seen in years, and all the man talks about is child support.

The young widow goes to a P.T.A. meeting and people are curious: she's a *widow* and she's only twenty-six?

She not only feels lonely, she feels deviant.

One woman said, "I don't know women my age who are also widowed. They're all my mother's age. The other day, one of them asked me if I wanted to go to a luncheon with her and her friends. They're all older widows. I said 'no' politely, hung up the phone, and cried."

Situational Loneliness

After the death there is an ache. It's as if one's body has been assaulted. There is a gnawing inside of one's guts, as though there is a deep wound.

That's what *situational loneliness* does to people. It wounds them. It's the kind of loneliness brought on by a profound loss. It's what all widowed persons feel.

"It's worse than the crazies, the guilt feelings, the rage,

and the depression,'' one man said. "And let me tell you, it lasts longer than any of those feelings.''

It very slowly goes away. It dissipates when you've successfully invested yourself in a new person or new activities—when you've given yourself new and meaningful roles in life.

Being younger, there are more opportunities to eventually find someone who will be central to your life. But some persons are wary of this. A few don't want it. Some are sure they will never find anyone.

A man whose wife had died told me, "I have a hearing-impaired son, who has borderline intelligence. I'll always have to take care of him. What woman would want that burden? I see no end to my loneliness.''

Maybe he's wrong. I hope so, but if he isn't he will need to cope with chronic loneliness unless he relieves his pain through new passions; interests that become consuming. He may need to content himself with short-term relationships without commitment.

Situational loneliness is aggravated by loss of roles.

You were an active sex partner in your marriage and you lost that role. Sexual pleasure wasn't only sexual intercourse, it was touching and being touched.

You were the one your spouse confided in. You lost that role. Your husband was your best friend. You told each other everything. Your wife listened to your stories of your childhood and you told her about your problems on the job.

You've lost the role of companion. There's no one left to take that after-supper walk with you. No one left to share morning coffee or the Sunday papers.

You may have lost the role of homemaker. Who's left to care if your kitchen floor sparkles or if the dining table, set for company, looks elegant? (You don't even want to cope with the demands of having company.)

You've lost the role of social director. There's no one left to plan with or for.

You may have lost the role of gourmet cook. Now that your spouse has died, you've stopped baking. You've stopped making those special dinners.

Your role as parent has drastically changed. It's now a lonely role, where the children need and demand energy you just don't have. Sometimes you feel resentful that you have to take on this role alone.

More than anything, you've lost the role of the beloved. No one ever loved you the way your spouse did.

Not only have you lost multiple roles, you've lost status.

There is status in being married.

Our society gives value to the role of husband or wife.

Despite a lessening of pressure on people to get married, the pressure still subtly exists. Women may wait until they're in their late twenties or even late thirties to marry— there are career demands and times have changed since World War II days when two out of three women were married by the age of twenty-one—but many women feel an anxiety about being single after the age of thirty.

Men over thirty-five also feel self-conscious about being single.

Now that one is widowed, that uneasy feeling returns.

Status is lost if a spouse was important in the community.

Listen to Laura, who was the young wife of a minister.

"We had an important role in the community, no matter where we lived. When we moved to a new city, the parsonage was ready—the refrigerator was filled and people were in the house, waiting to greet us with homemade cakes and welcoming words. As the wife of a highly respected clergyman, I had status. Respect. Now I'm just another widow. That's hard to take."

I remember the wife of a well-known news broadcaster who told me, "We were always being stopped in the street because everyone recognized my husband from the six o'clock news. They'd ask for his autograph. They'd ask his opinion on everything. We went to at least three parties a week because David was so well-known. After he died, I had the big adjustment of no longer being special. It was very, very hard.''

Because men have more power in our society, and many wives still live through their husband's successes, more women than men suffer from loss of status after the death. However, I did meet a man whose young wife had been a highly visible state legislator before she died, and he did admit to feeling a keen loss of status.

''I feel sheepish, saying it out loud,'' he said, ''but it's true, I have lost a sense of reflected importance. I was very proud of Shelley. I didn't mind being referred to as 'Shelley's husband.' She was a brilliant woman. She was articulate and she cared about the right things. She had the gift of getting other people to care—about issues like housing for the aged and civil rights. I loved seeing crowds go wild when she spoke in public. I loved seeing her picture in the paper. I liked having people turn around in restaurants and wonder if I was her husband.''

This fortyish man, wearing jeans, leaned back, crossed his arms behind his head, and looked thoughtful. ''Maybe that's okay, though, huh? Maybe it showed I was the liberated male.'' We speculated on that and both agreed that, today, more men have wives in showcase careers, at least younger men, and many of these husbands are proud of their wives.

We talked about another loss that aggravates loneliness after the death: the sense of *time* being important. He said that on Saturdays he'd putter in his darkroom in the mornings and leave the afternoons free, so he and Shelley could go to a film or for a drive in the country; now, Saturday could be

Thursday or Monday, it's just another day to get through since she died.

Then there's the wife who got up at seven every morning to make her husband's breakfast. Now, there's no reason to get up at seven or ten. She lies in bed, feeling adrift.

Time has gone awry.

Losses of role, status, and time. These are major losses. And it takes a very long time before a widowed person replaces the roles, accepts the absence of status, and makes new sense of time.

Patience. That's what you want to cultivate now. Don't impose a timetable on yourself. Don't decide you'll be your old self in four months and then you'll get up and resume living. Everyone has their own individual timetable.

Ride with some of the loneliness instead of always fighting it. The worst that can happen? You'll feel bad. That's the worst that can happen. I remember Lorna, who deliberately decided to spend her wedding anniversary at the ocean. It would have been the third year of their marriage if Seff hadn't died. "I needed to remember," she said. "I needed to think. I didn't want to be distracted by other people." Lorna was using her situational loneliness creatively; to review her life with Seff, to selectively remember the good things about their relationship as she watched the ocean in the bleak of the winter. It was, she told me, a gift to herself, this life review in solitude.

Self-Imposed Loneliness

Self-imposed loneliness is when you deliberately distance yourself from others in self-protection, so you won't be hurt. You're playing it safe, removing yourself from situations where you'll see couples. You avoid weddings. You refuse invitations to couple's homes.

42

Situational loneliness is inevitable after the death. Self-imposed loneliness isn't.

Harry Stack Sullivan, the eminent mind healer, believed the need for human intimacy is as driving a force as hunger. If he's right, then we can't allow ourselves to indulge in self-imposed loneliness. It's self-destructive. Having lost the central person in your life, you now need to achieve some degree of intimacy with other persons. You may not do this right away, but it means eventually reaching out and accepting social invitations. It means being open to meeting new persons. It means allowing yourself to get close to another person.

Maybe your inner dialogue goes like this:

"Who'd even want to be with me, now that I'm alone? No one, probably. I was a whole person when I was married. I feel crippled now. All of my self-confidence is gone. I don't even know who I am anymore."

Or—

"People loved Les. He was a great storyteller. He was warm and vibrant. Me—I'm the quiet one. People spent time with us because of him. I don't want their pity so I say 'no' when they invite me over."

Or—

"I feel like a fifth wheel, being with couples. No one wants an extra person around."

(A man said that. Didn't we always think it was the *woman* who feels like the fifth wheel?)

These feelings come from thinking you're nobody without a husband or wife—that you're worthless unless you're part of a couple. And when couples don't call as often, it validates your feelings of worthlessness, doesn't it?

Fight this feeling. Tell yourself, "All right, some people have stopped calling, but there are persons who do want a relationship with me."

Identify them. They're the couples who still call, even

though you've refused their invitations each time. They're couples who have singles as well as couples in their social lives.

Now call them. Say, "Forgive me for not having kept in touch, but I just haven't felt able to be with people. I now realize it's better for me to be with friends. Can we get together?"

Of course they will understand. They'll feel needed and important because of the way you've said it.

Coping With Couples

How can you be comfortable with couples?

As a woman who's alone, do not insist on paying your own way if the man is uncomfortable about it. Some traditional men just can't be nontraditional; they're used to picking up the check, and their discomfort at changing their ways is enormous. Respect this. Reciprocate their generosity with an invitation to your home for dessert. Or buy theater tickets and announce, "I happen to have two extra tickets and it would give me great pleasure if you would both be my guests."

As a man who's alone, return dinner invitations even if you don't know how to cook. One innovative widower invites married friends to dinner theaters; he says there's built-in entertainment while they're dining, and even though it might not be a memorable performance, it means a pleasant evening. Other ways to return dinner invitations: buy a deli tray and serve a paper plate picnic lunch on your dining-room table (a nice Saturday afternoon or Sunday evening touch); hire a caterer to bring in an elegant dinner; buy lox and bagels and cream cheese, prepare a pot of hot coffee, and serve Sunday brunch; bring home ethnic dinners, already prepared, from a restaurant—all you need to do is set the table. However you do it, don't be like John. After two years of widowhood, he admitted he had never returned any dinner invitations. He looked baffled when I suggested it. "I never thought about it!" he said.

If you feel like a fifth wheel, tell yourself, "*I have my own identity*. I don't have to be part of a couple in order to be interesting. I can be accepted for myself, not as an appendage to my spouse." Just empty words at first, but after you repeat them enough times and after you do join coupled friends enough times, you'll begin to believe it.

Women sometimes have a very special problem with other persons' husbands or lovers. Let Marion tell you about it.

"I was stunned the first time I went out with Toby and Bert after my husband died. What happened was that we went to dinner and a movie, and then Bert said, 'Toby, wait for me. I'll walk Marion to her door.' Fine. It was terrific of Bert. My parking lot is dark, and I appreciated it. When we got to my apartment door I took out my door key and all of a sudden he made a grab for me. Bert! My best friend's husband! I guess my instincts took over, because I quickly turned on my heel, opened my door, sang a good night, and slammed the door in his face. Did I ever tell Toby? No. And I wouldn't."

(Marion also made sure she was never alone with him again.)

Why would this happen to any widow? A lone woman may be considered a challenge. A man could be angry at his wife, and he's getting back at her. The man could be a womanizer.

Sometimes another problem arises—only it's with your best friend. She's acting differently. She's eyeing you warily when her husband is around. You feel her distancing herself from you, she doesn't call as often. You sense distrust. She thinks you're interested in her husband! Naturally, you feel hurt and betrayed. You have always respected their couple relationship. You would never do anything like that. And besides, you care about her.

Realize she's saying more about herself than she is saying about you. She is emotionally insecure, and any lone woman would feel like a threat to her.

Avoid being alone with her husband. When you are with both of them, make as much eye contact with her as with him. Direct remarks at both of them.

You've unfortunately become a symbol to her. You are being stereotyped as the "merry widow," available and hungry. She is making the silent statement, "I feel bad about myself, and my self-esteem is low." If you care enough about her and you have the emotional strength, you can say, "Look, I get the feeling you no longer are comfortable with me, that you think I'm interested in breaking up your relationship. I would never do anything to hurt you, I care about you." She may become defensive at first, but she'll think about what you have said.

Be selective: choose couple friends who are nurturing. Be wise: return all social invitations, even though your energy level is low. (Coffee and cake is as hospitable a gesture as dinner.) Be perceptive: if your couple friends don't call as often, it could be because you've turned down every invitation, or they just don't know how to relate to bereaved persons. You can help with that. Refer to your marriage and your spouse, so they know they can, too. If they act uncomfortable when you cry, save your crying time until you're alone, or when you're with persons who can tolerate pain.

Many widowed persons report their couple friends are still calling after six and nine months and a year and that they're still being included in most of their social activities. That's great. I'm delighted for you; but who are you going on vacation with next summer?

Sooner or later you might want to establish new relationships with single persons. This doesn't mean you're giving up those good couple friends, it means you're expanding your social life to include persons with whom you *can* vacation and spend Sunday evenings.

Widowed Persons Support Groups

Making new friends takes a lot of energy, you say, and you're short of that right now. An answer: join a widowed persons support group that includes widows and widowers in their twenties, thirties, and early forties.

It means immediate contact with persons who have gone through the same loss as you, who are your age, and who are as lonely as you are.

This kind of group is primarily a discussion group, but it evolves into an informal social group, too. It meets weekly, on an ongoing basis, or for eight weeks. The participants address topics that are important to all younger widowed persons: what grief is all about, how to handle unwelcome feelings, how to deal with loneliness, changing relationships with family and friends, overprotection from parents, changing relationships with in-laws, finances, work, where to live, and feelings about sex and remarriage. If there are parents in the group, single parenting is addressed; especially, the task of dealing with a child's grief.

Where is this kind of group found?

In hospitals, social service agencies, and in churches and synagogues.

If you cannot find a group, how about organizing one? It's really not difficult, and it can give you a sense of purpose at this difficult time when you've lost your sense of purpose.

Place an ad in your local newspaper, inviting other younger widowed persons to join you, every week, in your living room. Ages? Under forty-five. If you don't want to use your home each week, rotate: meet in each other's homes. Also have rotating chairpersons. Establish a kitty for simple refreshments. Organize a car pool. Both sexes? Of course. It helps women to hear a man's point of view. It nurtures men to have women in the group. And this kind of group is especially helpful to men. Many of them have no one with whom to share their distress.

A support group will give you a safe place in which to cry and express your sad feelings. You'll be able to share private feelings and thoughts that you don't want to share with your family. It's a place where you can test your reactions to your loss—to see if others are also reacting in the same ways. It's a place to share solutions to problems.

Solid friendships develop. By the second or third meeting, someone (an organizing type) asks, "Who wants to go out for coffee after the meeting?" Women plan to get together for Sunday night supper. A man and woman discover they have the same problem with their teenagers, so they exchange phone numbers. If you're feeling bad at night, there is someone to call.

Use the first meeting as a sharing time. Have each person tell the story of the death and what they have been feeling. There will be crying, so have tissues ready, but crying is healing.

In the following sessions, have an agenda: a topic each week. No lectures. Just everyone sharing.

(And develop a telephone roster, so people can call each other during bad moments.)

If you don't have the energy or the self-confidence or time to organize a group, ask your clergy person for help. Your priest, rabbi, or minister need only provide free space for a meeting room and some publicity (a few announcements from the pulpit and a blurb in the newsletter). A widowed persons support group is an innovative program for a church or synagogue to sponsor: your clergy person might even want to open it up to the larger community.

Restrict your group to widowed persons. Separated and divorced men and women have a different life situation. Also, be sure the participants have been widowed no more than four years. After that, needs are different.

Are you a reluctant man who isn't a joiner? Give this group a try. If there's no one in your life with whom you cry, this is a group you need. If you're not a cryer, is there someone with whom you *talk*? (That is, talk about your loneliness and your innermost feelings.) You may never have talked to anyone except your wife about feelings, and you need to talk in order to heal. You'll feel safe in this kind of group; you'll feel encouraged to open up and express the full range of your distressed feelings. If you're a man who is already open, all the better. A support group, as you already know, will give you a forum for your questions and your comments. You can help others as well as yourself.

Make Your Home a Social Base

You can use your home as a base for enlarging your social life.

I sat in Betty's living room, a cozy chintz and plump pillow room, and watched her slice cake. There was the warm aroma of brewing coffee. "There," she said, handing me a plate, "we were talking about overcoming loneliness. Well, after Bernie died, I didn't want to see anyone or go anywhere. My family doctor finally gave it to me. You can't stop living, he said. Bernie would have wanted you to build a new life. Make yourself move your muscles, he said, make yourself start a new life. He said, you're only in your thirties, you can't lie down and die. All right, I told myself, get off your duff, Betty, he's right. I had been getting bad headaches since Bernie died, and the doctor said it's depression. I had enough of a sense of self-preservation that I didn't want it to get worse—I have to be well enough to go to work every day. So I made myself call old friends.'' She excused herself and returned from the kitchen with a tray. "But," she continued, "I played it smart. I felt safe in my own home so I arranged to have everyone come here.''

"Safe?"

"Emotionally safe," she said, pouring the coffee. "This house was and is part of whom I had been for the past ten years. I wasn't yet ready to test new territory, to forge a new identity. I hated the word *widow*. I was insulted when anyone wrote me a letter addressed to *Betty* Davidson instead of Mrs. Bernard Davidson. I still considered myself a wife. So I had friends come here, in the home where I had always been Bernie's wife. I invited friends over for pizza while we watched TV. I had them for dinner, or for dessert if I didn't feel up to cooking. I was safely surrounded by pictures of Bernie and the trophies he had won bowling. Now, for the first time, I'm finally beginning to venture out more and accept friends' dinner invitations. I go to the theater with them occasionally. I feel okay about doing it, and I guess I'll do it more as time goes by. But I do think I did a smart thing, using my home as a social base. It's okay to use a crutch at a time of crisis.''

I agree. I believe in crutches. When you are ready to throw yours away, you will.

A note: If you've been used to having your husband greet guests at the door and hang their coats, ask one of your male guests to fill this role. If your husband used to play bartender, ask another male guest. If your wife used to see that guests mingled and took great pains at artfully setting the table, ask a woman friend to complete these tasks. This will make home entertaining easier, now that you are alone.

Use Your Family to Combat Loneliness

If you've had good relationships with at least some members of your family, see them often during this bad time. Use your father as a surrogate daddy for your two-year-old. Ask your brother to take your eleven-year-old to a baseball game. Use your family for yourself. You need all the love you can get right now, and families are often the best source for this. A woman told me, "My father can't stand seeing me cry, so I don't cry in front of him, but he does sit in the kitchen with me for hours, playing cards. It gives me a lot of comfort."

A good thing about families, they usually don't stand on ceremony. You can visit without a formal invitation. If they live a day's drive away, arrange to visit during the weekend, when you aren't working. (This takes care of lonely Sundays.) Call them, long distance, when the rates are lower. If they live on the same block or in the same city, drop in when you feel blue.

If you have a good relationship with your in-laws and you enjoy their company, you can give each other support.

Loneliness Is Distressful but Not Dangerous

When your friends and family aren't available, use *yourself*:

Get out of your house during lonely weekends. Go anywhere. Drive to a shopping center to people watch. Walk to the drugstore and eavesdrop while you're drinking your soda (it's a great distraction). Being around people and life makes you feel more connected to the world.

Renew some of your old interests. Enroll in an art class or take up swimming again.

Buy a pet if you enjoy animals. (That is, if the management of your apartment house allows it.) Did you know that touching a pet lowers your blood pressure and slows your pulse? A pet gives companionship. (And while walking your dog, you'll make new friends!)

Finally, tell yourself on bad days: "I can't avoid this loneliness so I'll just let it happen to me—today. Tomorrow, I'll be with someone I like, because I'll plan for that today. Meanwhile, I'll sit on my balcony (or front porch) so I can watch people, so I'll feel life around me. This will pass, this anguishing lonely feeling. I'll get through it."

And you will.

5. Children and Death

Approximately 1.5 million children lose one or both of their parents to death by the age of fifteen. Sooner or later, these questions nag at all of them:

"Did I cause it to happen?"

"Will it happen to me?"

"Who will take care of me now?"

Some children articulate these questions. Others wonder about them, never asking them aloud. And the age of the child is irrelevant. Each of these questions raises anxiety in the preschooler and the adolescent. If the questions aren't answered, children find their own fantasy answers, and that can be more frightening than reality.

"Did I Cause This to Happen?"

This question is on every bereaved child's mind.

A perceptive woman saw that her small son became withdrawn after the death of his father. She knew he wouldn't actually ask, "Did I make him die?" So she said, "Daddy died and we all feel very sad about it. No one knows exactly why he died, except that we know he was very sick, a grown-up sickness. It was no one's fault that he died, because no one can make another person get sick and die." She didn't expect a reply and she got none. But she knew he heard. She later decided to reinforce what she had told him. Holding him in her lap, cuddling him, she softly said, "No one can make another person get sick and die. Daddy knew you loved him and that you could never make him die. You couldn't make him get sick and die, even when you were angry at him.'' He looked at her searchingly and then nodded his head. She nodded, too.

A teenager lost her father to death. She and her dad had argued a great deal, and the morning he died in a car accident had been a morning when they had a big fight over breakfast before he left the house. This teenager acted out a great deal of anger after the death, and the mother suspected she was angry at herself, that she possibly felt she was responsible for her father's death. In fact, the daughter once muttered, ''If I hadn't upset him over breakfast he might have paid more attention when he was driving to work. He might not have crashed the car and died.'' Her mother, hearing that, sat down on her daughter's bed and took her hand. ''You don't have the magical power that it would take to make a person crash a car and die. You just don't have that kind of power over anyone else.'' Her daughter turned her head away. The mother added, ''All teenagers fight with their parents, it's part of growing up. Your father was very proud of your strong spirit and your independence. He loved the way you were developing strong opinions of your own, even if he did disagree with some of them. Sometimes, after the two of you would argue, he'd come into the bedroom with me and grin and say, 'That girl! She's something!' ''

Both of these women were addressing the spoken and unspoken question, ''Did I cause it to happen?'' in their own ways, appropriate to the ages and understanding of their children.

"Will It Happen to Me?"

Your child may actually ask this question, or if he doesn't, he may act out his concern. It's a question that can come up again and again after the death because a child often over identifies with the deceased parent: unconsciously, he sees the parent and himself as one. This over-identification makes him worry. Will he get sick of the same illness and also die? Will he die when he's the same age as his parent when *he* died?

Brett was fourteen when his dad died suddenly of a heart attack. Five months after the death, Brett awakened in the middle of the night with chest pains. Panicked, he called for his mother. He had never had chest pains before. His mother suspected he was over-identifying with his dad, but in order to reassure him and herself she took him to the emergency room of the nearby hospital. No, the physician said after examining him and giving him an electrocardiogram, there's nothing wrong except anxiety. Brett wasn't convinced, he still worried. The next time he suffered the same chest pains his mother made an appointment with a cardiologist. All the tests were negative. The specialist spent some time talking to Brett. He told him it's very rare for a child his age to suffer a heart attack. He explained the dynamics of over-identification in a fourteen-year-old's language. His mother sat listening so she, too, could use the same language if it was later necessary.

Many children worry, "Will it happen to me?" because anything could happen to them, now that the unspeakable has happened. They feel vulnerable. Their anxiety level is very high.

No matter what the age of your child, you can do these things:

- See that your child gets a thorough physical examination soon after the death. Ask the physician to reassure your son or daughter about the results.
- Do frequent hugging, touching, and kissing. If your teenager is going through a time when he feels private about his body and doesn't want to be touched, show your love in nonphysical ways.

"Who Will Take Care of Me?"

A big fear—will the surviving parent also die? After all, the worst in life did happen to one parent, why not to the other? Every child is concerned about this, younger and older, but the younger child is most concerned because he not only feels helpless, he *is* helpless; he is very dependent.

The underlying questions are: "What will happen to me if you die?"; "Who will feed me?"; "Where will I live?"; and "Who will love me?"

It's the fear of abandonment that is the bottom-line issue.

Reassure your son or daughter that you're in good health and you'll probably live for a very long time. Ideally, you should have a physical checkup to reassure yourself: share your good findings. If the physician finds anything wrong, tell your child what you're going to do to correct your condition. And when the condition is corrected, immediately share the good news. (This tells your son or daughter that illness does not necessarily lead to death. That we *can* get well!)

But there's something else you want to do, and that's to let your child know that if anything does happen (which is very unlikely, you'll add), someone else will definitely take good care of him until he grows up. (Make caretaking arrangements before you talk about this, so you can actually name the person for further reassurance.)

Do you really have to do this? Yes, I think so. Your child

has gone through the final abandonment—death. *He needs to know he will not be left alone!*

Is it a morbid thing to do? On the contrary, it's a loving and rational thing to do. You're giving your child a gift by reassuring him there *always* will be a central person in his life who will take care of him.

Perhaps your child already has a godparent who expects to take on this parental responsibility if necessary. If not, ask for this care from a family member who loves your child, and who has your values. If there isn't an available family member, how about a loving family friend? And you might want to do what many caring parents do—have a legal document drawn up between you and this other adult. (Ask your attorney about the procedure, once you find a person who will take on this role.)

After the death, the surviving parent might seem very vulnerable to the child; he sees his mother crying, so he often leaps to unrealistic conclusions: "Now she could get sick and die, she cries so much!" That's when children need to be told, "Crying makes me feel better. It's a way of getting rid of my sadness."

The Ways Children Grieve

Each child in a family grieves differently. Many don't show their feelings, others are verbal, and others act out distress instead of asking questions. How *you* grieve can influence the way your child grieves. If you bravely smile all the time, it's confusing to your child: "Why is mommy happy now that daddy has died?" Glad. Sad. Bad. Mad. All these feelings get mixed up in the child's mind. It's appropriate that you now act sad. It's appropriate that your child acts sad. He learns his appropriate feelings from you.

If you're not comfortable with crying, you can verbalize your sadness. Here are effective things to say to your child:

"I loved your mother, too, so I know how much you miss her."

"We both feel very sad, don't we?"

"I know you hurt, because I hurt."

"We'll both feel better eventually, and right now we still hurt."

A child's reaction to the death has a great deal to do with his chronological age and social development. The three-year-old can't understand death or that death is final, so she shows her distress in different ways than a fifteen-year-old. The nine-year-old grieves in different ways than the nineteen-year-old, because there's less cognitive and emotional understanding.

Children Under Three

Not only can't an under-three child understand the concept of death, she can't understand it's forever—her concept of time is not yet developed. That's why the toddler will keep asking, "When is mommy coming back?" even after repeated explanations.

Try to keep your explanations simple, brief, and concrete. This very small child can relate only to what she can see, touch, feel, hear, and smell.

One mother took a dry leaf from her backyard and said to her little girl, "This leaf is like daddy. Look at it." Her child peered at the leaf. "Now the leaf is going to die, watch it die." The mother crumbled the leaf into tiny fragments. "It's all gone now. That's what dying is, when something or someone is all gone and won't come back."

"I want the leaf to come back!" the child protested, then reached for the fragments. The mother said, "We both want the leaf to come back but it's dead, it can't. Here, try to make the leaf come back together again. Can you?'' The child tried. Tearfully, she looked up at her mother. ''See,'' her mother said gently, ''we can't put the leaf back together again. It's like daddy. We want to put him back together again and bring him home, but we can't. He's like the leaf.''

Then the mother added, ''I'm big and I can't do it, either. Let me show you.'' She crumbled another leaf into fragments and showed her daughter that even she couldn't put the fragments back together again. There was a silence. The child asked, ''Who's going to feed daddy now?'' The mother pointed to the crushed leaf and said, ''This leaf has died, it no longer eats food. Daddy is like this leaf, remember? He also died. He no longer needs food.''

It's very hard to translate the abstract into concrete terms for the very young child. It takes a lot of repeating.

I think I'd stay away from saying, ''Mommy went to heaven.'' Some children want to join their parent in heaven—right now. I worry when parents tell small children that daddy is ''asleep.'' It can make children afraid to go to sleep. They're afraid they will disappear. Some children feel confused: they're taken to the grave and told daddy is in the ground, and they're also told daddy is in heaven. Now, where is he? A three-year-old heard her mother tell someone, ''I lost my husband,'' and she worried: will her mother also lose her? (Children are *literal*.)

Died. Can't we use the word *died*?

Euphemisms are confusing to children.

What small children really react to, since they can't understand death, is separation. Fortunately, the under-three child reattaches herself to other persons relatively fast. (This might make *you* feel sad—you feel she's forgetting her daddy—but it makes her feel less sad, having someone love her as much as her daddy.)

The Four- and Five-Year-Old

Listen hard when your four- or five-year-old asks questions about death. Usually, the questions show a need for reassurance instead of an intellectual answer—reassurance the death wasn't his fault, that *he* won't die, and that he'll always have someone to take care of him.

If your child's goldfish, turtle, cat, or dog dies, you can have your child participate in the burial, which gives more reality to death in your child's mind. Grieving for the pet, as he buries it, helps him grieve his parent as well.

Anxiety over the death can become acute and show itself in regressive behavior: thumb sucking, bed wetting, bowel incidents, or stammering. Don't try to correct your child, you'll only make him more anxious. Instead, ignore these regressions, for the time being, and give him a lot of loving. In time, regressions will probably reverse themselves.

The Child From Five to Nine

It is during these ages that children finally understand the finality of death. However, they don't relate it to themselves. In their world, death and the finality of death happens only to others.

This is an age when a "memory book" can be of tremendous value. Buy a large scrapbook. With your child, choose snapshots and photographs of your spouse to paste in the scrapbook and include pictures showing child and parent together. Leave room under photographs so you or your child can write a little story about the photograph—where it was taken and what the parent was doing at the time. (Print, for the very young child.) Your son or daughter can even dictate the story as you write.

The "memory book" can be kept in your child's bedroom so he can pick it up and look through it any time, or it can be kept in the living room, so you can look through it together. Going over the stories and pictures allows him opportunities to ask questions and vent his feelings about the death.

If you have your spouse's voice on tape, it can be therapeutic for your child to hear it from time to time (especially if he's talking to his parent on the tape).

The Child Over Ten

After the age of ten, children can better understand the causes of death and that the body actually stops functioning. This is when intellectual explanations can be given as well as emotional reassurances. (Kids over the age of ten enjoy using children's encyclopedias; you can use this tool, with its accompanying pictures, to show the human body and relate it to what happened to your spouse.)

Despite the growing ability to intellectualize and cognitively understand the reasons for the death of a parent, there is still a great deal of difficulty dealing with the actual separation from the mother or father. Some kids can't stand facing the fact of the death, so they don't talk about it.

If your child is able to be open and expressive, you might want to suggest she write a "good-bye letter" or poem and read it at the grave. (Of course, you'll step back and give her the privacy to do this alone; but stay in the background, so she knows you're there for emotional support.)

Good-bye letters are a wonderful way of finishing up unfinished business; it's an effective vehicle for expressing grief, anger, hurt, or anything a child feels. One child wrote, "I wish I would have been there when you died, daddy, instead of being home."

If your child wants to write a good-bye letter, but doesn't want to go to the grave, that's fine. Just writing it can be helpful. (Then your son or daughter might want to read it aloud to you.)

*   *   *

The years before and during adolescence are filled with deep hurt after the death. Some kids can cry, others can't. One mother reported her daughter would deliberately misbehave so she could be punished, and this would give her a "legitimate" reason for tears. (Of course, her tears were for her loss, not the punishment.) Another parent reported his daughter, eleven, would have temper tantrums; she'd lie on the floor, kicking her legs, and wail, "I want my mommy!" He'd sit on the floor beside her, holding her hand, and say, "I know you do. I want mommy, too." He'd stay on the floor beside her, holding her hand, until her sobbing would subside so she'd know he cared.

It's hard to know how to help, isn't it? You hurt for your bereaved child and you try hard to help, but you feel you're not helping enough. Well, what *is* helping enough? Is there ever "enough" after the death? You're doing the best you can, and that's enough.

The Teenager

A teenager is experiencing many changes and losses in his life at the same time he's lost a parent to death. It's a period when there's much inner turmoil. Self-consciousness makes it difficult for him to appear different to his friends, and teenagers *are* different if a parent has died.

The loneliness every teenager feels is accentuated by the death.

It is during the adolescent years that the recognition of one's own impending death becomes real for the first time. The fifteen-year-old's mortality hits her with a sudden hard bang and this can be terrifying. Fortunately, her healthy defenses go up quickly where she denies (as we all do!) and she has a reprieve (as we all do) until the next time her mortality confronts her. Being hit for the first time with her own mortality is difficult enough, but since it's happening at the same time her mother dies, it's devastating.

School performance often drops. Girls sometimes turn to sexual relationships for comfort and a sense of connection to another person. Boys become afraid of crying over the death in front of other persons. Idealization of the deceased parent sometimes happens. The leftover anger at the dead parent is often transferred to the surviving parent as the child feels too guilty to remain angry at the parent who has died.

A mother may turn to her son for her own comfort: he's taller than she is, his voice is now deeper, and he's worried about her, so she translates this into viewing him as the adult who can give solace. He can't. He is still a child. The father may inadvertently turn to his teenage daughter for comfort; she looks like her mother so she gives the illusion of adulthood and nurturing. However, she's a child and she needs the nurturing.

If there's a support group for adolescents who have lost a parent to death in your area, consider it a valuable resource. Being in that group will help your teenager. It will allow him to feel more normal, and it will give him an opportunity to meet other children in the same circumstances. He won't feel so alone. He'll also learn better coping skills.

And consider using rituals for comfort. There are the traditional rituals following a death, where you can include your child, and there are creative rituals you can develop. One father designed his own ritual for himself and his daughter. Several months after the death of his wife, he and his daughter chose a small tree to plant in their backyard as a memorial. After he brought the tree home, he suggested they plant it in front of the breakfast room window, where they could watch it grow through the years. Every time it blooms, they drink to "the tree"—he drinks champagne and she drinks club soda. It's their way of saluting the memory of her mother and his wife.

The Child Over Eighteen

Because many grown children are busy with their own lives (they're away at college or they're living on their own, building careers, or they may be newly married, building their own families) one might assume they are not grieving as hard as their parent. It's true they might have more diversions in their lives, but that does not mean they are not grieving hard.

Some grown children are overwhelmed; they're trying to cope with their own *and* their parent's grief. One twenty-year-old man said, "I feel guilty about moving out of the house now that mom is alone, but I *want* to move. I'm angry because I can't. I just got out of community college and I want to go away to finish college, but how can I? She's dependent on me. She expects me to always be with her, to stay home a lot. I'm angry about that, and I also feel guilty because I'm angry."

One grown child who is married said, "My husband tries to protect me from my mother's demands since my father died. He tells her I'm asleep when she calls late at night. I'm grateful for that, because I do feel put upon and exhausted from trying to comfort her, but I also feel guilty. I should be there for her."

Are you asking more of your grown children than you used to? Should you? Can you? How much can you ask?

I think you want to avoid reversing your roles: putting them in the parent role while you become the child.

You'll find something paradoxical happening. The less you ask for, the more you'll get.

Do as much as you can for yourself. Try to understand, they are in pain from their loss, and they have the large task of working through their own grief. And allowing yourself to become emotionally dependent on them will make you feel *more* helpless.

*　　　*　　　*

Some older children find the pain of the death so crippling that they literally flee the scene of the death. Some leave college in the middle of the term and go away as far as possible. Others join cults. Some simply go off, with or without a note, and you don't know where they've gone. This is called "flight syndrome."

Of course you're very upset about this. How can you not be? You're confused and you feel guilty and you're bitter and angry. Think about getting professional help for yourself, in order to sort out your upset and mixed feelings. Try at least to stay in minimal touch with your child and let him know you're always available, no matter what he's done or how he feels. Say, "I'm here for you, whenever you want to talk or visit." Many children do eventually return to some kind of relationship with their surviving parent, either through phone calls or visits or both. Try hard not to take what has happened as a personal attack: it's really a reflection of your child's very deep and private pain.

I've talked about kids who find the pressure of helping a parent through grief too much to cope with and I've talked about grown children who must flee. However, I haven't mentioned the children who have mustered the emotional strength to deal with their own grief as well as their parent's. If you're that lucky to have a child that intact, be glad. (But avoid blaming the other kind of child!)

Different Kinds of Death Affect the Way a Child Grieves

Children of all ages find it easier (not easy!) to deal with an anticipated death than a sudden one.

Violent death is a crisis for the entire family, including the children. Many bereavement specialists feel that suicide is the most difficult death of all, because the child inevitably feels so rejected.

Some persons were mentally ill before they killed themselves, and there is often a shameful feeling of relief after the death because trying to cope with the irrational behavior of the person caused so much tension. It's normal to feel this relief.

If there were repeated attempts at suicide, the child lived in an atmosphere of terror.

There is tremendous rage. The suicide is perceived as a deliberate leaving, that the parent didn't love the child enough to stay. Shame is felt because of the social taboos around suicide. The neighbors, the relatives—they're shocked and then sometimes blaming.

Often a child blames himself for the suicide. If he was repeatedly told before the death, "Be quiet! You'll upset your mother," and then the mother killed herself, he may silently berate himself. There's more feeling of shame if the surviving parent acts ashamed, or makes up a story that indicates a different kind of death. ("My husband had a heart attack," or "My wife had an accident in the bathtub.") Sometimes doctors conspire in this cover-up, in order to "protect" the family.

And how does a child answer the question, "Why did your mother do that?"

Children and adults who are suicide survivors need support groups especially for suicide survivors. (See the back of this book for listings.)

Trauma hits hard when a child is a murder survivor. I remember an eleven-year-old boy who was watching TV on a Saturday morning, alone in the house, when the news flashed on the screen: he not only heard about the murder of his mother, he saw her body, covered, being taken away.

If your child is a suicide or murder survivor, please seek

professional counseling for your family. Family therapy will give you the support you need at this terrible time and will help you and your child understand each other's feelings. You'll learn how to handle your child's distress at a time when you're feeling like you can't handle anything, and that will give you some feeling of control over your life.

Reaching Out to Your Children When You Feel You Can't Reach Out

How does a person whose life has been shattered by death pick herself up and be a capable single caretaker for a grieving child? It is very hard.

Your energy level is low. Your patience wears thin. Your preoccupation with yourself is so overpowering that you can't see outside of yourself to see your child—at least in the first months after the death.

Please ask everyone in your life to help. Your kids can use the attention and caring of your clergy person, doctor, family, friends, neighbors, scout leaders, teachers, guidance counselors, and in-laws. Say to a neighbor, "My son is pretty lonely since his father's death. Do you mind taking him when you take your son bowling on Wednesday nights?" Ask the scout leader, "Can you get my daughter a scholarship to girl scout camp this summer? My income has dropped since my husband died, and she needs to be with other girls." Say to your sister, "The death has been so hard on the kids, would you take them to lunch occasionally?"

You can't do it all by yourself. Ask for help directly. In most cases, you'll get it.

6. Single Parenting

A school in an affluent suburb held an after-school discussion group for children of divorce and children who had lost a parent to death. The counselor who led the group said, ''There are big differences between the two groups of children. The ones whose parents are divorced can still talk about what they're doing with the noncustodial parent— where they go together, and what the relationship between them is like. The kids whose parent has died—they withdraw. They don't say much when they're with those other kids.''

A woman I hadn't seen for several years told me, ''Remember that couple who lived on the end of our block? Well, he died several months ago. I asked my daughter, Heidi, to reach out to their child. Heidi is her age but Jenny won't talk to her about her father's death or how she feels. I was sure she'd open up with Heidi. After all, Heidi went through a lot when I got divorced. They have so much in common.''

There *are* big differences between the child of divorce and the child whose parent has died. The child of divorce may have a weekend daddy, or a mother who writes and visits even though she doesn't have custody. The background sounds of a child of divorce could be the bickering of the two parents over visitation and custody and alimony and child support, but there are two parents. The child of divorce knows other children like herself—divorce is so common. The child of a parent who has died knows few or no kids like herself. The child of divorce will feel tension in the house—there's a great deal of tension following the separation—but if it was her mother who left and she feels powerful and in control of her life because she was able to leave, there could also be laughter and pleasure in the house. The child of death awakens to gloomy silences and hears muffled crying.

We cannot compare these two groups of children. I hope, someday, all schools throughout the country will offer discussion and support groups for each. Separately.

Your Feelings As a Widowed Single Parent

You not only have to deal with your own feelings over your loss, you have the huge task of dealing with the feelings of your grieving child. You also have to do all of the parenting by yourself, which is a lonely and exhausting task that never seems to end. Self-pity and anger as well as resentment are feelings single parents report, especially widowed persons. "I love my kids but I feel overwhelmed and I'm often mad," a woman said. It's a long difficult job, single parenting.

Sharing your feelings with other parents in the same boat helps. This is a function of a widowed persons support group, where many parents can be found.

Respite from child care is important to your mental health. I'm not suggesting you act like Stephan, who went out every night and left his kids with a baby-sitter. He justified this by saying, "If I'm not happy I can't make the children happy, and I have to get out of this house every night in order to stay glued together." I am suggesting you establish an adult world along with your child-inhabited world. This can mean leaving your children with your parents once a week, while you go out with friends. It can mean hiring a baby-sitter one night a week. If you have money problems and can't afford baby-sitters you can join your neighborhood baby-sitting co-op, where you baby-sit for each other at no cost. If you don't have a co-op, you can start one by merely putting a notice up at the corner drugstore or in the apartment house laundry room. (It can read, "Mother with five-year-old wants to organize small group where we'll baby-sit for each other. Call———for more information.") Another idea? If you have an extra bedroom you're not using, consider calling your local college (call the dean's office) and offer your room to a responsible student in exchange for baby-sitting. (No, you don't have to cook or clean for her. You don't even have to change her bed linen. This is a time when you're very tired and you don't want to take on the task of taking care of other adults.)

Feelings of guilt and inadequacy are common to single parents after the death. They're expressed in thoughts like these:

"If I hadn't let him work so hard he wouldn't have had the heart attack and the kids would still have a father."

"I can't do it all by myself, I'm not up to taking care of the children. When they talk to me I don't hear. I'm going through the motions of being a parent like a robot. I'm not a good father."

Children, however, are resilient. If they feel loved, they can survive almost anything. Reach out and touch them. Tell them how much they mean to you.

They might get scared when they see you cry or withdraw. Make it a point of letting them know that you're not going to have a breakdown just because you're crying, that crying makes you feel better. Give yourself a "private time," a time when you go into your bedroom by yourself. Let the kids know you need private time and that between the hours of three and five in the afternoon mommy isn't available unless it's an emergency. Allowing yourself this private time is another respite from child care, and it gives you a time to be preoccupied with your own feelings, not the feelings of your kids.

Even though you're feeling empty and sluggish, try to maintain family schedules (except for your private time and your time out of the house with adults). Children need the steadying influence of continuity. It might be tempting to burrow beneath the blankets in the mornings to forget what happened to your life and let the kids fend for themselves for breakfast, but don't give in to this temptation. They need the reassurance and comfort of knowing you still get up and call "Breakfast!" That you still sit with them while they're eating and talk about their school day.

You can maintain family schedules and cut down some of the physical work (which is important, since you're low in energy). Continue the Sunday dinners, but serve fewer courses or cook simpler recipes. Have the kids pitch in and help cook, serve, and clean up. (Children want to be close after the death. Sharing household tasks brings parents and children closer.)

Later, as the months go by, you can attempt to *replace* some of the familiar schedules if they feel overwhelming. Suggest Sunday dinner at a restaurant. Tell them, "Kids, we're going to have pizza tonight. Mom's not cooking!" The key word is *replace*. An immediate replacement will give them reassurance.

You can even make them part of the decision-making process, as Ricky did. "Look, kids," she said, "I'm beat from all this chauffeuring and working full time and cleaning and cooking, and we need to see where I can cut down some of the work. Let's talk about what's important for us to continue without any changes and what we can modify or change. Who wants to talk first?" After several discussions with shouting and yelling and laughing, it was mutually decided that going out for ice cream on Sunday evenings had to be continued, but Chinese takeout was fine for Saturday nights so mom wouldn't have to cook. That bowling on Wednesday evenings had to continue, but the kids would be responsible for having supper ready when mom got home from work.

Don't feel guilty about giving them chores. Feeling *bad* for your kids is understandable. Guilt is irrational. Guilt gets in the way of good parenting. "My father died when I was twelve," a woman said, "and my mother was so depressed she slept most of the time. *I* was the one who had to take care of the younger kids and do the housework and cooking. Now that I'm widowed I'll never do what my mother did to me. *My* children's lives won't be changed in any way."

This is guilt speaking, isn't it? Her children's lives have been changed, she has no control over this (as her life has been changed). If she allows her children to know her feelings about the death, and if she encourages teamwork in the family—all of them sharing chores—it will bring the family closer. Of course she's not going to dump all the responsibilities on them, as her mother unfortunately did with her, but bringing them into the decision making that's necessary on an everyday level after the death and giving them a sense of responsibility about their home will be good for the kids. She'll be giving them a feeling of control over their lives. They will not be passive, they'll be active members of the family, and that's what will give them a feeling of control at a time in their lives when they've lost control.

Who was the disciplinarian in your family before the death? If it was your spouse, you may now feel inadequate in that role. "I get terrible headaches after I have to holler at them," a woman said. "I hate being the bad guy," a father said. "Then they get angry at me and life is so hard right now that I just can't take their anger."

Are you feeling intimidated by your kids? "I had always left the punishing up to my husband," a woman told me, "and here I was, suddenly having to take on this new role of the stern parent. I felt self-pity. I felt life just isn't fair. Well, I finally came to the conclusion that life *isn't* fair or my husband wouldn't have died at the age of forty-four. That's when I stopped the self-pity and I got on with my job as their mother. And that included being the disciplinarian." (And I'm sure her kids feel more secure, now that she's no longer intimidated.)

You may never have been the one to say "no" to your children (your spouse did). But now you're thrust in that role. And there are times when you need to say no. Your lowered income might now mean no more designer jeans for your daughter; if she wants designer jeans she'll have to earn some of the money herself. When your son pleads with you to change your mind about grounding him, it's important to be able to say no. The secret to saying "no" without discomfort is saying it firmly, not changing your mind once you've said it, and avoiding big discussions on why you said no. (They already know why.)

Most single-parent widows and widowers worry. Can they make it as single parents? Will their children make it? Take one hour at a time. Take one day at a time. Easy does it. These time-tested rules work.

The Child With Special Problems

Most kids get through the death intact, even though they suffer. Some children, however, become self-destructive. These are the kids who turn to drugs, vandalism, shoplifting, or drinking. If you have a child who is doing any of these things, of course you'll get professional help for him. But you'll need help, too. Your feelings and your life—everything's in turmoil, isn't it? You don't know how to stop your child and when to turn your back on what's happening (be-

73

cause that's what you're sometimes tempted to do, life is so difficult). You question your own behavior: are you sitting on him too hard, as he says you are? Or are you too soft, as your sister insists? And you're full of guilt feelings—if the death hadn't happened, he wouldn't have turned into a kid who makes trouble, you tell yourself.

Sit in on a meeting of Toughlove. It's a national organization with chapters in many cities for parents who have troubled children who are acting out. It's an organization that helps parents make decisions about what behavior they won't accept from their teenagers and to stick to these decisions, no matter how hard. For more information, write or call:

Toughlove
P. O. Box 1069
Doylestown, Pennsylvania 18901
Ph: (215) 348-7090

You need a lot of support during this time. I know you're feeling apathetic. It's hard to go for help, but make yourself get it. It will make life more bearable.

Informing School Personnel About the Death

It's very important that you tell your children's teachers about the death. Also inform the school principal, the school nurse, and the guidance counselor. This will allow all school personnel to be more sensitive to your child's needs.

When next fall comes and school is ready to open, inform those new teachers, too. Grieving takes a long time.

Schools are usually oriented toward the two-parent household. Class discussions are often centered around the premise that there are two parents. Before Mother's Day and Father's Day, teachers may ask the kids to make gifts or cards. Schools sponsor father-son and mother-daughter events. All of this can make your child feel lonely and alienated. Active intervention, on your part, is important. Call the teacher and inquire, "Can my daughter bring her aunt, instead, to the mother-daughter banquet?" Tell the teacher, "My son is going to feel terrible if you ask the kids to make cards for Mother's Day. I know it's two months from now, and that's why I'm calling you ahead of time, to see if there's an alternative you want to consider. Can we think of something?"

Caring school personnel want to be sensitive to your child's changed needs, but you have to at least let them know about the death. Don't assume they already know, just because you live in a small community. And don't expect your child to tell them. It's too big and painful a task for a child.

Are You Comparing Your Child and Your Spouse?

"Your father was ambitious!" a woman screamed at her teenage son after the death. (Her son didn't want to go to college.)

A man looked at his daughter in her jeans and shirt. "Your mother was so feminine," he said. "Can't you be more ladylike, like she was?"

Comparisons hurt children. Many kids tend to think of the deceased parent as perfect, and when they hear how they're not measuring up in comparison, their self-esteem suffers.

Perhaps *you* need help in separating your son from his father or your daughter from her mother. If your teenager looks exactly like your spouse and has the same gestures, it might be difficult for you to separate the two of them in your mind. Think about this.

It's very important that children of all ages be encouraged to build their own identity. This makes them feel more valuable.

*   *   *

Kids whose deceased parent was well-known in the community or nationally have a particularly hard time, because the grieving is prolonged through concrete ongoing reminders. There may be annual ceremonies, commemorating the death. The surviving parent might continue to represent the deceased spouse at official and formal functions, or make the home a shrine to the deceased parent: framed letters on the wall from other well-known persons; trophies, awards, and photographs of the deceased shaking hands with other dignitaries. But even if this isn't the case, strangers as well as friends constantly say things like, "Oh, you look just like your father!" People often expect the son to *be* like his father, and a celebrated act is hard to follow. You need to let your child know verbally that his separateness is respected. That you value his unique and special qualities and that you don't expect him to be a replica of his father or live up to the community's expectations.

There is another difficult situation: the parents who were in difficult marriages and unconsciously sabotage their children. A woman watched her son carefully after the death to see that he didn't drink. "Your father was a drunk," she often told him, "and I won't have you turn out like him." She would suspiciously grill him after he'd come home from a party: "You didn't drink anything, did you?"

Her son felt battered from her negative expectations. He'd sulk or he'd yell at her, and he'd feel guilty when he did. His yelling would accelerate her anxiety, and she'd act out more of her negative expectations. A nonproductive unending circle, and the mother never did realize what she was doing to him.

Then there was the recently widowed woman who sat in her living room with me and her son. She was red eyed from crying. "He ran around from the day we got married," she said, oblivious of the fact that her twelve-year-old boy was

glaring at her. "He had an affair with his secretary and she had the nerve to come to the funeral!"

Your deceased spouse may have been an alcoholic, an absent father, a compulsive gambler, or a womanizer—it doesn't matter to your children now that he's dead; they're torn with conflicting feelings of anger, loyalty to each of you, love for both of you, and more anger. You don't realize it, but you are increasing your children's conflicted and pained feelings by openly airing your anger at your spouse, and by talking about his failings. I know you don't want to increase your children's pain. Seek professional counseling for yourself, where you'll have an appropriate place in which to vent your upset feelings; a person to whom you can talk without having your kids included; a setting where you may even be able to resolve some of these feelings and become more comfortable yourself.

Relating to Your Son After His Father Has Died

Relating appropriately to your opposite-sex child isn't always easy. Mothers often feel anxious about this. Here's what you want to avoid:

- Making your son "the man of the house" isn't fair. He's too young for all of that responsibility.
- Asking him to be the disciplinarian to the younger children also puts too much responsibility on him. It can shape his personality in ways I know you don't want: the child who prematurely assumes taking care of others internalizes a "stern parent" personality and grows up to be an adult who is full of shoulds and oughts. An adult who is rigid in his expectations and relationships.
- You want to be his mother, not his girl friend. Don't ask him to light your cigarettes or get your drinks. Respect his right not to be physically touched; most teenage boys

have conflicting feelings about being touched by their mothers (they're unconsciously aware of potential sexual arousal). Ask yourself: "Am I flirting with him, even subtly?"

A man whose mother was widowed when he was sixteen remembered, "I felt angry when she flirted with me. I felt she was betraying my dad. I felt she was being unfair to me. I felt sexually aroused and that made me feel guilty. I was one confused teenager."

Bring males into his life who are willing to be part-time parent surrogates. It provides role modeling, companionship for your son, and it gives you some private time. Grandfathers and uncles and friends of the family are appropriate persons, if they're nurturing men. Scout leaders are sometimes willing. These men should be males your son looks up to and wants to copy. They can be men in whom your son confides. Many surrogate fathers have sons of their own; what they do in their role as a surrogate parent is include your son in their family activities. How do you get a responsible, caring man to take on this role? Ask him! Reassure him it won't be a full-time demanding role. This is a flattering request: you'll usually find a positive response.

(Think twice, though, before you ask your new boyfriend to take on this role: your son may feel threatened by your relationship.)

Relating to Your Daughter Now That Her Mother Has Died

As a father, relating to your daughter can be complex. Traditional men sometimes put their daughters in "the little housewife" role. If you were in a role-defined marriage where your wife stayed home and cooked and cleaned, you may unconsciously expect your daughter to assume this role because *females* do these chores. Or because you don't have these skills and your daughter does. There are pitfalls: she's using a great deal of psychic and physical energy grieving, and she has to use a lot of time doing schoolwork. Without realizing it, you may be asking too much of her.

Taking on "the little housewife" role can feed into fantasies of wife replacement. I observed a teenage girl scolding her widowed father for not staying on his diet, and, having known the family before, I was able to see a re-enacted scene: the daughter was using the same words and body language her mother used! Was she feeling like his wife instead of his child? If she was, it was inappropriate and unhealthy. Her father had innocently set her up, though. She never would have assumed the role or the expectations if he hadn't put her in the kitchen wearing her mother's apron (literally!) and cooking her mother's recipes.

Sharing household tasks is another story. It's legitimate to expect all of your kids, boys and girls, to help in the house. Why can't boys learn to bake? Why can't girls do outside work in the garden—the hoeing and mowing? It's good for children's self-esteem when they know they can tackle all kinds of chores, and that chores aren't sex related.

How to comfort your daughter is an important question. Taking her into your bed. Well, I know that if you're doing this, it's with the best intentions: to quell her fears and to reassure her that she still has a loving parent. You may even find yourself comforted by having her so near. But it's *not* the same as when you and your wife took her into your bed to romp on Sunday mornings when she was only two. Whether she's four or eight, sexual feelings can be aroused. Comfort can be given, instead, by holding her in a rocking chair; by sitting by her bed, reading a bedtime story; or by just sitting nearby while she plays and you read.

Surrogate mothers help. A caring aunt can tell your teenage daughter about birth control. A sister-in-law can take your daughter shopping for her first bra. Your mother can spend time with your preschooler. (She can teach her how to make Jell-O and she can do a lot of hugging and touching and kissing and loving.)

Surrogate parents help reconstruct family life. The "normal" family consists of a mother and a father, and now that your child is no longer part of a normal family, she's lonely. Of course the introduction of the surrogate parent into your child's life doesn't actually make a new family, but it gives the illusion of a reconstructed whole family, and that can give a great deal of comfort.

Learn About Child Development—It Can Help

You'll find it reassuring to learn that your child is developing normally at this time, even though he's undergone a massive trauma by the loss of his parent.

Reading about grief and how it affects children can help. Reading about child development can help. This doesn't mean you'll open a book on child development, read what the normal five-year-old is able to do, and literally expect your five-year-old to be able to do exactly the same. Motor control varies depending on the individual child. Social development is dependent on many variables: the sex of the child, what birth order your child is in, the cultural and economic conditions of your family life, and your level of anxiety at this time. Also, your child might have regressed because of the death; it's not unusual that a three-year-old revert back to bowel accidents, that a six-year-old starts to cling, and that an eight-year-old begins to whine.

But reading about child development can give you a useful and general guide on what to expect later, and that can be very reassuring to a single parent.

An example: the "terrible twos." If your baby is eighteen

months old, and you're reading about the terrible twos, you won't be upset, later, when your two-year old says "no" at least ten times a day and is resistant to every suggestion. You'll understand that she's acting out conflicting needs of dependence and independence through her behavior, and that it's not only normal, it's healthy. You won't start feeling guilty: "She's acting this way because of the death!"

If you have teenagers, ask your librarian for the titles of good books on child development that focus on adolescence. Kids suddenly make a leap from pleasant little girls and boys to demanding, angry teenagers with stony expressions, who seem to hate you. (Adolescents are dealing with a stormy time of their lives as well as their grieving, and that is very hard for them and you.) Books can be of help.

Be Kind to Yourself

You're taking your children through the rites of passage alone—if you have very small children, from infancy to puberty to adolescence. Maybe you'll remarry and have some help. Maybe you won't. But right now you're doing it all by yourself and you deserve a bunch of red roses, delivered every day, and self-affirmation. Tell yourself, "I'm doing a very good job, even if it's not perfect."

Ways to be kind to yourself: don't center your entire life around your children, leave some time and energy just for yourself; don't become dependent on your kids.

And slowly learn to let them go. That way, when they reach the age when they pack the suitcases and go away to college, you won't be left with the empty-house blues. Well, maybe a couple of weeks of the blues, but then the nice feeling that you now have time to nurture yourself and become the person you never had time to become before.

I wish I could send you that bunch of red roses every day. As a single parent, you deserve it.

7. Changing Family Relationships

There were eight of them, in this group of widowed women and men in their twenties, thirties, and early forties. We were sitting in my living room, talking about how relationships with their families have changed.

"In the four years I was married, I never talked to my mother as much as I do now," Alison said dryly. "She never misses a morning. When the phone rings at eight every morning I know it's my mother. And the conversation is always the same."

"Tell us," I said.

"Okay, it starts this way. 'Alison, are you up?' If she awakened me, which is usually the case because I'm not sleeping well since my husband died, I say 'Mom, if I wasn't up I'm obviously up now.' Then she says, 'What are you doing?' What would I be doing at eight in the morning? Then she says, 'What are you going to do today?' I tell her, and I get the editorial comments: 'Alison, why are you having lunch with Bernice? She's so much older than you, she can't introduce you to anyone,' and 'Alison, tell your hairdresser not to cut it so short this time, you look like a prison matron when it's too short in the back.' "

Charlene, a blonde who looks like a cheerleader, said, "I like it when my mom calls every day. We're very close."

Alison started to say something, her cheeks were flushed, and, instead, she looked at her nails. Sherry, sitting next to her, noticed her discomfiture and sympathetically touched her arm. "I bet you had your own apartment before you got married," she said. "This is a new thing to you, having your mother in your life again, isn't it?" Alison nodded. Charlene sounded pleased as she said, "They couldn't *kick* me out. I lived at home 'til I got married."

Alison's ambivalence toward her mother isn't surprising. She left home at the age of eighteen to go to drama school, and even though she returned to the city to work after graduation, she was on her own; she lived with two other actresses until she got married. Her contact with her mother during her marriage had been limited. Phone calls a couple of times a week, and occasional visits back and forth. Now that her mother is calling every day, asking personal questions, and giving advice, she feels like a child again. At the same time, she's vulnerable—her husband has just died, acting jobs are irregular, she's living by herself—and she needs nurturing.

Younger widowed persons need the support of their families, and parents don't always know how to give it. Sometimes they're overprotective, and other times they're interfering. Some do worry about how to balance caring with necessary distancing—how to establish and maintain an adult-to-adult relationship. It's hard.

"My mother acts like I'm not capable of being a parent," said Fred, a thirty-eight-year-old accountant who's attractive in a solemn way, wearing rimless glasses and a careful haircut. "She calls me every evening after I've put my daughter to bed. 'What did you give her for supper?'; 'How's her rash, what are you doing about it?''; and 'Is she still sneezing? Is she wearing warm pajamas?' No one believes a man can be a capable single parent."

"Oh, no!" exclaimed Ginny, an executive secretary who always wore dark glasses to the group because she didn't want people to know when she was crying. "Being a man has nothing to do with it. My mother's insisting I move back home just because I've been widowed. All of a sudden, in her eyes, I'm helpless. Come home, you'll have all the privacy you want, she says. Every night you'll come home from work to a hot cooked meal, she says. You'll have a free baby-sitter, she promises. Who's knocking at my door that I need to go out? The only place I go is here and work.'' She flicked the ash of her cigarette in the ashtray. "No," she said to Fred. "It's not because you're a man, believe me."

A woman said wistfully, "I wish my parents would give me all that attention."

"No, you don't," another woman said. "You'd go crazy. You'd feel like a dependent child."

"I wouldn't. I'd keep my independence."

"You can't have it both ways. We're either on our own or we aren't."

I asked the woman who had sounded wistful: "Has your relationship with your parents changed at all since the death?"

She thought. Someone poured a cup of tea from the pot. The air conditioner hummed. She answered, "My parents own an employment agency. My mother was always a busi-nesswoman, first and foremost. She never was a cook or a housekeeper or even a mother—I mean a mother in the tra-ditional sense. The housekeeper took care of me when I was sick."

"I'm sure she loves me," she added, leaning back against the sofa pillows. "It's just that she's a tough business-woman, that's her whole world. *She* made the agency the big-gest one in the city."

I asked, "How has she been with you, now that you're alone?"

There was resentment in her voice. "If anything, she's less accessible. Sometimes I get the feeling she's afraid I'll ask her for something, or that I'll become dependent on her.''

When no one said anything, she softly said, her voice trailing, ''She loves me, I'm sure.''

After the group left, I thought: nothing stays the same in life, and this also goes for family relationships. As a member of a family changes through loss, the family changes in its behavior. The equilibrium of the family has been disturbed. The tension the widowed person feels affects every other family member. Some parents change in ways that are helpful. A mother learns how to touch—she now hugs her daughter frequently. A father now talks about his feelings to his son and asks him about *his* feelings. When parents do become overprotective or interfering, it's because their anxiety level has been raised by the death. The woman in the group who's wistful—her mother *does* feel threatened; she never learned to be a mother, and now she's terrified. Will she be expected to be someone or something she's not? How parents react can also depend on the culture in which they live: some ethnic families expect a widowed daughter to wear black until she remarries, and their expectations, if not met, can become loud demands.

Overprotective Parents

Are you sending your parents signals, ''I can't take care of myself,'' and ''Take care of me like you did when I was little''? Courting protection courts overprotection—there's such a fine line. ''What's wrong with expecting some protection?'' a woman asked. Nothing. *If* they're able emotionally to give it and not cross that fine line. ''What's the difference between protection and overprotection?'' that same woman asked.

Protection means giving you emotional space and privacy

while they're quietly keeping an eye on you, to see if you're okay. It means offering options, instead of telling you what to do—and, even then, offering options only when you ask. It means not being judgmental. It also means offering concrete help if you're having trouble functioning. (Financial help, if you're out of work and they can afford it, is one kind of concrete help.)

Overprotection? That's when parents constantly probe your innermost thoughts, or call you several times a day; when they push you to date or remarry; when they tell you how to raise your child; also, when they tell you it's time to stop crying.

If they are overprotective, take new small steps to care for yourself. When you see yourself succeeding it will give you the self-confidence to take larger steps.

1. Stop sharing every thought and feeling with your parents. Children do this, because they haven't yet separated themselves from their mothers and fathers. Adults retain much of their privacy, because, through the years, they've developed a sense of self.
2. Trust your own decisions. If you're anxiously asking your mother what she would do, and you're asking frequently, stop. The worst that can happen? You'll make a wrong decision. However, most decisions are reversible.
3. Learn how to take physical care of yourself and your child. Women *can* fix leaky faucets, with the aid of a simple manual. Men *can* nurse sick children, with the advice of the pediatrician.

Overprotection from parents is common after the death of a spouse, but it's usually not deliberate or even conscious. Most parents mean well. They just don't realize how they're behaving, or that their behavior weakens self-confidence.

Moving Back Home

Sometimes, just sometimes, moving back home is a financial necessity. But it's risky. Your parent's home can become an emotional womb, where you're seduced into snuggling in closer, donning your Doctor Denton's, and weakly calling, "Mamma." I'm being facetious, but moving back home does mean adhering to your parents' rules, adjusting to their idiosyncracies, and being viewed again as a child. After all, it is their house.

Their rules: how are they going to react when you stay out all night? And if you're not doing that and wouldn't do it anyway, will you be expected to be home at a certain hour?

Their idiosyncracies: have you forgotten how crazy-clean your mother is; how she went out of her mind when you didn't use a coaster? How your father lectures? You, also, have idiosyncracies. We all do, but it's easier living with our own instead of other people's.

How will you be viewed as a child? Scenario: your friend is visiting, and your mother pokes her head through the door, "I have some freshly baked apple cake for you!" (Aren't you saying that to *your* child?) Or, she asks before you leave the house, "What time will you be home, dear?"

Re-creating the family home is re-creating the family roles. It's difficult to avoid.

Having Your Parent Move In With You

Michael, whose wife had recently died, was left with two children, a ten-year-old daughter and a seven-year-old son. His mother is a widow who lives across the country. "She's telling me she's ready to retire from her office job, so it would be easy for her to move in with us. She says my kids need her, that we're probably eating garbage food, and that the house must be a mess," said Michael.

87

I asked, "What was your relationship with her when you were younger?"

Michael scratched his head and grinned. "Well," he said, "I must say she doted on me. I'm the only son. I guess I sort of liked getting more attention than my sisters."

I suggested a trial period, since Michael was so tempted. That he have her visit for the summer, with the mutual understanding that they wait and see how the visit goes before making any commitment to permanent change.

The first week was perfect. Grandma cooked her delicious pot roast and it had been a long time since the last pot roast. She taught her granddaughter how to crochet a scarf. She played Fish with her grandson every day. She even said, "Go out already, Michael. You've been in the house with me every night. Go out, and I'll baby-sit."

The second week—that's when grandma became critical. "The children's manners are atrocious!" she fussed. "This house is full of dust. How come you keep that cleaning woman? She's watching soap operas instead of cleaning."

The prying began shortly after that. "Michael," she told him one evening after he got home from work, "a woman called you a little while ago. She said her name is Sheila. Who's this Sheila? She sounds older than you! Is she divorced, or what?"

The climax came a week later. Grandma threw a temper tantrum because Michael announced Sheila was coming to dinner on Sunday. "I won't have a strange woman in this house, so soon after the death," she exploded. "I'm not cooking for a woman who's ten years older than you and who's divorced with a grown child!" She warned, "Michael, I won't be here if she comes, I promise you."

The next day Michael firmly told her it wouldn't work if she moved in with them. He loves her, the kids love her, but . . .

*　　　*　　　*

88

On the other hand, there was Jerome, who installed his mother in the carriage house on his grounds. That worked very well. She had her privacy. He had his. Every evening, they ate dinner together—she, and Jerome with his children. She did the cooking, and Jerome and the kids cleaned up after dinner. That's the only time they spent together, the evenings and occasional weekends. Daytimes, Jerome's mother built her own life. She joined a senior center, and she became active in a church group. They had intimacy at a distance and nurturing when needed. Grandmother is present at all holiday dinners, she's there when the children have birthday parties, but they respect her right to change that, too. (Who knows, Jerome's mother might meet an interesting man who takes up all her time.)

Meanwhile, she is a surrogate mother for the children.

Sometimes parents are no problem, and it's the grown child who is. You know if you're the one who starts most of the arguments, or if *you* are critical.

But it really doesn't matter who's difficult. The important thing is knowing whether or not you'll enjoy living under the same roof and whether you can retain your independence and adulthood if you do.

How Do Your Parents Expect You to Grieve?

I asked the members of the younger widowed persons group that met in my living room how their parents expect them to grieve.

Alison: "She thinks if I don't talk about my husband I'll keep my mind off my loss. She says all this crying isn't good for me."

(Translation: Alison's mother is uncomfortable with open signs of grieving. *She* wants to avoid talking about the death, so she wants her daughter to avoid the subject.)

Fred: "My mother expects me to fall apart, maybe even have a breakdown. I can tell, she's so anxious about me."

(Translation: Fred's mother suffers from acute anxiety. She cannot cope with crisis, so she projects—she assumes her son can't.)

Ginny: "My mother is angry because I want to start dating. I want to meet someone. I can't understand her anger. And yet she says she'll baby-sit!"

(Translation: Ginny's mother never dated after she was widowed at the age of forty. She avoided relationships because she really doesn't like men. She wants her daughter to be a mirror image of herself, to validate her own feelings. But it's even more complicated. She denies all of this—these are her subconscious needs and feelings—and, instead, has this self-image of the mother who *does* want her child to date and remarry. Her anger is a reflection of subconscious wishes.)

Your parents' expectations reflect their own needs, so if you're not grieving the way they want you to, tell yourself, *"I am a separate person from my parents."*

Are They Pressuring You to Remarry?

Your parents grew up at a time when marriage seemed the permanent answer to everything: enough money, a lifetime companion, respectable sex, children, and visibility in the community. It's no wonder if they're pressuring you to date and eventually remarry. Also, they worry about your children: they want them in a two-parent home, and you can understand that. Or your remarriage might mean they come out looking better: if you're desirable enough to land someone, it means they were successful parents.

Do you feel like they're loading a guilt trip on you as inadequate because no one is interested in you and that means you've failed your parents and yourself? Do you feel they're betraying the memory of your wife or husband by pushing you to remarry?

If the answer is "yes" to either question, tell your parents, "I know you love me and you're concerned about me, but I'm uncomfortable with your expectations. Let's not talk about this anymore, please." If they act defensive, don't address the defensiveness; instead, repeat what you've already said. If that doesn't work, change the subject. After you've cut that conversation short enough times, they'll no longer bring up the topic because there's no payoff for them.

Try not to internalize their expectations. Their hopes don't have to become your expectations.

Parents-in-Law

If you're fortunate you have a good relationship with your parents-in-law. They'll be a significant part of your support system. However, even good relationships can change after the death. They may feel betrayed when you start dating— after all, it was their daughter or son. They may be afraid they'll lose their grandchildren if you remarry.

It's the unusual parents-in-law who experience no mixed feelings and no fears when you finally "let go" of your deceased husband or wife (their child) and reinvest yourself in a new person.

Also, they're grieving while you're grieving, and this can be complicated.

Take Sarah, for instance. She sat in my office, tears welling. She searched for a tissue in her pocketbook and I handed her the box on my desk.

"When I knew my in-laws were coming in for the holidays I was so glad!" she gulped. "I was looking forward to their visit, I wanted to talk about my husband, I wanted to hear what he had been like when he was a little boy."

There was a silence while she tried to contain herself. Then she said in a mournful voice, "My father-in-law didn't mention Jimmy, not even once. When I would talk about him, he would turn away. My mother-in-law would put her finger to her lips, shushing me. When he wasn't in the room, she warned me not to mention Jimmy. She said her husband couldn't take it. But I couldn't get her to talk, either."

"I think your in-laws are in too much pain to talk about their son," I said.

"*I've* lost a husband!"

"It's not the same," I said. "The two kinds of losses are different. Each of you feels immense pain. *They* feel guilty because they survived their child—parents aren't supposed to live longer than their children. Losing him means losing their future. He was going to carry on their family name. They would be remembered through him. They would go on through him, even after they're dead. When he died, their hopes and dreams also died. It's like they lost part of themselves."

A year later, when Sarah had become seriously involved with a new man in her life, I saw her in a shopping center. We talked, then I asked: "How are your in-laws doing?" Her face clouded. "Not too well. Jimmy's dad had to be hospitalized for depression this year. He's still grieving very hard." A few minutes later, while we were talking about something else, she interrupted herself: "Do you remember that conversation we had in your office? When I was complaining that his parents wouldn't talk about Jimmy to me? Well, I finally understood. Now that I've met someone, I realize that *I* could get to the point of putting the past behind me, even though I'll never forget him, but Jimmy's parents may never be able to do that."

Past relationships with a child can color a parent's relationship with a daughter- or son-in-law. I met a woman who

92

stopped seeing her daughter-in-law because she couldn't resolve the rage she still feels toward her deceased son. Before his marriage, he went to prison for dealing drugs. He had been a difficult adolescent, abusive to his mother. He had been an alcoholic since the age of fourteen. She still couldn't forgive him after he died in a motorcycle accident. Today, she turns her back on his memory by never contacting her daughter-in-law and ignoring the existence of her grandchildren—his children.

Sometimes in-laws distance themselves because they never approved of the marriage. The death gives them the excuse to sever the in-law relationship.

Occasionally in-laws blame a younger widow or widower for the death. Mickey's wife died of cancer. His mother-in-law cornered him after the funeral: "*You* killed her. If you had gotten her to the doctor sooner she'd be alive today!" Mickey felt devastated. He tried talking to her but she walked away.

Some parents-in-law had counted on their son or daughter—usually an only child—to take care of them. These in-laws are frequently elderly and in poor health. Terrified since the death, they look to their son- or daughter-in-law to carry this on. Sherry, who's in this situation, told me, "I can only do so much. I want to help but suppose I remarry and move out of the city? All I can do, later, is find a good nursing home for them."

You may never have liked your parents-in-law. They might have been critical or interfering. *You* might want to sever the relationship. "Do I need them in my life?" a woman said. "No! They never liked me. No one could have been good enough for their son."

Rejection. Anger. Certainly, these strong negative feelings are sometimes part of the in-law relationship. If they were, it's natural they carry over after the death. But time often heals, and that's good, especially if there are grandchildren.

Be kind to yourself if your in-laws are doing the rejecting. You feel enough guilt, you don't need more.

You also can't stop living because of your in-laws' expectations. You can reassure them that dating does not, in any way, diminish the love you had for their child or the value of your marriage, that their son or daughter would have wanted you to continue living. Life is for the living. You can show your in-laws, if you remarry, that they will continue to have a close relationship with their grandchildren by initiating that relationship yourself.

Don't rub it in, though, like a man who unwittingly told his mother-in-law about all of his dates. He just didn't realize how much it hurt her, until she told him. "I guess I was using her as a mother figure," he said. "My own mother is dead. I was asking her advice on how to get a particular woman more interested in me, and I was giving her all the details—where I'd go on a date, what movie, what restaurant. Sure, when I look back, I know I unintentionally hurt her."

Brothers- and Sisters-in-Law

If you had a close relationship with your brothers- or sisters-in-law before the death, it will probably continue. They might include your kids in their family activities. (Ask them to, if they don't!) But, occasionally, even close relationships deteriorate. Rosy, an attractive widow in her thirties, told me, "My brother-in-law made a pass at me three months after my husband died—my married brother-in-law who's my husband's brother. What a louse." Florence told me, "My husband had been business partners with his brother. After Marcus died, his brother tried some shady things so he could cheat me out of my rights, out of what money I was supposed to get out of the business. That way, he'd pocket what was mine and the children's. I'm no longer speaking to him or his wife, even though I was very fond of her.'' Larry says his relationship with his sister-in-law is tense because he didn't wait an entire year before he began dating. She feels he's not honoring her sister's memory. Vernon is angry at his sister-in-law because she never visited his wife at the hospital while she was dying and she didn't come to the funeral. ''We had all been so close, and she never showed up. When I finally asked her about it, a few months after the death, she said, 'I'm a nervous woman. I couldn't have handled it.' I'm sorry, I can't accept that.''

Expectations. Assumptions. Different values. All of these factors can get in the way of the in-law relationship. If you have children, *attempt* to heal the relationship. Your kids need it.

Your Sisters and Brothers

Alice is a friend of mine. We had gone to Antioch College together. A few weeks after her husband died, I visited her. ''Sit down'' I said. ''I'll make the coffee.'' Carrying our mugs into her living room, I asked, ''How are you doing? Tell me.'' Shrugging, she made a noncommittal noise. I sat beside her on the sofa. We sipped. ''I'm not doing too well, but I guess you're not surprised,'' she said. I asked, ''Has your family been helpful?'' I know Alice's family. A divorced mother living in town. A father who's remarried and now lives in Phoenix. A sister who's younger. Alice and her sister had always been close. She shrugged again. ''Okay, I know you never got along with your mother,'' I said, ''but how about Selma?'' (Selma's her sister.) Alice didn't look at me. She took a bite of her Danish before she answered. ''I don't want to see Selma right now.'' Oh? ''Is the coffee hot enough?'' I asked. She nodded. I plunged in. ''So why don't you want to see Selma?'' Abruptly Alice got up. Hugging her arms close to her body, she paced back and forth, her face pinched and angry. Then, stopping short, she looked directly at me. ''I don't want to see my sister because I'm so damned jealous that she has a husband and I don't!'' she wailed. Her face crumpled, then, and she cried like a baby. I got up and hugged her.

It's very hard to be around couples after the death, and when it's your sister or brother who's part of a couple it's even harder. There's always that leftover sibling jealousy from childhood. (I don't think we ever free ourselves completely from it.) A young widow sees her sister pregnant and it hurts. She and her husband never had a chance to start a family. A man visits his brother and he can't stand watching him and his wife get ready to go on vacation—if his wife hadn't died, this was the month *they* were to have gone away. All the unfinished business that younger couples never finish when one partner dies.

A man reports he feels jealous when he and his kids go over to his sister's house to eat dinner. He feels left out of family life, and he knows his kids do, too.

A woman said, ''I can't stand being around my married sister. She and her husband squabble over the most trivial things. Don't they know *nothing's* worth fighting over?'' Her priorities have changed. She now knows what is important. Health. Loving. Being together. ''If she wasn't my sister she wouldn't dare fight over which restaurant to eat in—not in front of me, when I've lost my husband.''

Fred, the widower in my group, says that his sister is pushing him to get rid of all of his wife's clothes. ''When she comes over she marches into my bedroom and pulls the closet doors open. 'I see they're still here,' she says, and she gives me a meaningful look. She means well, but if she wasn't my sister she wouldn't dare go in my closet, she wouldn't dare tell me when I should give Gwen's clothes away.''

This is Fred's oldest sister. He tells me she was always bossy, even when they were kids. She's continuing the same role she assumed with him decades ago. He's allowing this, but he can lock the bedroom door before she comes, or say, ''That's private territory!'' He's playing out his old role, too.

Relationships with siblings are complex when we're small *and* when we're adults. An oldest child continues to command; she's been the rescuer, the caretaker, and the high achiever. The middle child, sandwiched between siblings, is used to being invisible; he's quietly good or bad. The youngest was always babied and still expects to be babied by brothers and sisters. There are exceptions, but the order in which we were born has a lot to do with our behavior in the family. (Whether we're male or female also determines our behavior within our families.)

Families—Then and Now

At the turn of the century, and for some persons, more recently, families lived together under the same roof—cousins, aunts, grandparents, children, and parents. Everyone in the extended family took the bereaved person's emotional temperature every day. Aunt Gail's having a bad day? Give her some soup. Sit, Aunt Gail, have a good cry. Maybe a game of cards to take her mind off herself? Today, widowed persons are apt to live alone. Their families may live in a different city. To compensate, some use other people's families, or close friends to replace their own families. Others use caring neighbors, or groups (church, synagogue, or singles groups). All of these replacements for family are valid.

Everyone who's been widowed needs warm, continuing support.

And if your family is accessible, you may use their support differently this year than you will next year. You'll be at a different place in your grieving. Today you might not be able to handle being with your sister, you can't stand seeing her happiness. Next year, you can handle it.

Nothing stays the same. Your grieving. Your family relationships. When you become aware of this, you're more able to handle family relationships and your grief.

8. Changing Relationships With Friends

Making new friends is easier when we're very young. It seems much harder when we're past our teens. As a person who's been widowed, you're apprehensive. You don't know where to find new people. Your skills at starting new relationships are rusty. At the same time, you know you should try. You hate the loneliness, and some of your relationships may have changed, especially with your married friends.

Facing Your Feelings

Perhaps you feel resentful because you have to deal with this task when life is hard enough. I understand how you feel. Life is unfair.

Weekends are the pits. If you're employed, your job takes care of the weekdays, and after work you're too tired to go out anyway. But Saturdays and Sundays—you dread weekends. You hate holidays. Your birthday's coming up, but who cares? They've scheduled you, at the office, to take your vacation next month, but there's no one with whom to go.

And now, in order not to suffer this intolerable loneliness, you have to make new unmarried friends who are available weekends, holidays, and vacation time. Doing it feels overwhelming.

You Have a Choice

You can decide to burrow in, that is, not establish new relationships. You can make the choice to center your life totally around your children, career, or family.

(I know someone like that. She stays home every evening and watches TV, and once in a while she goes with her sister to Atlantic City for the day to gamble. The characters in the nighttime soaps have become her friends and family. She has no children.)

Or you can decide to use your strengths to build a second life.

Burrowing in means no risk. Nothing lost and nothing gained. Building a second life means taking scary and unfamiliar routes and acting in unfamiliar ways. But it eventually means living again.

If you decide to build a second life, even with mixed and terrified feelings (and that's normal), first identify what and who you want to retain of your old life. Then realize the building of a second life is a process. It takes a great deal of time and effort.

(Pat yourself on the back for making this decision. You're showing strength!)

Friends to Keep and Those Who Drift Away

What can you retain of your married life? Who will stay around? What friends do you want to keep?

Sometimes old friends surprise us. The ones you didn't expect anything from, one or two of them startle you with their continued support. The ones you counted on—some are still calling and others have disappeared.

Friends who have experienced profound loss in their own lives tend to be empathic and can better tolerate your pain. They're there when you need them. (These are the persons who lost a spouse to death or divorce, or they've lost close

100

family members. They may have suffered the death of a very close friend. Losing a lover might have meant a profound loss.) If they do disappear from your life, it says something about them, not you: they haven't yet worked through their pain.

Couples. Their behavior varies. Some do stay in touch. Others drop out of sight. I remember Zenia, who told me, "A couple of months after my husband died, I saw that my neighbors were having a party. I felt so hurt. This was the first time I hadn't been invited to any of their parties. We always invited each other!"

Other widowed persons say their married friends haven't deserted them, but they feel uncomfortable, like a fifth wheel. Milly quit the play-reading group she and her husband had belonged to because she doesn't want people's pity. "Everyone puts on their coats at the end of the evening and walks out the door in couples," she said. "I wave good-bye and walk out alone. I catch pity on their faces and I shrink inside. So now I'm looking up friends who are divorced or who have never married. I'm twenty-nine, and I realize I don't have to limit myself to only the married persons who were part of my married life."

This is a time when you have the luxury of terminating your relationship with couples you never liked. Your spouse enjoyed them, and you only tolerated them.

Here are people you *don't* need right now:

THE SCOLDERS—They insist you stop crying and get on with your life. They scold, "Be glad he didn't suffer!" They lecture, "You have a long life ahead of you, you're young, you'll be married before you know it."

THE BULLDOZERS—Not only do they scold, they barge into your life and house and try to take over.

THE "I DID IT SO YOU CAN DO IT TOO" PEOPLE—They smugly tell you how strong they are; they've overcome adversity, so you can do it, too.

The "My Story Is Worse Than Your Story" People—
They can't stand it if you're suffering as much as they are.

Limit your time with these people until you're feeling better.

Many widows and widowers report they feel the need to act "up" in front of their friends. "No one wants to hear sad stories more than once," they say. So they smile, smile, smile, while they're weeping inside. But it's a terrible strain, holding in pain while grieving. Don't punish yourself: parcel out, in bits and pieces, the time you spend with persons like this. But first ask yourself, are you sure you're expected to act "up," or is this behavior what you expect of yourself?

Occasionally, friends run away. Rhona was very upset about a friend she and her husband had known for years. They had been very close. "I called him the week before my husband died," she said, "and I told him that if he wanted to say good-bye, now was the time to do it. He never showed up, he never called. I haven't heard from him since.

"I feel like calling him and saying you bastard, you uncaring bastard," she said.

Well, she didn't. It was too hard for her. But she did write him a letter in which she told him just how she felt. The letter writing was for *her,* not to bring him back into her life. After she dropped it in the mailbox, she felt instant relief.

Letter and journal writing is a catharsis. It can purge you of rage and hurt.

Letters can also be a tool for renewing a relationship at the same time you're airing your feelings. Sally was crushed because her best friend stopped calling after the death. She wrote an honest and tactful letter because she wanted to preserve what was left of the relationship as well as be open about her feelings of hurt. She started the letter with a positive statement, telling her friend how much she cared about her. Then she expressed her feelings of rejection. She ended the letter saying that despite those feelings, she does love her, she does want to continue their relationship, and can't they now contact each other without any reminders of what occurred.

Her friend was able to return to the relationship without losing face and without feeling shame. At the same time, she felt free enough to later tell Sally that she just hadn't been adult enough to face the death and she was sorry she hadn't been there to give her support.

Professional and Business Colleagues

Will your husband's colleagues continue their relationship with you? If you saw them in couple situations only—dinner parties at the boss's house, for instance—let that give you a cue. There were no lone women present, so there will probably be no more invitations. But is this so hurting? Were you really intimate friends? Wasn't it a relationship of convenience, meant to cement the bonding of bureaucracy or help husbands move upward? Those affairs were part of the politics of work. You're no longer a part of his work world.

If your colleagues—other women—have stopped including you in their out-of-the-office couple activities, it's because you're no longer part of a couple, and I know that exclusion hurts. They've internalized the couple ideology. They also don't know what to do with a woman who is alone. They feel they can't get up from the table to dance and leave you sitting by yourself. They don't always feel like going out of their way to pick you up and take you home. Also, you're a younger single woman. You may be a threat. Of course that hurts.

Trudy, who's a psychologist as well as newly widowed, said, "I think the exclusion is because we compartmentalize our lives. We're either 'professional colleagues,' 'business friends,' 'golf buddies,' or 'widows.' God forbid anyone mix categories at a party.''

I can understand Trudy's caustic tone. She's being left out of her colleagues' couple affairs. But most of us compartmentalize. ''Old friends from college'' may not mix well with ''church friends,'' we think. So we don't invite the two groups together to brunch.

It's too bad. We limit our lives and the lives of our friends when we compartmentalize. We hurt people. I know your hurt.

People Who Never Mention Your Spouse

You're irked when people never mention your spouse. Of course you are.

Dominique is a thirty-nine-year-old woman whose husband died a year ago. She called me after Thanksgiving for an appointment. ''I'm falling apart,'' she laughed nervously, pulling a strand of her hair, sitting in my office. ''I never should have gone. I should have stayed home with my girls.''

''Where did you go?''

''I couldn't hack being alone during the holiday. So I called a woman friend I had lived with before I was married. We had been roommates in San Francisco. She and her husband now live near here, and both of our families had become very close. They came to the funeral, and we've been in touch. Well, a week before Thanksgiving, I knew I couldn't sit at that table alone with my daughters and eat turkey. I have no family here, so I called Marie and her husband and I practically invited myself and the girls, I was so desperate. They immediately said, come.''

She hid her face in her hands.

Her voice was muffled. ''It was horrible.''

She looked at me.

"We were there three days and no one mentioned Louis! It was like he had never existed. I felt like I was in a bad dream."

After talking more, I better understood the situation: her friends were speechless because they didn't know what to say. They were afraid Dominique would cry if they talked about Louis, and they didn't think that would be good for her. (They also didn't know what to do if she cried.) They didn't want to upset the girls—they wanted the girls to be happy during this visit.

But Dominique needed to talk, and crying would have been healing. The girls needed to hear stories about their father, they miss him so. Reviewing their life together as a family would have validated the years they had together. Hearing the affirmation of Louis would have made them proud. It would also have helped Dominique maintain her identity as his wife. She isn't yet ready to relinquish that role and think of herself as a widow. (Later, when she is ready to give up that role, she will. It takes a long time.)

Dominique could have initiated the conversation, but she didn't know how. She could have remembered the good times the two families had together. ("Remember that inn with the Victorian dining room in New Hope?") Her openness would have given them permission to be open also. Her comfortableness would have made them comfortable.

"It's not too late," I told her. "Why not invite them to *your* home for Christmas? It's only a few weeks away. While they're visiting, bring out your photograph albums. Use them as a tool for talking about your husband. Point to a photograph where he's being affectionate with the kids, or where he's being funny. Remember happy times. It'll open up communication between all of you, because they'll be in some of the pictures."

She hesitated. "I don't feel up to houseguests."

"Make it just for Christmas Day," I suggested. "They live close enough for a one-day visit."

"But—"

"Don't play the 'but' game with yourself. There can always be a 'but,' " I said.

Dominique called me after Christmas. It *had* worked.

Not all bereaved widows and widowers want to talk about their spouse. It's too painful. Looking at photographs can also be painful. Are you practicing avoidance? It's all right. The time will come when you *will* be able to talk and look.

"Lunchtime" Friends

These are old friends who invite you to lunch but never to their homes for dinner when their husbands or wives would be present. Instead of lunch, it might be an invitation to have a drink after work, at a bar. Maybe they do feel threatened. You're now single and you *are* attractive. But it's just as possible they feel alienated from what they assume is your new lifestyle and they're sure you'll find theirs stodgy. "Lifestyle!" a woman exclaimed. "What new lifestyle? All I do is go to work, come home and cry, and go to bed." They don't know the emptiness of being widowed. They read the magazines that tell how exciting the single life is, and they believe it: singles sit around in hot tubs laughing and bantering; singles spend their Saturday afternoons getting their legs waxed so they can look good trying new and different sexual positions with new partners. They, like all of us, are not taught about grieving in school, so they grow up knowing nothing about how you're really feeling. There's also the myth that all widowers have scores of women calling them for dates, and that they need no people from their past in their new lives. Or they might assume a widower only wants to come to dinner if there's a woman present. A single, beautiful woman.

One widower banged his fist on the table. "My best friend tells me he knows I want to meet someone nice, so he's waiting 'til his wife comes up with the right woman before they have me to dinner." He rubbed his knuckles and, with anger, said, "Did I ask him to fix me up? I don't want a matchmaker. I don't even want to date, for God's sake. I've only been widowed three months!"

He added, "It would be so damn good to sit at a dinner table with a family right now."

Maybe he should tell them. They'd probably be grateful, hearing it like it is.

Joining Groups—A First Step

The first time I heard a very young widow tell me she now reads the obituaries, I was taken aback. Later, much later, I discovered that many widows and widowers in their twenties, thirties, and early forties regularly read the obituaries—obsessively. To see if there's anyone else like themselves who's a survivor of an untimely death. To see the cause of death in someone also young. To see how many other persons there are like themselves.

To feel less isolated.

This reading of the obituaries is a cue. It tells us that younger widowed persons feel particularly isolated. That, in order to feel less alone, they eventually need to make new friends. That they need to reach out.

The quickest way to meet new persons is through joining groups.

Parents Without Partners

If you have children of any age, Parents Without Partners (P.W.P.) is an organization that caters to the needs of the single parent as well as her or his child. Members explore the challenges of raising children alone through moderated discussion groups. There are parent/child events, such as ice-skating parties and holiday dinners. For persons who are interested and ready, there are adult social functions— dances and wine-and-cheese parties.

Paul Moses, an International President of P.W.P., said in the *Parents Without Partners Sourcebook* that he had to force himself to join, he was so shy. He joined because he needed to find out how other single parents were managing their lives after the loss of the other partner. He developed deep friendships in the group with both women *and* men.

There are chapters throughout the country. If you can't find a chapter nearby and need more information, write or call the national office:

Parents Without Partners
7910 Woodmont Avenue
Suite 1008
Bethesda, Maryland 20814
Ph: (301) 654-8850

Singles Groups

Whether or not you have children, singles groups can be settings for the development of new friendships. We stereotype. We assume singles groups are exclusively for dating, mating, and eyeing potential sexual partners. You can use them for these purposes, or you can use them for only one purpose: to establish new friendships.

If all you want to do right now is make new friends, stay

away from the dances. Instead, attend the lectures. That way, you'll avoid feeling like you're in a meat market and you won't be giving out the wrong signals.

An excellent way to feel comfortable immediately at your first meeting is to introduce yourself to the program chairperson and tell him or her you'd like to serve on a committee. Right away, you're made part of an inner circle.

Realize you may not like everyone there, but you don't have to. Meeting one or two persons you enjoy is enough.

There are different kinds of singles groups. Some focus on issues. Singles Enjoying the Arts (SETA), located in Washington, D.C. and Baltimore, Maryland, focuses on cultural events, where members attend concerts, theater, ballet, and museums. Some groups are age related. A particular group might attract down-to-earth persons where another group might appeal to fashionable men and women. There are sailing and skiing singles groups.

Where can you find your kind of group? See if your Sunday newspaper has a singles page. Some big-city Sunday papers now feature a singles page to list calendar events and group meetings.

Here's advice from a widow who's active in the singles group scene:

"Comparison shop. Visit several groups before you decide on one. If you're shy, take a friend. If you hope to meet someone of the opposite sex, go by yourself. You're more apt to be approached."

This same woman said she used singles groups to make new female friends at first, and later she started going to the dances.

Volunteer Work

Theresa said, "I became a volunteer for Meals-On-Wheels. It's a nationwide group that delivers cooked meals to home-bound persons. I work in the kitchen several hours each week, packing the food, and all of us talk while we work. It's been a terrific place to meet new people."

Max, a widower who felt at loose ends for months, now volunteers in the coffee shop of a local hospital. He works behind the cash register. "I volunteer on weekends because I work during the week," he said, "and you'd be surprised how many people I meet. I'm now becoming very friendly with a dentist who works here in the dental clinic. When he heard I own a dental lab, we started to talk. We've been out to dinner twice."

"I volunteer at the Y.W.C.A.," said Elizabeth. "I teach a class in aerobic dancing. I've become friendly with the woman who teaches yoga, and we're going hiking this Saturday."

It's true that women have a long history of volunteerism; they've had more leisure time to give. However, more men than ever before are now volunteering in all kinds of settings.

Meeting new persons when you volunteer is easy. You're working alongside each other, week after week. If you're doing something with your hands, you won't be self-conscious about silences.

Most cities have a central agency for volunteerism, where you can inquire about openings in various institutions. Or you may already have a preference. Choose the kind of work where you can use your skills or personality. If you love teaching, you might want to tutor inner-city kids. If you are outgoing, you might want to be a tour guide.

Widowed persons are under a great deal of stress. In the beginning, don't rashly commit yourself to more hours than you can comfortably handle. You can always expand your hours.

Since you are ready to make new friends, avoid the kind of work where you'll be isolated in a room by yourself.

Not only does volunteer work help you make friends, it's good for your self-esteem at a time when your self-esteem is low. You *know* you're helping people.

If you find you don't like your volunteer task, ask the director of volunteers to change it. You're doing them a favor. At least enjoy what you're doing.

A tip: Newly widowed persons are sometimes so grateful to the hospital staff for taking good care of their spouse that they want to volunteer at the hospital. If you're one of these people, don't be disappointed if you can't handle the assignment, or being there. Seeing sick persons, or going to the same place where your spouse died, might be too hard for you right now.

Classes

School is an excellent place in which to meet new people. Take a noncredit class, though, because the demands of a credit course are too much to handle when you're newly widowed. (Do you really need tests and term papers?)

In many cities, the public school system sponsors a free or low-cost night school adult education program. You can take classes in everything from Beginning Spanish to Watercolor Painting. Classes are also offered in Ys. Community colleges offer moderately priced classes in pottery making, gourmet cookery, swimming—anything and everything. And in the

111

past years we're seeing the development of independent programs, where the teaching is done outside of an institution—in the teacher's homes, for instance. This is cozy and provides an intimate place for new friendships.

What already-learned skills do you want to sharpen? Square dancing? Sculpture?

Maybe you'd like to take a zany class, like "How To Conduct Yourself In A Singles Bar." (Yes, some of these independent programs offer these kinds of fun classes.)

The 1960s saw the beginnings of Free Universities, an idea borrowed from Europe. Offering free or low-cost courses in everything from backpacking to poetry writing, the classes are usually held in homes. Call your local university and ask if they sponsor a Free University.

Later, after you've been widowed at least one year, you might want to continue your formal education in credit courses, but start slowly.

Day Trips

One-day trips, sponsored by organizations or travel agencies, where you meet at a certain place in the morning and take a chartered bus to your destination, can be a very good way to meet new persons. (It's a myth that only persons over sixty take these trips.) Not only is it a cheap way to see another city or go skiing, it's a convenient way to visit a museum, go to the theatre, or go discount shopping. In the summer, it's a quick way to escape the heat and see the ocean. Wherever you go, it's a diversion, and diversion lifts depression.

It's almost impossible to sit next to a person on the bus for two hours and say nothing or be with the same group all day and not meet someone interesting.

You'll see these trips advertised in the Sunday papers, and you can also call your local travel agencies.

Vacations

I highly recommend college-sponsored tours if you have no one with whom to vacation. You'll meet interesting people before the date of departure.

The particular department of the college sponsoring the trip offers a mini-course before the trip date, teaching you about the place you'll be visiting. During the weeks of the mini-course, you'll make friends, and by the time you're at the airport you'll know who you're going to have dinner with every night in France. You may even find a trip roommate while you're taking the course.

Most colleges and universities sponsor trips. They open them up to the community so you don't have to be one of their students. (Most participants aren't.) Call the continuing education department of the college.

(Don't take a trip to a place where you and your spouse vacationed together. You'll spend the entire vacation crying.)

Following Up on New Friendships

New friendships are tentative; they need nurturing. Take the initiative. Call your new friend. Don't wait for a call.

During your first contacts, you'll get to know the person better. If you're lucky, she is the kind of person you enjoy. Sometimes this isn't the case.

Avoid:
- "Poor Me" and "Isn't Life Awful" persons
- Passive people, who wait for you to plan everything

Cultivate:
- Persons who share your lifestyle and values
- Life-loving persons

And once you do choose a new friend, force yourself to say "yes" to all invitations, even when you don't feel like going out. Invite him or her to *your* home.

One new friend leads to another. Before long, you'll have developed a circle of friends. Pat yourself on the back. No one has done this for you, you've done it for yourself!

9. Getting Back Into Dating

This chapter is for persons who are ready to date, who are already dating, or who are thinking about it.

A woman said, "It feels sacrilegious, even talking about it." Well, she's only been widowed two months. It would be unusual (not wrong!) if she were thinking about it. Wait another six or nine months. By then she may be wondering what it will be like. Or she might even be dating.

Dating is one of the big differences between younger and older widows. There are more opportunities to meet men when you're in your twenties, thirties, or early forties. The older woman finds a shortage of men her age. Also, younger women are sometimes more aggressive. They've grown up at a time when women are expected to be assertive and aggressive. Older women may find it difficult to go out alone on a Saturday night. This usually isn't even an issue with younger women. The woman over fifty may find it hard to dine alone in an elegant restaurant. Most younger women find this surprising. Vacation alone? Many older women are frozen at the idea, but younger women do it all the time. Self-images are different when one is younger. Older women are victims of the youth culture. Many feel unattractive even if they're not. Younger women are *part* of this culture that is so valued. All these differences make a difference in dating.

And men. Many widowers have made these remarks: "Women seem to be more interested in me than before I was married. Maybe, now that I'm in my thirties (or forties) I seem more self-confident. Certainly, I've had more life experience.'' The younger widowed man does find it easier to meet and interest women than he did when he was in his late teens or early twenties, perhaps because there are so many women out there and they *are* aggressive.

The question is—are you ready to date?

Readiness

Ask yourself:

"Do I get angry at friends who want to fix me up?"

"Do I insist that I'll never meet anyone as wonderful as my wife (or husband)?"

"Do I feel guilty when I even think about dating?"

"Am I avoiding being with people of the opposite sex?"

If you're saying yes to all of these questions, you are not ready. If your answer is yes to some of the questions, you have mixed feelings.

Anytime we get ready for a major life change we have mixed feelings. We're torn between holding on to the old life and reaching toward the new one. Eventually, the mixed feelings resolve themselves. This can take a long time, so usually men and women begin dating even before they're completely resolved.

Guilt Feelings

Widowed persons often feel guilty when they begin going out. Even persons who were in bad marriages, who have put a halo around their marriage, revising their relationship history, feel guilty. They remember the marriage as having been good! They're not being deliberately dishonest. They need the halo in order to validate the years invested in the relationship. (It's hard to admit one stayed in a bad marriage.) Survival guilt, suffered by every widowed person, lends to the halo.

After the end of a good marriage, the guilt comes from feeling you are betraying the memory of your spouse and diminishing the value of your relationship by dating. Some persons feel guilty because they're being blamed for dating so soon—usually by their spouse's family or friends.

A remembered conversation can bring about guilt feelings. "I feel guilty when I remember what my husband always said," a woman told me. "He would always say he was the one who would die first. 'I'll die first and you'll be dating within a few months,' he'd say. Teasing, you know. Well, here I am dating, and he's been dead only a few months. I feel so guilty!"

Guilt also comes from feeling you are still married. How can I date, you ask yourself, if I'm still feeling married?

I've talked to men and women whose spouses urged them to remarry; the husband or wife was terminally ill and they were very concerned about what would happen to their mate after they died. One dying woman even approached one of her female friends, asking her to consider marrying her husband after the death. "He needs to be taken care of," she pleaded. "He'll be so lonely. And he's a good man!" This gives the surviving spouse "permission" to date and later remarry, and it alleviates guilt feelings.

Some religions alleviate guilt by requiring that widowed persons begin building a new life by a certain time. In orthodox Judaism, there is a given length of time to mourn and a time to build a new life. It is one's duty to meet these time requirements.

Awkwardness

There's guilt, and there are also feelings of awkwardness.

Robin said, "I felt like a teenager, sitting at the restaurant table during my first date with this man. I felt so awkward."

The woman she was talking to, a married friend, was astonished. "You were the sweetheart of that fraternity in college. You were always so popular. Why would you feel awkward?" Robin gave a short ironic laugh. "Popular? Shall we call me the popular widow? Seriously, you know how close I was to Carl. I adored him. I hate being in the position of having to begin a new life without him. I resent it. I detest having to go out with strangers and make small talk, when Carl and I had five years of deep and meaningful communication—spoken and unspoken. I hate being looked over, like an object, when I had a husband who accepted and loved me, no matter how I felt or looked. And," she added, looking annoyed, "I hate the role playing. I remember that horrible role playing from years ago, before I was married."

"Did you role play with men in those days? I don't remember us talking about that at college."

"Sure. We all role play when we're dating someone the first few times."

The other woman looked uncertain.

"We all do!" Robin said. "We pretend we're so interested in everything he's saying. We try to be what the other person wants us to be. It's a strain."

Her friend twisted her wedding ring, maybe a reassurance to herself that she was married. "What did you think this guy you went out with wanted you to be?" she asked.

"Who knows? I guess I do know. He no doubt wanted to be with a woman who was sexy, feminine, intelligent but not too intelligent, and very interested in him."

The other woman laughed. "It sounds like advice given in those women's magazines from the 1940s where they told you to be sexy, but not blatantly sexy. The ads told you what deodorant to use so you'd be 'feminine.' "

"Exactly. And I've been socialized like the rest of us, despite the women's movement. Even after five years of a great marriage where I was always myself, I'm reverting back to the girl who must please. Maybe in different ways than back in the 1940s, but I still have to please.''

Robin is typical of many younger women who have been widowed. The death had left her feeling shaky and unsure of herself. On that first date she felt like she was being thrown into a pool of ice-cold water and she had to sink or swim. And she had forgotten how to swim. She's resentful; she doesn't want to swim.

Men, also, feel this way. ''First of all,'' Will said, ''I lost some of my hair in my thirties. My wife died when I was forty-one, and after that I started to feel self-conscious about my round bald spot. When I thought about dating, the big question was—should I buy a hairpiece? I did get one and I felt like a fool in it. To top it off—no pun—that first date of mine didn't ask me one question about myself, she was so wrapped up in her divorce. I sat there listening to her troubles and I was resentful. Not one question! I remember that when I got home I looked in the mirror and I felt like I was seeing a stranger with that hairpiece. I was disgusted with myself for spending so much money on it, and I felt guilty about cheating on my wife. If I hadn't felt so awkward—it was my first date—I would have asserted myself. I would have turned the conversation to me.''

He added wistfully, ''My wife never minded my bald spot. She even liked it.''

What are *you* expecting on your first date?

The feeling Robin had, ''What am I doing here anyway?'' is to be expected. You were part of a couple, loved by a special person. You could read each other's thoughts. You laughed at the same things. Silences were comforting, not threatening. Now your spouse has been forcibly taken from you and you're sitting with a stranger.

''That first date was so bad for me,'' one woman said,

119

"that I told him at the end of the evening I couldn't see him again. 'Why?' he asked. 'I'm not ready to date,' I said. Fortunately, he had enough ego strength that he didn't give up. He kept calling. Eventually I did go out with him again and it was better that next time."

It is easier, the more you do it.

The first time you're out, though, can be very different than the first time you ever dated.

"I never had an evening like that and I don't think I ever will again," a woman said. "We went for a couple of drinks, and I felt stiff and self-conscious. Then he drove me to his apartment and we had more drinks. In a fuzzy daze I let him lead me to bed, like a robot. I don't think we said one word to each other during our lovemaking, if you can call it that, and it really didn't matter because I was so hungry for sex. I was like a starved kid who—well, all I remember was grabbing and groaning and yelling. Afterward I was so embarrassed because of all the noise I had made and how easy I had been. We didn't talk afterward, either, and he drove me home in silence. I felt ashamed and dirty."

I said, "Don't be so hard on yourself. Remember, your husband had been very sick. He hadn't been able to make love to you for almost a year."

"But the noise I made!"

"He's heard it before. Look at it this way: you met an important need that night, and even if you didn't meet it in just the way you would have liked, it was met."

"I wouldn't go out with him again, even if he asked me!"

"I understand. You felt exposed. But don't blame yourself for acting on your urgent need. Be kind to yourself."

Blaming yourself is so easy when you begin dating. "Why did I act so boring?" "Why was I so over eager?" and "Why did I talk so much about my husband?" It's a fragile time for you. *Be kind to yourself.*

How Much Should You Talk About Your Husband or Wife?

Marcie nuzzled her baby daughter's neck. The child giggled and slid down into her mother's lap. Marcie's mother appeared in the kitchen doorway. "Can I take the baby?" she called.

"It's okay, mom," Marcie answered, kissing the top of the baby's head. Sotto voce, she said to me, "Now you can see why I appreciate having my mom's help."

I looked around, it was a small house, a row house on a modest street. Marcie had been in one of my groups, and I had stopped in, being in the neighborhood.

"Guess what!" Marcie smiled triumphantly, "I've been asked out." Oh? She nodded. "I've been baby-sitting for this man who's divorced," she said, "and he drops off his child when he goes to work in the mornings. He has custody. Well, we always talk when he gets home, and one thing led to another, I guess. He asked me out for this Saturday night."

"Are you nervous?" I asked.

She pondered the question. "I am about one thing. It'll be my first date since, you know, and I don't know how much I can mention Ken. I'm nervous about that." We were silent while she buttoned her baby's sweater. "My whole life was Ken!" she exclaimed. She put the baby in the playpen. "I got married when I was eighteen, and before that I was a kid living with my parents. Everything I did and thought was a result of being married to Ken. I still think in terms of 'we' instead of 'me.' "

I asked Marcie what interests she has that belong only to her—that weren't a part of her life with Ken. She looked blank. I asked, "Are you interested in politics?" (It was an election year.)

She grinned wryly, "I always voted the way Ken did." Then she brightened. "Running!" she exclaimed. She seemed suddenly energized. "I run every morning. I'm addicted to running. Remember how depressed I was after the death? Remember that psychologist I went to? Well, he told me to run. He said it would help the depression go away. It did, and I'm still running."

I felt as though I was now talking to a different person, a self-confident woman.

"I get a high when I run," she said. "I'm a passionate runner!"

"Talk about running."

"He might not be interested," she said.

"Possibly," I answered, "but it's a way of starting the evening. It will lead to what he's interested in, won't it? Talk about running, you light up when you do, and it'll give energy to the evening."

As Marcie's new life develops and she gets into other activities she'll have developed more of her own identity. Right now, she's still "Ken's wife." Each new interest will belong only to her. It won't be part of her former life with Ken. She'll no longer be worried about how much she can talk about her marriage, because she'll be full of her new life and that's what she'll talk about.

"I already have decided what I'll say about my husband and how much I'll say," a thirty-four-year-old woman said. "On a first date, when I'm asked if I've ever been married, I'll simply say 'yes.' The man will probably take it for granted that I'm divorced—how many younger widows would he have met?—and then I'll briefly correct him. I'll just say that my husband died."

"Suppose he asks how he died?"

"Oh, I'll be honest, but I won't make a big deal of it. I won't dwell on it. That would only make me feel bad, remembering everything, and what good would it do the new relationship?"

"In fact," she added, "I imagine some men might identify with my husband's death. They would feel very threatened if they heard the details. He dropped dead on the golf course from a heart attack and he was only thirty-five. He never had been sick. They could feel, 'If it happened to him, and he's around my age, it could happen to me.' "

She's right. Younger men *do* feel threatened when they hear of a man their age dying. "But later," she said, "if the relationship develops, I will feel more free to talk about my husband and our married life, because, by that time, this new man and I will be sharing much more of each other."

As we talked some more and explored her feelings about dating and relationships, she told me she has other people she can talk to about her husband—good friends and loving family. "Tell widows and widowers," she said, "to definitely limit their references to their spouses at first. To try out the waters before they go on and on. It would only make their dates feel 'What am *I* doing here?' "

What About Your Wedding Ring?

"Should I remove my ring before I go out?" a woman asked. There's no law or custom about this issue. You don't have to remove it completely. You can move it to your other hand. If you don't move it, it can be very confusing to your date. He'll be getting silent mixed messages. "I'm out with you so I must want to be but I still feel married so I'm not really with you."

If you're not ready to remove the ring from your person, consider wearing it on a chain around your neck. Many widows do, and you can tuck the chain inside of your blouse or dress while you're with your date.

One widow had her ring reset so it no longer looks like a wedding ring, and she wears it on her right hand. Another woman gave her ring to her twenty-year-old son, so he can, someday, give it to a new wife. A man gave his ring to his son, for any future marriage. "Giving the ring to my child," he remarked, "gives me a sense of continuity."

Whether you're dating or not, there's no set time frame for when you'll remove your wedding band. Strong mixed feelings accompany this. It's a symbolic act. Some widows remove their ring, and two weeks later, in guilt, put it back on again. Others resolutely take it off a few months after the death, even if they aren't dating yet, and never put it on again. Follow your feelings, even changed feelings.

"Do I Put Away Photographs of My Husband?"

"My living room is filled with photographs of my husband," a woman said, "and I have my first date next week. Should I put away the photographs before he comes?"

Viewing all the photographs will give her date a signal: she's not really going to be with him that evening. Rather than have the man flee (why should he get involved with a woman who still feels very much married?), she might want to move most of the pictures to the den, or her bedroom.

Eventually, when she develops an intimate relationship with someone, she'll want to also remove them from her bedroom. Nothing turns a person off more than viewing a family picture gallery from the bed: a spouse smiling down at a wife, a woman kissing her husband, or a formal wedding portrait.

Moving the photographs doesn't mean discarding them. Lovingly swath them in protective covering and place them in a drawer. Put them in photograph albums. (If you have children, develop a family project: purchase an album and have the kids decide, with you, how to compose the photographs on each page.)

You can also consider placing the photographs in your children's rooms. It's a loving thing to do.

Has Dating Changed From Before You Were Married?

If you're in your twenties or thirties, and you were married a short time, you'll probably find dating mores and customs the same. However, if you are forty-five and you had been married since your early twenties *and* you lived with your parents before that, expect changes:

- Some men might expect you to pay for your own dinners.
- Many women are more aggressive than you remember.
- Casual sex is more common.
- Some men might expect you to meet them; they don't expect to pick you up and deliver you home.

How you'll react to these changes depends on your lifestyle preferences and your values. There's no right or wrong. Women who feel their worth is reflected in how much a man spends on them will look for more traditional men who still pay a woman's way.

Men who were married to passive women might feel threatened by the assertive woman who acts out her expectations. Traditional men who feel strongly about being the ones who call the shots also feel threatened. Fortunately or not, there are still plenty of women out there who are willing to let a man lead. There's someone for everyone.

Recreational Sex

Many women report that they feel a strong sexual drive. They were in their thirties when their husbands died, at the peak of their sexual interest, and they're now going into dating with a high degree of desire and more sexual experience than they had before they were married. Society has given them permission to act on their desires. Some of them have been deprived for a long time because their husbands were too ill to be sexually active. Recreational sex fits their needs.

Some widowers, however, find casual sex threatening. They feel the demand to perform, and guilt feelings about betraying their deceased spouse make them nervous; they may become temporarily impotent. Others say they married a young inexperienced woman, as inexperienced as they, and now very experienced women are expecting them to be great lovers. Not knowing if they can measure up, they become impotent. This frightens them. Once they have a bad experience, they're often afraid to try again. But as time goes on, most of them become more comfortable. They change, learn, grow, and adjust.

Finding People to Date

How can you meet persons to date?

There are the traditional and nontraditional ways. If you're conservative, you may prefer the traditional route of being introduced through friends. If you're a risking person, you might consider traditional and alternate ways.

There's the growing industry of dating services. If this is a possible option for you, here are some tips:

- Comparison shop. See what's available, and the differences between dating services, before you buy.
- Ask how they screen their clients.
- Use only services that interview their prospective clients in person.
- Ask if and how the service guarantees that none of the people you meet are married.
- Ask what kind of persons the service attracts. Professional women? Businessmen?
- Ask its procedure for having you meet people. Be sure you're going to be comfortable with that procedure.

- Ask the fee, and ask for details; a small initial fee could build up into an expensive bill.

Video services, where you're able to see your prospective date, are expensive. The charge could be $250 for six months, or more. But it might be worth it to you.

Some cities offer the kind of dating services where a lunch or dinner at a restaurant is prearranged by the service, and it is in this safe environment that you meet your date. "If I meet a creep," a woman said, "I can eat my lunch and run. Also, he's not going to make a lunge for me in a restaurant."

The Personals are another alternative way to meet someone. Choose a newspaper or magazine that reflects you. If you run an ad in the *Village Voice*, you may get replies from bright and interesting persons but some will also be offbeat. Pick a tabloid newspaper, like the *Globe,* and you're more apt to get answers from blue-collar workers rather than corporate types. A literary magazine, such as *The New Republic,* attracts intellectuals. City magazines, glossy and expensive, are filled with ads from upwardly mobile professional and business people who want to meet upwardly mobile professional and business people.

If you're running an ad in a magazine that has a national circulation, state what part of the country you're living in. Request answers from persons living only in that part of the country. (If you live in New Orleans, say so.)

Watch for telling phrases: someone asking for a "discreet caring daytime relationship" is already in a relationship, probably marriage. A person seeking "sensual pleasures" wants instant sex. The words "passive" or "dominant" say a sadomasochistic relationship is being sought.

After these warnings you may be asking yourself, "What kind of crazies run or answer these ads, anyway?" Some perfectly nice persons use the Personals. And they can be very effective. A woman who had been widowed two years placed an ad in a local magazine and she received seventy letters. Carefully screening each one, she came to the conclusion that thirty were from responsible persons. (The ones that appealed to her were from men who didn't call themselves "handsome"!) She further screened the thirty and narrowed it down to ten. Her telephone contacts led to four dates. She is still dating one of these men, an attorney who's new in town, and who felt a personal ad was the quickest and most efficient way to meet a woman who also loves hiking and classical music.

Newspapers and magazines that run Personals do not print addresses or phone numbers. They reserve the right to edit or reject any ad. You rent a mailbox for a given length of time, and if you don't renew your ad after that time, your replies are discarded.

To protect yourself further, once you run or answer an ad, always make arrangements to meet the person in a place that is not your home—in a restaurant or a bar. On your first date, go home alone. (And if you're wary, once you meet the person, do not give out your last name or your address and phone number.)

"How about singles bars?" some people ask.

I'll quote from some younger widowed persons who are dating:

"I always am afraid the men in those bars have a disease. Obviously, I can't ask any of them to get a blood test."

"I met my wife in a singles bar!"

"It depends where it's located. Pick one in a nice neighborhood, where everyone knows each other, and you'll find yourself emotionally comfortable."

"I went, and no one talked to me."

If you do prefer the traditional route, meeting someone through friends, *tell* friends you're now ready to date. They may have been hesitant to introduce you to someone because they didn't know you were ready. Or they just didn't think of it.

What Kind of Persons Are Not for Permanent Relationships?

These persons are *not* good bets for long-term relationships:

• Multiple marriers
• Persons who desperately need to be taken care of
• Married persons (Who needs the problems?)
• Anyone who drinks too much or takes drugs

This is all basic stuff, this information, and you may be wondering why I'm even talking about it. You're now very vulnerable, that's why. Newly widowed persons are emotionally needy. Lonely. Hungry. It can be tempting to say "yes" to the first person who comes along. Or you may have gotten married right out of high school, you might have married your childhood sweetheart, so you have little experience with persons of the opposite sex, and you *are* naive.

Multiple marriers aren't usually good bets for relationships; many continue marrying, divorcing, and remarrying. Even if they swear they're now ready to settle down, wouldn't you wonder why they couldn't make it on three tries? Persons who desperately need to be taken care of are in no shape to take care of *your* emotional needs. (Later, they might be, but not when you meet them.) Married persons? You're going to get pretty angry when he can't sleep over, and when you can't be with him on weekends or holidays. Alcoholics or drug addicts—isn't life hard enough for you right now?

"I'm just dating him. I'm not going to *marry* him!" a woman exclaimed, when she admitted her new friend may be an alcoholic. Attachments can grow. She doesn't know how dependent she'll become on the relationship.

It's Not Easy

Getting back into dating is not always easy. You're not the same person you were before your marriage, so you have to figure out the kind of person you *now* need and find him or her. The tendency to compare your dates with your spouse is strong. Children complicate the issue: you have the task of helping your kids not be afraid they'll lose you, too (even grown children). You may feel self-conscious because your waist has thickened or your thighs are flabby. It's not easy, but you're doing it or you're getting ready to do it, and that is courageous.

10. Sex and Relationships

I sat at my desk, reading a long letter from a woman who had been widowed fourteen months. I reread the first page:

"When I went to a lecture on relationships a few months after my husband died I wasn't ready to listen. I left before it was over. Now, however, I'm dating and I'm looking for a committed relationship. I'm seeing a man who has never been married. He's forty-three. Do you think a man that age, who has never been married, is a high-risk person? Would he be able to cope with the demands of a relationship *and* my daughter, who's thirteen? She is withdrawn. She's still grieving the death of her father, and she looks at this man as an intruder."

I put the letter down, thinking: she was married at nineteen; she lived in a small town and her only concerns were which dress to wear on a date and whether or not to go to the beach on a Sunday. Men who were bachelors at the age of forty-three? She wrote that she never met any, besides her middle-aged uncle who had been a strange duck (according to various aunts and her mother), given to wearing a toupee that didn't fit, hoarding old newspapers, and "keeping" a woman from across the tracks. Now she was facing a new world of never-married forty-three-year olds as well as men with quirks and kinks that she had never heard the likes of: a man who had begged to rub oil all over her body and a man who belonged to a spanking club. She now lives in Los Angeles, but she had never heard of spanking clubs and she had only read about men with bottles of oil. This new man in her life, he *is* forty-three and has never married, but at least he's traditional. He, like she, attends church every Sunday morning. He lives in the house his parents owned. He is passionate about his rose bushes. He wears three-piece suits and carries a briefcase to work. The thing that nags at her— could he handle an upset kid who's scared someone will take away her mother and a woman who doesn't know who she is now that her husband has died?

It worries her. And she's typical—a younger widow finding it's a very different single world out there.

Men, too, find it's different. "I don't meet women who are like my wife," a man told me. "We got married when we were both twenty-one. She lived at home with her parents before our marriage. She was a virgin. I was a virgin. She wanted me to make all of the major decisions after we were married, and I did. I'm just not meeting anyone like her."

He probably won't.

In talking further with this thirty-one-year-old machinist, it turned out he has a bad girl/good girl mind set. He expects to meet another virgin. I reminded him of the obvious: he'll only find a virgin if she isn't divorced or widowed, and even then it's highly unlikely. "Look," I said, "you're thirty-one. You'll probably be meeting women in their late twenties or early thirties. Do you really think they'll be virgins?" (I felt silly even saying the word.)

He was stubbornly quiet.

"You don't expect to meet an eighteen-year old, do you?"

His eyes flickered. I suddenly realized—he did. Later, as I reflected on our talk, I speculated that it wasn't that he was really looking for a virgin. He was attempting to recreate the past. He was resisting being a widower. He wanted desperately to go backward and to recapture the earlier years

132

when death hadn't hit him. He's also afraid of more sophisticated women because he doesn't know if he'll measure up.

So here we have a woman who is faced with the kinds of men she had never met before and a man who is looking for the impossible. She is more flexible, so she has already met someone. Time will help her discover whether her friend can cope with her complicated life and feelings; whether he'll be able to tolerate the grief of a bereaved child, who sees him as an intruder.

The name of this game is called being selective. But you need to understand what you really want (that's what my machinist friend has to do) in order to be clear on who you want.

Are YOU Different?

Listen to this woman:

"I had been a dependent wife. I had never worked because we had children right away. I had never used my college education because I got married right after I graduated. After my husband died, I slowly put the pieces of my life back together. After a year of being preoccupied with my grief and myself, I went to work. I went into real estate, and I eventually got my broker's license. I found I was competent! I was so competent that by the third year, I was selling commercial properties, and I was soaring. I was now considered a hot shot. My income was more than my husband had ever made as a teacher. But I was feeling very anxious throughout this entire growth period and I couldn't figure out why, unless I was still grieving and I didn't know it. Well, I looked through some photographs recently and it hit me. I saw pictures of my husband protectively holding me and I realized—if he could come back from the dead he wouldn't like me. He detested aggressive career women. I had turned into what he would have called a man-eater."

She paused, and then she said, "I'm not a man-eater. I can outsell any man in my office but in my private life I'm not a man-eater." Another silence. Then she said, "I loved my husband very much, and I'll tell you something I've never told anyone. I could never get involved with someone like him again. I've changed. I need a man who respects and admires and likes strong women." Her eyes filled with tears. "He didn't."

This woman reflects the new opportunities women now have since the advent of the women's movement. Her whole life has turned around, and her new material conditions have changed her self-image and her expectations. She's not the first widow who has started a successful career since the death and now sees herself differently. Many do. Their behavior changes. They are now more assertive and self-confident. They not only have become competent and respected businesswomen or professionals, they have also grown in their personal lives: they have had to learn how to manage their business affairs and family finances; they've had to be both mother and father to their kids. Briskly moving through their weekdays, controlling time and motion, they're in control of much of their lives.

These women now want a relationship with a man who isn't afraid of them. They want and need men who are strong enough themselves that they are not wary of strong women. These are women who can now discuss tax shelters and the Bach Festival in Madeira (their incomes allow them to travel). They're not inclined to seek men who want them to be waiting with a drink at the end of the day, asking, "What happened at the office, honey?" They're more apt to meet a date at a bar at the end of a hectic business day and expect to discuss their latest business deals—the date's and theirs.

A woman summed it up, and she sounded poignant: "I had a great marriage, but it was a marriage that belonged to a special era in my life, when I was a sheltered wife. I've grown from that sheltered wife to an anguished widow to a very independent woman. Would I want the past back again? It's too simple a question. I would give anything if my husband wouldn't have had to die, but I'm no longer that same woman who was his wife. I would hope he would be proud of me and my accomplishments, but I'm not sure.''

I asked her if she found it easy to meet men who don't see her as a threat. She thought. Then she laughed, and it was a grim laugh. ''Younger men don't see me as a threat, probably because they were brought up differently than an older man. Younger men have mothers who are career women. But I don't think I want a man in his twenties. I'm thirty-seven. I remember different songs, different wars. My income would probably be larger than his, and I'm not sure I'd be happy about that.'' She drummed her fingers on the table, thinking. ''Also,'' she said, ''a younger man would have to be comfortable with my teenagers and they'd have to accept him. I can't see my suburban neighbors inviting us to dinner. I can't even see my *friends* accepting this kind of a situation.''

She grinned at me and said, ''So I'll continue to seek that elusive man who's made it, who's not a multiple marrier, who's not bisexual, who's not tied to his mother, and who likes kids. Know anyone?''

''*I'm* not different than I was before!'' a woman told me after one of my lectures while we were milling around the refreshment table. ''I'm pretty much the same. Don't think we all changed so much. I still want the same kind of life I had before. I still want to be a wife in the traditional sense. Give me a man like my husband and I'd be ecstatic.''

''Are you finding anyone?''

She grimaced. ''They're all married.''

135

"I've tried singles clubs and singles bars and there are far more women out there than men," she said. "It's not easy. But wouldn't you think some eligible man would appreciate a woman who is a terrific hostess and a great cook and reasonably attractive? I have a goal. I want a meaningful relationship one year from now. I'm putting all of my energy into that goal. I'm putting a hell of a lot of time into that goal!"

Her husband was a businessman. She still lives in the sprawling rancher. She still belongs to the country club, and she still moves in the same social circle. She sits in the club bar after her tennis lessons, eyeing any man with graying temples who walks in. She knows exactly what kind of man she wants. There are no confused feelings in setting her goal, so that will make it easier for her to meet someone.

And she's right. Not *every* woman starts or renews a career after they're widowed. The kind of man she'll attract will be a traditional man who wants what her husband wanted—a competent, attractive woman who centers her life around her man. A woman who drops what she's doing if his needs are urgent. A woman who has time to do that, and who is willing to do that. The trouble is (she's right again) many of these traditional men are already married. They're domestic creatures.

So it isn't easy, establishing a relationship whether you're involved in a career or not. But it's possible, even with the accumulated children and years that come with widowhood.

And then, when you find a relationship, you have to ask yourself: "Am I willing to give it the time and energy it needs? Am I willing to share enough of myself?"

How Much of Yourself Are You Willing to Commit?

Let's look at Rita. She's a rangy woman who looks very good in those suits with padded shoulders, the kind Joan Crawford wore in her earlier films. She's in her thirties, and she is the executive director of a health agency. She aspires to be the national director. Rita was working before her husband got sick. She had always worked. The death seems to have accelerated her career goals. She says the loss has made her acutely aware of time and of her own mortality. She says she's in her thirties. If she really wants to make it in the work world, she'd better move fast. Not having children, she has the time to devote to her career. No problems with baby-sitters when she goes to conferences. No guilt feelings when she has to work overtime or on weekends (which is most of the time).

She got involved with George. He, too, is an upwardly mobile executive. George is divorced, and he has his two kids with him on weekends. She had met the children, and she was casually friendly while they were wary. After a while, George started urging her to spend more time with the children on weekends. "Come skiing with us!" he pleaded. "They'll grow to love you when they really get to know you." "Sorry, George," she said, "I really can't, I have to work Saturday." Another time he argued, "You don't have to go into the office every Saturday. At least give me week-ends!" "Sorry, George," she said, "that's the way it is. These are important career years for me."

She's not willing to fully commit time and self and energy to the relationship, and there's no right or wrong about this. It's her decision. She's trading off a committed relationship for a career. That's her priority.

And there's Jody. She had a good marriage, and then her young husband got Hodgkin's Disease. Flare-ups. Remissions. More bad times, and then he died. She was physically and emotionally exhausted from taking care of him. After the funeral, she felt unexpected feelings of relief. She didn't tell anyone about the relief, she felt too guilty. How could she feel relief when she had loved her husband? (Jody didn't know that relief is a very normal feeling after the months of a terrible terminal illness are over.) The relief was quickly followed by the despair of grief. A year after her husband died, she met Roger, who had also been widowed. At first the excitement of that new relationship was exhilarating. They were constantly together. Movies. Theater. Dinners. Weekend trips. Rides in the country. They even went to Greece. Jody felt like a desirable woman again and she loved it. When Roger suggested they move in together, she panicked. Share that much of herself? She pictured herself taking care of him if he got sick. She had fantasies. He was in bed, tubes stuck in him, and she was hovering over his body. He was out of bed, bald from chemotherapy, and she was hovering over him. He was dying—and there her fantasies stopped. Her panic increased. She abruptly withdrew from the relationship and Roger never knew why. She wouldn't talk about it, she felt too guilty about being selfish. That's how she saw herself: selfish because she didn't ever want to be a caretaker to a dying man again.

Now her friends notice she never allows herself to get that close to a man. She dates but she avoids any relationship. She claims to be lonely. When a man gets too close she always finds something wrong with him and that's the end of that.

If Jody sought counseling, she'd learn that there are no guarantees in life, but we must keep living or we have no quality in our lives. She'd possibly learn a basic truth: *she's* the one who could get sick. And the sadder and even more basic truth: we all eventually die, and loss is inevitable, it is part of life.

After learning these truths, and learning to live with these truths, she may become strong enough to *live*.

Meanwhile, Jody is evading a task of bereavement: reinvesting oneself in a new relationship or activities. (Rita is different. She's reinvesting herself in her career.)

It's Tricky, Dating and Grieving at the Same Time

Coping with a relationship while you're still in deep grief can be very tricky. I remember Dick, who was in a support group I led. An attractive man in his thirties, successful in his banking career, he found it easy to meet women. Dick became involved with Karen, who had never been married, when he was in his sixth month of bereavement. Deeply grieving, he turned to Karen for solace and companionship. He told the group members that they were going to Mexico for a week, so he could escape his mourning for a short while—a respite. When he returned, he stormed into the meeting, fuming with rage. What had happened? "She became angry when I talked about my wife!" he exploded. One of the group members asked, "How often did you talk about her?" A silence. "Look," he blustered, "I'm still grieving, remember? What am I supposed to do, put on a happy face when I feel lousy? My wife and I had gone to Mexico on our honeymoon. Being there brought it all back." One of the women said, "You really can't blame Karen for feeling left out. She probably feels used. Maybe you shouldn't take up so much of one woman's time until you're finished with most of your grieving." Dick looked confused and pained. "I need her," he said. "I'm too lonely to give her up. Besides, I need sex in my life. Can't you understand that?"

As the group facilitator, I certainly could understand. I also knew Dick was attempting something very difficult— building a new relationship with all its demands while he was still in the depths of his grief.

If you're seeing someone while you're still experiencing anguishing waves of grief, be honest about your feelings: tell that person you know you're not ready to begin a committed relationship, you don't yet have enough of yourself to give. Friendship? A sexual relationship within the context of your friendship? That's different than a committed relationship. Your honesty will relieve you of feelings of pressure and give integrity to the relationship.

Your Children's Feelings

If you do have kids, chances are they're still living at home, or at least some of them are. They may be small. Chances are they may react to your new relationship. You are their only surviving parent, and they are afraid of losing you, too.

Children don't say this, they act out their fear.

Here are some ways they act out:

"My son mumbles 'hello' when my friend comes over and then he disappears until he leaves. I tell him how rude this is, and he doesn't seem to hear me. His eyes glaze over."

"My daughter has a temper tantrum just before I go out. I'm a wreck when the doorbell rings, and she seems to gloat over this."

"My daughter is nasty to this woman. Really nasty! We've taken her with us to dinner twice, and she insulted my friend, she was rude, and she seemed to deliberately ignore her when she was asked a question."

"It's funny, when I first started to date, my boys seemed to want me to go. 'Go, mom,' they'd say. Now that I'm in a relationship, they find all kinds of bad things to say about Norman. They ask me how I could even want to be with him, he's nothing like their father. They criticize the way he eats, they criticize the way he talks and what he says."

"My little girl wants all my attention when Sandra visits. She crawls in my lap, she cries a lot, she wants to eat, or she has to be taken to the bathroom. When Sandra and I planned to go out for the day and I was going to leave my child with the baby-sitter, she suddenly got sick. I had to stay home."

*　　　*　　　*

140

There are exceptions. There are the children who ask, "Are you going to get married?" or "Is he going to be my father?"

But is this really an exception? There may be more anxiety in this question than hunger for a father replacement.

Kids desperately want to be like other kids. They want a family again, they want to be able to say they have a mother and a father, but they feel they're betraying their dead parent when they are friendly to this new person.

There are other concerns.

A teenager told me, "My mom's going with this guy who has kids my age. If my mom marries him, what about *his* kids? Will my mom love them as much as she loves me? Will she love them more?"

A ten-year old said, "My father's new girlfriend told him he should spank me when I'm bad. My daddy has never spanked me. Who does she think she is, my *mother?*"

And another teenager said, "My mother's boyfriend stayed over the other night. She doesn't know I know it, but I do. He sneaked out of her bedroom around five in the morning and left the house and I heard him. I hate her for doing that. I thought she loved my father!"

A wistful child of eight told me, "My mommy used to take me to the shopping center with her on Saturday afternoons. We'd shop, then we'd stop at the restaurant for supper, then we'd go to the movies at the shopping center and we'd have ice cream before we'd go home. She doesn't do that anymore. She's always with Stanley. If she does take me, she hurries home to go out to eat with Stanley. My grandmother comes over to sit with me and I try to wait up for my mommy but she gets home too late. I fall asleep. I don't like Stanley. I wish my daddy was here."

A lot of hugging and kissing and reassuring is important at this time. That's hard to do, though, if you're the parent

of a teenage boy who no longer wants to be hugged and kiss-
ed. Instead, you need to spend a great deal of time with him.
This is the way you're silently saying, "You'll always be
very important to me." (And why not say it aloud?)

Have you included your child in some of your couple activities? Don't make it a dinner at an elegant restaurant.
Your thirteen-year-old son will only squirm and be bored.
Go bowling, or ice skating or roller skating—something he'll
enjoy. Don't take your daughter at the same time your girl
friend is taking her daughter—at least not right away. Give
the relationship time to gel.

One woman told me she occasionally suggests her son invite a friend along, too. That gives her son a respite from
being "good," while he clowns around with his friend, and
he doesn't feel left out of the couple relationship, because he
has his own friend.

Instant acceptance. It's highly unrealistic if you expect
your child to accept this person or the relationship instantly.
Acceptance is a process, it takes a long time. Initial resistance is normal, and it doesn't mean there can't be eventual
acceptance. The more you push instant acceptance, the
more you'll find resistance.

"But," a woman asked, "what do I do about my son's
rudeness? When he hardly speaks to my friend?"

"I am not rude to your friends," you can say, "and I will
not tolerate rudeness to my friends." A child needs limits,
especially a child who has lost a parent, because that child
has lost all sense of permanence and safety. Limits give
boundaries, and boundaries give the illusion of safety. You
not only tell your child you will not tolerate certain behavior,
you let him know what the consequence will be and you act
on this. You must be consistent. That, too, gives the illusion
of safety in a world that is no longer safe to him.

Your Sexual Relationship

I get so many kinds of responses when I talk about sex to widows and widowers. One woman said, "Sex? In my head I'm still a fourteen-year-old girl who's a virgin. I started to date my husband a year after he was bar mitzvahed and he's the only one I ever slept with. When I finally do get into a relationship, I won't know what to do."

She will. She'll feel strange and self-conscious and confused the first time, but by the third time she'll be fine. She'll be fine because she isn't fourteen; she's a twenty-eight-year-old woman who's had enough life experience to give her a strong sense of self. It's that sense of self that will allow her to walk from the bed to the bathroom, naked. That will enable her to not feel like a failure if he can't sustain his erection.

Many younger widowers do have a temporary problem getting and maintaining erections right after the death or even later. They feel they're in the wrong place with the wrong woman—a displaced feeling. Or they feel guilty, as though they've betrayed their wives. This passes.

Because you have been married, you're used to being direct in telling your spouse what you sexually want and need. (At least, I hope this was your way of doing things.) What do you do now that you're in a relationship? The same thing. Will he think you're forward or will she think you're kinky? Well, do you want a man who would have that reaction, or a woman who thinks that is being kinky?

Do you allow this man with whom you're in a relationship to sleep over if you have kids?

It's easier to answer the question, "Do I go away with him on weekends?" (Why not?) I think the answer depends on many things: how committed the relationship is (you don't want a parade of men passing through your bedroom during the next years—that confuses children); how persons in

143

your social circle behave (if this is not uncommon in your circle, and your kids' friends are used to their parents' live-in lovers, your child won't feel like you or he are deviants); and how secure your child feels at this time (insecure kids feel especially displaced if a new person moves into the house). You might also want to consider the neighborhood in which you live. It's harder to be accepted with a live-in lover if you live in suburbia, but then, I don't have to tell you that. And will your family shun you? And does it matter? (It may not matter to you, but it might matter to your kids.)

If you have teenagers, ask them how they feel about it. One woman did, and her daughter replied, "It's okay, as long as I don't hear both of you at night." Her son asked, "Why don't you get married instead?" (He did move in, and they did later get married.)

But not all relationships turn into marriage. And many of them shouldn't.

The Function of Relationships

Long-term intimate relationships give you a base on which to test your own growth and development: how you relate to this person shows you what you want now. This gives you a better idea of what and who you want later.

These relationships are good for teaching you how to relate to someone different than your husband or wife.

Out of necessity, you learn to be more flexible.

If you've picked someone emotionally healthy, you can do some role modeling; you will become even healthier.

A successful relationship will raise your self-esteem.

But be selective. That's called being good to yourself.

11. The Complexities
of Remarriage

A second marriage is very different than the first one. It's more complex. There are issues that need to be worked through that didn't exist before and many mixed feelings around these issues.

Having come to remarriage after suffering great loss, you may be apprehensive as well as hopeful. You're not the same person you were before—no one is after the death of a spouse—so you feel differently; you might even behave differently.

Tina, who is thirty-two with a Renoir face, handed me a mug of hot chocolate and looked around her living room decorated with folk art and primitive portraits of children. "Sure, it's more complex this time," she said, sitting down. "I had to decide what to do with this house, put it on the market or rent it—it's a bad time to try to sell—and I have to get rid of a lot of my furniture. Ted's place is completely furnished. I hate selling my furniture. I love everything in this house." She sighed and there was a silence. Then she continued, "Ted has children and he wants us to go to our attorneys and have prenuptial agreements drawn up. I don't know how I feel about that since he has so much more than I do and he's concerned about his kids, maybe more than he's concerned about *my* financial security—who knows. I don't have children. Why do *I* need to draw up an agreement?" Her voice was grim. "Now I have to think about changing the beneficiaries on my insurance policies and my other papers. It's not like the first time. My husband and I were very young, we had just finished college, and we didn't have a cent besides our salaries."

Tina's right. The issue of property and assets usually doesn't exist before a young first marriage.

Lenny and Marilyn invited me to their home for drinks. Both of them had been widowed. They've been married four years. The furniture was bamboo and off-white cotton, the paintings splashes of bright colors. They were tanned from many hours on their boat. Their kids from their marriages were playing Monopoly on the sun deck.

"We're happy," Lenny said, "but don't think it's been easy. Remember, each of us came to this marriage with two children. I had done a lot of reading about the so-called blended family before we got married, but the blended family isn't so blended in that first year."

His Scandinavian-looking wife, with her long, blond hair tied back in a ponytail, raised her eyebrow at her husband. "Honey," she said, "think back. How about that ghastly second year?"

"Oh, yeah," he laughed. "That was the year Marilyn's thirteen-year-old daughter threatened to run away, to go live with her grandmother. She said she hated all of us. We went into family therapy."

Marilyn said, her voice very even, "That was also the year your son finally stopped being so polite and let me have it. I was the wicked stepmother. It was a year full of name-calling and yelling."

They eyed each other with ironic smiles over their drinks. The glass sliding doors to the sun deck opened and a gangly boy with freckles peered into the room. "Hi!" he said. "Can I call Bryon to sleep over tonight, Dad and Marilyn?" Lenny looked at Marilyn. She nodded. "Okay," he said to his son, "but be sure he asks his mother first."

Marilyn and Lenny are typical, a couple who went into re-marriage with children and found that blending is a long process.

It's not only property and children that can be hot issues; it's also getting through the comparisons you were so sure you weren't going to make. It's getting used to living inti-mately with another person when you were just getting used to living alone. It's deciding which set of in-laws to have for the Fourth of July barbecue, the ones from before or the new ones. It's learning not to cringe when your husband talks about his deceased wife to the neighbors, and you're sitting there like a lump as they're all remembering the good times together. It's swallowing your resentment when your new wife's friends keep telling you how great her husband was. It's rearranging the living room and having your husband get home from work, look around, and exclaim, ''What's wrong with the way Norma fixed it? I think we should put it back the way it was.''

It's silently worrying about whether you should be buried next to your deceased spouse or your new one. The plot was already purchased for you, next to your deceased husband's plot. When your children grow up they're going to have to travel from one cemetery to another if you're buried next to your new husband. Then you come to your senses: why are you eating your heart out, you're only in your thirties. Then you realize why. Death is real now. And a little round part of you, way inside of you, feels guilty, thinking you may not be buried next to your deceased husband.

It sounds very complex, doesn't it? But it may also be all the good things you hope it will be. You're part of a whole family again, whether it's just the two of you or there are children. You are again the center of someone's life. There's now someone waiting when you get home, who worries

147

when you're late. You have a purpose for living. You've found someone again with whom to laugh and make love and make plans. You can finish the unfinished business of living that was cut off so quickly.

Just be sure you're getting married for the right reasons: because you love *and* like this person; because you laugh together; because you enjoy the companionship; because the sex works; because your rhythm and pace of everyday living is pretty much the same; because you share the same values; and because you enjoy sharing your space and your time with this particular person.

Are You Sure You're Finished Grieving?

It's not fair to yourself or your new spouse if you're still in deep grief. This doesn't mean you won't have brief sad interludes during the anniversary of the death, or when you see your son graduate from Harvard you won't feel bad, knowing that for your son it's not the same having his stepfather there instead of his father who also graduated from Harvard. But your deep grieving should be over before you consider remarriage. You should be finished with the waves of *anguished* grief. If you're still experiencing them, wait.

If the person you're marrying has also been widowed, is he still grieving? I don't mean those fleeting sad moments of remembering, I mean the crying and the depression. If your relationship has basic strengths, it can stand some waiting. Talk about it together.

Perhaps you're marrying someone who's divorced. If she left instead of being left, she probably did her grieving before the divorce took place. (A divorced woman told me she felt powerful after she left; for the first time in years, she felt in control of herself and her life.) However, if she was the one who was left, she may still be in deep grief. Being very needy, she'll have little to give to a marriage right now.

She'll need *your* emotional care. She's at the stage that you were in before, remember?

If you're marrying a person who has never been married, will he understand the grief of your children? Will he feel threatened by your occasional sadness?

Some persons jump into remarriage very fast because they're so lonely. Remarriage within the first year of bereavement is potential trouble: there's no way grief can be completed and resolved within one year. In fact, it usually reaches its highest peak in the latter half of the first year, or during the second year. It's very hard to build a new relationship while one is still in deep grief.

Getting Rid of Ghosts

All right, you've made the decision: you are getting married. But get rid of the ghosts before the wedding. Now is the time to clear the closets as well as the air, to clear the bureau drawers as well as your thoughts.

It may be hard to do, but put away all the photographs of your deceased spouse before the wedding. (Give them to your children for their rooms or apartments. If you have no children, put them in the attic.) Take down the framed award your husband won. Put away your wife's golf trophies. It won't be easy, you might feel some guilt, but it's a necessary thing to do in order to say good-bye. Your newly married home cannot be a shrine to the past, not even one room. It's not fair to your new spouse.

Ask your future wife if she wants the cookbooks and the file boxes of recipes to stay in the kitchen. It'll be *her* kitchen now, and those cookbooks and recipes are part of your past.

That king-size bed—it's an overwhelming ghost. Buy a new bed and do it before your marriage.

There will still be reminders: houseplants, a chair covered with the needlepoint your wife worked on, the workshop your husband built in the basement. Talk to your future spouse, ask him what he'd like to keep. Be sensitive to his hesitations or his silences. They're as eloquent as words.

Before you discard or give anything away, ask your children if they want them. Maybe your teenage daughter would like that needlepoint-covered chair in her bedroom—it's a loving reminder of her mother. You're walking the thin line between being sensitive to your future spouse and your children's needs; that's why you want to offer everything to your children before you dispose of them.

Ghosts are sometimes experiences, not objects. If you and your wife always vacationed in Cape Cod during the month of August, don't take it for granted your new spouse will want to continue that custom. Those neighbors in Truro, the ones you walked the dunes with every summer, they're going to be very curious about your new wife; they may act reserved with her out of loyalty to your deceased wife. Ask your future spouse if she wants to try it once, and if she doesn't, if she wants this to be part of your old life, over and finished because she wants new beginnings, respect how she feels.

Ghosts are hard to live with. They're hard to give up, but they're harder to live with once you've remarried.

Property and Credit

Making the transition from "mine" to "ours" isn't always easy. A woman said, "My husband and I loved auctions. We bought a beautiful chest at an auction in Pennsylvania and we refinished it together. I love that chest. It has sentimental value to me. After I remarried and I moved into my husband's apartment, he wanted me to put it in the den, and I wanted it where people could see it in the living room. We had a fight about it—isn't that silly? But we did. I felt resentful that he was telling me where to put *my* chest."

*   *   *

"After I moved into my wife's home," a man said, "we had a hard time and it was over her furniture. She's very particular, every piece of furniture in her home was chosen with care and she thinks of it as *her* furniture. Well, when I'd unthinkingly put my feet up on the cocktail table or rest my head against the sofa pillows, she'd yell, 'You're dirtying my furniture!' It was always *her* furniture. Now it's easier. I have my own study, and I bought some things—a sofa, a desk, you know, but everything is mine. When I want to relax I go in there."

Most persons come into remarriage with assets much larger than a chest or a houseful of furniture, though. Then there are decisions to be made: how do you divide up what you each have, and what do you leave to whom?

Prenuptial agreements, what the woman in the apartment filled with folk art was talking about, is something you might want to consider if you have considerable assets and children. You expect your marriage to last, you wouldn't be going into it if you didn't, but you know that divorce can happen. A prenuptial agreement is a legal agreement stating what you're going to give to whom if your marriage ends and is drawn up when each of you goes to your respective attorney *before* the wedding. If you do consider this kind of agreement, choose a knowledgeable attorney (some lawyers know little about prenuptial agreements) and be sure each of you uses a different attorney. Your future husband's lawyer might be his best friend, he might play handball with him every week, and if you also use him—well, how objective will he be about your needs?

You need to review your existing will before you remarry. You may need to write a new will. If you're hesitating about writing a will because you're superstitious, your common sense may overcome your superstition once you know some facts: wills are governed by state laws; if you die without a will, the state in which you live will decide how your estate will be distributed. These state laws vary. In some states, if you have no will, one third of your estate goes to your spouse and two thirds to your children, or half of everything goes to your spouse. Is this the way you want it? Lawyers' fees plus court costs can be much more expensive when an estate is distributed without a will. Your heirs might have to wait much longer for their money.

Before you remarry, discuss your new or changing insurance needs with your insurance agent, and, if necessary, change the beneficiaries. Review all of your important papers and see where and if you want to change beneficiaries.

Women need to have credit in their own name as well as joint accounts after remarriage. You might have been one of the many women who found, after the death of your husband, that you could no longer use the credit cards that were in his name only, and establishing credit in your name took longer than you expected; meanwhile, you had no credit, despite an excellent credit history (in your husband's name!).

It is different this time, isn't it?

Your Children

Sometimes widowed persons coming into remarriage strike it lucky: their children immediately accept the marriage. More often this doesn't happen. Acceptance takes a long time—it's a process. Here are some ways to try to make the process easier:

- Inform your children, once you know you're getting married. Share your plans. This way, your kids aren't left uncertain about their future.
- Give them opportunities to be part of the planning of the wedding. Ask them to play a role in the ceremony.

- Verbally reassure them that they'll be as important to you as before. *Repeat this.*
- Spend time alone with them, before and after the wedding.
- Include them in activities with your future spouse. Choose activities that appeal to everyone.

Children resist a parent remarrying because they're afraid they'll lose their surviving parent. After all, they've already lost one parent. Children resist a parent's remarriage because they feel they're betraying the memory of the deceased parent by their acceptance of this new person. If your kids are still grieving, this can slow down the process of acceptance.

As adults we can understand this, can't we?

It is also helpful if you realize your remarriage means many changes in your children's lives. A new parent figure, welcome or not, is physically in their home. Their space, privacy, and time will be impacted on and changed. New stepsisters and brothers might be in the picture, sharing their bathroom *and* their time with you. They're faced with a new side of you, the part that's seductive and flirtatious, and this is difficult for some children who need a parent to be strictly a parent and nothing else. Activities in the house could change for them—maybe added chores. If your new spouse is very structured, new demands could be put on them. If your new wife is gregarious, and their mother was private and quiet, it could mean a household that suddenly changes: many new, strange people floating in and out of their lives; all those new aunts and cousins planting moist kisses and leaving lipstick on their faces; all those new uncles chucking them under the chin and saying things they never heard before from adults, "How're you doin', kiddo?" This can be upsetting to quiet, private children.

But there will be payoffs for your kids. Your teenager might have felt she had to stay home with you most weekends, even though you never told her she had to (you didn't even know she felt this way!). She'd see you looking forlorn and she didn't want to leave you alone, but she really wanted to escape and be with her girl friends, away from death and grieving and loneliness.

She'd hang around the house on Sundays and feel resentful; then she'd feel guilty because she felt resentful.

Now she finally feels free to build her own social life. (Yes, I know you never intended for her to feel this way, but many adolescents feel responsible for their alone and bereaved parent.)

The heavy gloom and the tense quietness that followed the death is now gone. You do things together as a family. You *are* a family. Your kids might be fighting this new person and your new marriage, but deep inside of them, they're glad they're part of a whole family. They feel normal again.

Your New Spouse's Relationship With Your Children

Discuss your feelings and philosophy about child rearing before you remarry. One of you could be more permissive than the other; one of you might have different ideas about what children should be like. You might have to compromise.

I really think you should be the one who punishes your kids, and not your new spouse, until there is a large degree of acceptance of him and the marriage. As the relationship develops between your spouse and your children, your husband can begin to take on a more active role, and then later, an equal role. When that time comes, be sure you always present a united front.

Names: what should your child call her new stepmother? Whatever is comfortable for her. Calling her "mom" will possibly stick in her throat; she'll feel she's betraying her real mom. (Your future spouse might want to suggest a name.)

If you're marrying someone who has never been married, he has a big job ahead: learning to share you. At times you might feel conflict. Who should you spend Saturday afternoon with? Your daughter who insists the two of you be alone, or your new husband who wants to go to a movie? Your eleven-year-old and your new wife both demand your attention at the same time and you suspect they're competing; then you think, "Oh, that's silly." (Is it?)

Here's a way of handling this situation. Set aside a time of the evening when the kids know you and your new spouse are to be left alone; perhaps a wine-and-cheese hour, from six to seven every evening before supper, in a room by yourselves. (This can be the time when your kids are preparing the salad.) And then let your spouse know that your kids will have you all to themselves in the hour before they go to bed, for bedtime stories or just plain talk.

If you're moving into your new spouse's home, it won't be an easy time for your children. They're going to feel displaced. Not only do they have to get used to the new house and neighborhood, they have to make new friends and get used to the new schools at the same time they're mourning the loss of their friends from the old neighborhood and getting used to sharing you.

This is a time when ground rules for living in the new place should be limited to as few as possible. That will make life a little easier for everyone.

Your children, no matter what their ages, are torn between accepting this new person and holding on to their dead parent. The holding on takes a long time to complete before they let go. Time. That's the key word in their eventual acceptance of your spouse and the marriage. Give yourselves time.

Your Stepchildren

You're going into the stepparent role with centuries of mythology behind you: you have been cast as the mean stepparent. Sure, it's unfair. It's like mothers-in-law. They've come to that role with the baggage of mythology. (Have we ever heard a *father*-in-law joke?)

There are ways in which you can attempt to win over your stepchildren:

- Accept the fact you can never replace their biological parent, so don't even try.
- Be direct and honest when you want them to do something; don't be manipulative.
- Be sensitive—do they mind being touched? If they shrink back when you kiss or hug them, be content with a fleeting touch on the shoulder and caring words.
- Constant talking or fussing over them or nonstop activities are overwhelming, so slow down.
- Show interest in their lives not by talk only, but by doing: show up at the P.T.A. meeting and offer to take your teenage stepdaughter shopping.

If your new spouse was divorced, this may make acceptance more difficult. Your stepchildren feel a natural allegiance to their biological parent who is still alive. The letting go that eventually occurs with children whose parent has died does not occur with children who still have both parents living. And it shouldn't! What you can hope for is that your stepchildren will eventually grow to love each parent and stepparent in his own way. Kids are able to love many people.

The Relationship Between Your Kids and Your Stepchildren

Territory. That's one of the biggest issues between step-siblings. Each of the respective parents is territory. Their bedrooms are territory. The bathroom is territory. The house is territory. And each of them, in their own fashion, is fighting for his piece of turf. (There's the passive-aggressive fighter, the agressive fighter, and the child who doesn't seem to be fighting at all but is.) Each of the kids is very conscious of who gets more attention from each parent and stepparent. There are power grabs. Sibling rivalries. Wariness. Distrust. Temper tantrums. Withdrawal. Tears.

If you know all of this is normal to the process of building a stepfamily, you don't feel as defeated. You're more able to take one day at a time.

Your responsibility? To be sure you're acting fairly. You can't be responsible for your feelings. You can expect to favor your own children. You are responsible for your behavior: you can't play favorites.

Insist your parents also act fairly.

Ask your new spouse to be responsible in the same way.

Slowly your new stepfamily merges or blends. It's a zigzag road, as all growth is. Some moments are actually joyous. Eventually people and relationships fall into place. Trust begins. Loyalty within the stepfamily develops. Love begins.

If you'd like some help along the way, contact The Stepfamily Association of America, Inc. It's a nationwide organization that offers educational materials and support, social activities and conferences. Write or call:

The Stepfamily Association of America, Inc.
28 Allegheny Avenue, Suite 1307
Towson, Maryland 21204
Ph: (301) 823-7570

In-Laws

Some parents are very happy when their widowed son finally remarries, especially if there are small children. Others show concern: is this woman as wonderful as their deceased daughter-in-law? Will she be as good a mother to the kids? Will she encourage the children to stay as close to them?

Then there is the mother-in-law whose daughter has died. She may be very upset when her son-in-law remarries. This new woman is replacing her daughter, it's like her daughter is dying again. She is sure her grandchildren will forget their biological mother. They might forget *her*.

If you're marrying someone who has never been married, your new in-laws might feel it is not suitable for their child to have to be an instant stepparent and have all this responsibility.

And if you're very fortunate, none of this will happen.

If any of it does, realize that time is your ally. Their resistance and defensiveness will dissolve as they see you do want to include them in your new family. That you are encouraging their grandparenting. That even though your new wife has never been married and has been confronted with a demanding stepparenting role, you are sensitive to her need for time alone and respite from child care.

Expect This Marriage to Be Very Different

You're at a different time in your life, so this marriage has to be different. You and your new spouse will build your own family rituals. Christmas might be celebrated differently: in your first marriage your children were very young and you were a full-time homemaker; you had the time to cook a big Christmas dinner for twenty people, hang stockings on the mantel, invite neighbors in for eggnog, and trim a big tree. Your children, being small, expected these traditional rituals. Today they're older so they don't. And you're now a full-time career woman instead of a full-time homemaker; you don't have the time to shop and cook and lavishly entertain. Your new Christmas ritual may be spending the holidays as a family at a ski lodge.

You and your new wife may decide you're finished with the suburbs. You renovate a house in the gentrified inner city. Your new neighbors are professionals, like the two of you. Your lifestyle has changed radically.

Or you and your new husband quit your advertising jobs and move to Boulder, Colorado, where you open an art gallery. A big contrast to before, when you and your first husband lived in an apartment on West End Avenue in New York.

Or you finally do conceive your first child, now that you've remarried, and you move to the suburbs.

Nothing stays the same in life. Especially in a remarriage.

Look Forward, Not Back

A woman said, "If only I had shown this much love when I was married before! I feel guilty."

Regrets are like dead flowers. They should be thrown out. Try to look forward, not backward.

You're making a second life through remarrying. Maybe you didn't do everything right the first time. You were less experienced and less knowledgeable. You weren't as keenly aware of how little time we have. Now, because you do know more, you can try harder.

You do have a second chance. You are starting a new life. You've grown through your grief, and in the years ahead you'll have many chances to show you much you've grown.

12. The Choice to Stay Single

Remarriage isn't for every widow or widower. There are those who consciously make the decision not to remarry and others don't realize they've made that choice but they have. Their behavior indicates that they have.

Michelle

I first met Michelle in one of my favorite bar-restaurants where the oak paneling and the smoked glass is the same as it was at the turn of the century. She had called me when she heard I was writing this book; she said it was time someone wrote a book especially for younger widows and widowers, and if she could be of any help to let her know. We talked again on the telephone, and she let it slip that she was sure she'd never remarry. I remembered that later. And that's how we ended up sitting in my favorite bar-restaurant.

I reminded her that she had said this. I said, "Why are you so sure you'll never remarry? You're only forty-one. You're attractive. As a high school principal, I'm sure you meet many men." This self-contained-looking black woman folded long, elegant fingers and smiled in a self-knowing way. "I'm a loner," she said.

I waited.

"I don't think I realized I was a loner until I had been widowed three years," she said. "And I didn't find out until I got involved with someone."

Oh?

She leaned back as the waiter put shrimp cocktail in front of her. We unfolded our napkins. "Andrew—that's his name—really wanted to get married," she continued. "He's divorced, his children are grown, and he's a domestic creature. He's older than I am. He's in his early fifties, and he's rattling around in his big house by himself. This is a man who loves people. He really loves people. Once he said to me, 'Michelle, do you know my dining room table hasn't been used for over two years? I miss the dinner parties with a woman sitting at that end of the table, making conversation with all of my friends.' That's what he said."

She speared her shrimp and dipped it in the sauce.

"But what does that have to do with your being a loner?" I asked.

She stopped chewing and stared at me as though I should have understood. Then she said, "I didn't want to be that woman sitting at that end of the table," she answered. We ate in silence. Then she said, "It wasn't Andrew. He was fine. He's a dentist; he's financially secure; he's a gentleman; he's even courtly. It was me. I found that out when he wanted to spend weekends with me, when he wanted us to spend every weekend at his home. That's when I discovered I'm really a loner."

"How did you find out?"

"Even though his house is large, I felt intruded upon. It annoyed me, having him present twenty-four hours a day. After two weekends at his house, I decided to ask him to spend the next weekend at my house. Maybe it's because it's his place, I told myself. Maybe I'm uncomfortable being in someone else's home. But that wasn't it." She paused, then continued, "I felt the same way at my home. I didn't like having to share my space and my privacy."

I asked, "But what about when you were married? How

did you handle your feelings about sharing space and privacy then?''

She shrugged, smiling slightly. ''When you get married at nineteen you don't know what you're like. And when you're older you're different than you were at nineteen. And in between nineteen, when I got married, and the year my husband died, I was so busy raising children and going back to college and then getting my Master's and Ph.D. while I was working full time that I didn't have time to think about how I felt. It wasn't until my husband died that I realized I like my privacy,'' she said. ''Look, I never had any privacy before that. How would I have known? Women tell me they hate walking into their empty houses after they've been out at night. I love the quietness and the privacy. I noticed, the weekend that Andrew stayed over, that it annoyed me when he'd fill up my ashtrays with his cigars, and it bothered me when the noise from the television disturbed my reading. He loves TV and I don't, so he spent a lot of time watching it while I read. He mostly watched sports. I hate sports. I'd be reading and he'd want to talk, if he wasn't watching TV. I'd feel annoyed when I had to stop reading and listen to him, but I felt since he was my guest, I had to be gracious.'' She added, ''And I even resented sharing my bed every weekend. Before that, when he had stayed over intermittently, it was all right. But *every* weekend?!''

''What didn't you like about sharing your bed the whole weekend?''

She thought. Then she said, ''I'm a light sleeper, and his snoring bothered me. Not having the entire bed to sprawl out on bothered me. I wouldn't have minded if he had gotten out of bed at two in the morning and gone home—that would have been different. And then, in the morning, I felt I had to make him a big breakfast. He insisted I didn't have to, but how do you let a grown man nibble on a slice of dry toast?''

She played with her napkin. "That taught me a lot about myself, that relationship with Andrew."

I dared the question: "And how do you feel about being a loner?"

"Fine!"

And she gave me a quizzical look, like why shouldn't she feel fine.

Over a leisurely lunch, we made some desultory talk about her work, the public school system, and the politics of the city. I decided to give it another shot before we parted.

"Tell me," I asked, "since you plan not to remarry, what are you planning to do with the next few years?"

Without hesitation, she said, "I'm ambitious. I hope to move up in the school system, and since I now have my Ph.D., I think I can manage that quickly. I'm active in my sorority. I love traveling, and some of my divorced and widowed friends also love to travel. We just came back from Africa. We plan to go to the Holy Land in a couple of months. I have season tickets to the opera and to the symphony. I go to church regularly. As you can see, I'm a person who likes people. I just don't want to live with anyone."

I asked, "Do you see men playing a part in your future?"

She laughed. "I hope so. I enjoy men. I'd hate to think Andrew is the last man in my life."

"And what kind of relationship do you want with a man?"

She rose and pulled on her kid gloves. "Friendship. Companionship. Someone to go to nice restaurants with and maybe to go to a piano bar with—I don't like going to bars with women. If I met someone I was really attracted to we'd probably have a sexual relationship, but he'd have to accept the fact he couldn't sleep over." She laughed again, buttoning her cape. "Oh, if there's a blizzard he could sleep over. I'm not that rigid, but there aren't too many blizzards around here, are there?"

We walked to the door together, and I thanked her for having lunch with me, for letting me interview her. She asked when the book was coming out. I told her I would send her a copy. We shook hands and I watched this self-confident woman walk down the street; even from the back she looked confident.

We live in such a couple-oriented society, it's hard to believe that a woman would choose not to remarry. Michelle, though, has one of the best reasons in the world: she's a loner. We make a mistake when we feel sorry for loners. We're so sure they're lonely. And they're not. *They* pick and choose the times when they want someone around, and this suits them fine. Michelle cherishes her moments alone. She puts great value on her independence and privacy. She uses her time alone creatively: she reads, she listens to music, she writes papers for the course she happens to be taking—she's always taking a course. She calls her daughter who lives in another state, she calls friends and they chat. Sometimes, she told me, she just lies on the chaise on the porch and watches the way the light filters through the trees.

Phillip

I had never been in an apartment that had so many electronic gadgets in it. I didn't know what most of them were. I stepped over some scientific journals to get to the chair Phillip cleared for me. He sat down. He cleared his throat. He looked at me. "Well!" I said. We looked at each other. "Your mother suggested I talk to you," I said. (His mother is a friend.) He nodded briefly. I said, "I'm writing a book on younger widows and widowers." He nodded, looking at me. I thought: maybe he's like this because his loss has been so recent. Then I remembered what he had been like as a child—aloof, brilliant, and eccentric. This twenty-seven-year-old man had been a nine-year-old boy who had taken my record player apart and put it together again just because he wanted to see what the inside looked like; and he had been a boy who was admitted to Johns Hopkins University when he was fourteen (a special program for precocious youth). I decided on a frontal approach. He was not going to initiate the discussion nor was he going to indulge in small talk.

"I'm really glad you agreed to talk to me about your wife and the death," I said.

Pain flickered across his face. His mouth worked wordlessly. He said, "Maybe I can help other men by telling how I feel. I don't know. My mother says I can, that I should try."

Gently, I said, "I'm sure you can, Phillip."

He pulled at his fingers, cracking the knuckles, and looked at me imploringly. "I don't know what help I can be. I'm not the typical male, I know."

"You weren't the typical young boy," I said.

He nodded.

"But that doesn't mean you're not feeling what every other widower feels," I said. "I'm sure you can help. I'm jumping the gun, Phillip. It's so early—your wife only died five months ago, but do you see yourself eventually remarrying?"

He looked startled. "God, no!"

"Why not?"

A rapid blinking of the eyes, a licking of his lips, then, "Who'd I marry? Who would marry me? Nobody but Joell could understand me, or could stand to live with me. Did you ever meet Joell?"

I remembered their wedding. They were two kids—they were in their early twenties but they seemed like children—both wearing glasses, both looking scared and each of them with the same expression on their faces: "What am I doing here? What am I doing here with all these women with their gold chains? And these other relatives who are talking and eating and drinking with such gusto—they're in another world than I am. I don't even know them."

Phillip had never dated until he met Joell. He met her after he finished his postgraduate work, on the job. They were both physicists. According to his mother, *Joell* had never dated before. Both of them, his mother proudly told me, were in Mensa, the organization for persons with exceptionally high I.Q.s. "They'd come to dinner on Friday night and they wouldn't open their mouths," she told me. "But they loved each other! They'd hold hands like little children under the table while they'd eat. They'd sneak glances at each other like teenagers."

Then Joell was killed in a car crash.

"Do you think you want eventually to have children, Phillip?" I softly asked.

His shrug was impatient. "It's not important to me. No. That means remarriage. No."

I hesitated, then I said, "You might meet someone like Joell. It could happen again."

His eyes were accusing. "I don't want to meet anyone. No one could be like Joell. I just want to do my work, I want to be left alone to do my work."

We sat in silence for a few minutes. I said, "What will you have besides your work?"

"My work's enough!"

I looked around the room. The electronic gadgets. The piles of scientific journals on the floor and on tables. Maybe he was right.

I kept thinking about Phillip. For days, I kept remembering our conversation. I felt so sorry for him. Then I tried to sort out my feelings, and I realized something: to feel sorry that he has to go through such pain in his grieving is one thing; to feel sorry for him because he may never remarry—well, that's projecting my own feelings. I forced myself to picture him as a forty-year old, as a sixty-year old, and it wasn't hard. He would be engrossed in his work, as he is now, he would continue to publish in journals, he would go to conferences throughout the world, as he does now. Nothing would be very different. He is so sure he can never find someone like his wife, and he's possibly right. He's so sure he'll never find anyone who would *know* him as Joell did.

That's not much to ask, to have someone *know* you. And maybe Phillip is being realistic: he doesn't want to get married again, if it isn't to someone who would know him in the real sense of the word; someone who could appreciate his idiosyncracies, his intellect, and his uniqueness.

There are other Phillips. These persons do have a hard time finding kindred souls. Some of them feel like Phillip; if they cannot find someone like themselves, they refuse to settle for less.

Puffin

Can you imagine a person named Puffin? When I think of the name, I picture a girl (not a woman, a girl) who attended a finishing school in the South, the kind where all the girls become perennial girls, even in their thirties and forties; girls who have coming-out parties and their own horse. When they marry, these girls live in big houses on hills. They use their mother's cleaning woman. When they have the girls to lunch, they serve watercress sandwiches or eggs benedict. Their sons' names have Roman numerals after them, names like William II.

And that's exactly what this Puffin was like, except that she was childless. And her mouth was drawn and older than it should be, and you could see by the distanced look in her eyes that she was protecting herself.

I met her four years after her husband died.

He had been striken with multiple sclerosis and had been

sick for a very long time. After years of being confined to his wheelchair and bed, he had finally died at the age of forty-seven from pneumonia. Puffin had been his physical careta-ker since she had been twenty-five. She is now forty-two.

"Poor, poor Puffin," her mother told me over a glass of iced tea with a sprig of mint in it. "I swear, I don't know what's going to become of her."

I met Puffin while I was on tour promoting my book, *For The Woman Over 50.* She brought her mother to the lecture, and after I finished talking and signing books, her mother came up to me and asked if I had seen any of the gardens of their city—it was daffodil time. No, I said, but I'd love to see a Southern garden. Then she turned to introduce me to her daughter, Puffin. And that's how I came to be sitting on her mother's wraparound front porch, that same afternoon, drinking iced tea with a sprig of mint in it. After her mother told me the story of her daughter's tragedy and said, "Poor, poor Puffin," Puffin opened the screen door and smiled vaguely. "Sit down, dear," her mother said. Puffin sat next to me, on the porch swing. Her mother, with white hair tint-ed blue, got up from the wicker chair and said, "I must take a little rest. You girls just gab a bit," and she floated past us, the scent of lilacs lingering after she disappeared. We smile tentatively at each other, Puffin and I. I asked her what she does with her time in this charming city. "Oh, nothing much," she answered. We rocked. "I hear you're a widow," I said. She nodded and stared ahead. "Do you work?" I asked. "I volunteer," she said. I think I was ner-vous from this nontalk, because I asked a question I didn't expect to ask: "Do you think you'll ever remarry?" For the first time, there was strong emotion. She turned her head to stare at me, her eyes flashing, and in a cold, controlled voice, she said, "I have no intention of remarrying. I had enough of taking care of sick husbands, thank you." Thank *you,* I said a few minutes later when I realized our communication was finished as far as Puffin was concerned, over and finished as she stared ahead. Thank you for a lovely afternoon and please tell your mother her daffodils are lovely and I enjoyed the refreshment. Could you please call me a cab?

I can understand the Puffins and other women like her. They are victims: burnt out from taking care of sick, terminally ill, or disabled husbands. They are emotionally and spiritually and physically exhausted from months or years of lifting heavy men from wheelchairs to beds, spoon-feeding them, emptying bedpans, and sitting by their beds Saturday nights while their friends are dressing for parties.

I can well understand why they refuse to remarry. The idea is terrifying to them: it could happen again, and they feel they couldn't survive it.

The Persons Who Don't Articulate Their Reasons

Michelle and Phillip and Puffin—they know the reasons they don't want to remarry. However, many widowed persons don't, because they don't think about it. They aren't aware they resist remarriage; instead, they act out their feelings.

There is the woman who had been widowed five years. She centers her entire life around her eleven-year-old son and sixteen-year-old daughter. You see her son trailing after her in shopping centers. Her daughter's starting to date; the woman waits up for her at night and spends the evening watching television and looking at her watch. Not only doesn't she have any male friends, she has no close female friends. She's making a statement: she's absolutely avoiding the possibility of remarriage.

And there was the pretty widow I met at a pottery class we were both taking. We got in the habit of going out for coffee after class, and one night she confided, "This darling man visits when my kids are at school. It's strictly a functional relationship. He fills my physical needs. It's a wham-bam-thank-you-ma'am relationship and that's the way I like it. To be polite, we ask each other how our kids are as he's zipping up his pants—do I sound crude?—but I wouldn't have it any other way. I hope it goes on like this for years, it works so well. I'm not looking for anyone else. I'm too content with things just as they are. Married men do have their functions.''

She, too, is making that statement.

Articulated Reasons

How can we say a reason is good or bad, when a person avoids remarriage? We can make subjective judgments, that's all. In doing research for this book, here are some of the other articulated reasons I heard.

Some men and women said they just don't want the responsibility of another person. A few told me they suffer from a chronic illness and they assume no one would want a partner who is ill. Here and there, I found someone who has a disabled child, and they're sure no one would want that in their lives. One man confided he's now gay. Some told me they had bad marriages, and they're afraid to take another chance. A few, just a few, confided that they never enjoyed sex. (What courage! Most people, today, would never admit that.) More than a few said that after they were widowed, they found they like sex with a variety of persons and they don't want to go back to monogamy. Many men told me they're wary of starting a new family. It's the money and the energy that they don't want to expend, and they don't want to be the forty-year-old father of a baby. Many persons have said what Michelle said—they don't want to share time and space and privacy.

When you're doing research for a book, you talk to many people. Some of those people talk about other people, not themselves. There was the woman who told me about another woman: "She's a secret drinker. I know why she avoids remarriage. The bottle is her first and only love. If she remarried, a man might find those hidden bottles and either leave her or push her into a treatment program."

A woman said scornfully of a widower: "That man's so cheap, he would never share his money or property. The first time he got married, he had nothing. Money wasn't an issue. Now it's a different story."

Options

Fortunately, it's a time when there are more options, at least for many persons. Men and women who choose not to remarry aren't looked at as if they're eccentric or crazy (at one time they were so regarded). They can, if they wish, surround themselves only with other singles. There are even apartment complexes that are built exclusively for singles, and if there was a snowstorm and you couldn't leave your apartment complex for months (just suppose) you could be perfectly happy: there are built-in social activities, physician's offices, drugstores, food stores, saunas, hot tubs, indoor swimming pools, and outdoor pools for when the snow melts.

Singles are such a recognized layer of our society that many advertisements in glossy magazines are solely directed to them: they represent big bucks.

There was a time when a widow was called a "merry widow" (not a compliment!) if she openly enjoyed herself by smoking, going to bars, and loving men. It's now an obsolete term.

But—if you live in a very small town, and you don't remarry, you'll possibly be referred to as "the widow," as the years go by. (People in small towns, particularly the kind of town that isn't trendy and still looks like a setting from a 1930 movie, tend to look at older widowed persons in set ways. They stereotype. You're either the kindly grandparent who they assume is happy because all you need are your grandchildren, or you're the eccentric widow who snaps at children who play on your grass.)

Your particular religion might pressure you into remarriage, because of its position on childbearing. (Procreation is given a great value.)

Your parents, if they're traditional, could pressure you. They might assume no one can be really happy if they're not married.

You can leave the small town, change your church, or avoid your parents. Or you can say, "I am my own person. I shall make my own choices."

There's no doubt that widowed persons who have higher incomes can enjoy the single life more than persons on limited incomes. If you have enough money, you can afford to live alone and love it. You can enjoy mobility: travel, go to the theater, and take weekend trips on a whim.

And the single life isn't necessarily a dour state of loneliness. You can make it what you want it to be (and what you can afford).

Jacqueline Simenauer and David Carroll, authors of *Singles: The New Americans,* indicate that almost 40 percent of widowers say the single life is going well!

Nothing Ever Stays the Same

However, having made your choice, don't take it for granted that what you want today is what you'll want forever.

A woman who had been widowed four years summed it up well:

"After my husband died and I recovered from my grief, I

felt like I was a teenager again. All I wanted to do was get out and have a lot of fun. I had gotten married when I was very young and I had gone with my husband since I had been thirteen—I never knew or dated any other boy. I was only twenty-nine when he died, and I was so tired from nursing him through cancer. I realized, I felt like an old woman and I had never even had the chance to be a normal teenager with the dating and all. So after I finished grieving, I grabbed every chance to have fun. I took dance lessons. I started going to singles bars. I said 'yes' to every man who asked me out. I was having such a ball that I knew I never wanted to get married again and have all those responsibilities. It was a terrific time of my life. Then, earlier this year, I started to get tired of it. I had finished being a teenager. I had gotten all the kicks out of it and I was finished. I started to think: it would be nice to have someone love me again. Now, I *want* to get married.''

Nothing ever stays the same, at least for many persons.

13. Where Should You Live?

"Can you believe it," a man said, his tone bitter, "a woman asked me at my wife's funeral if I was going to sell my house. At the funeral!"

Sadly, this sometimes happens.

Wait At Least a Year Before Deciding

Even if you begin pondering this question, wait at least a year before you make any final decision as to where you'll live.

The first year after the death is filled with indecision. This is a time when not only can you not make up your mind about anything, you're constantly changing your mind. Your whole world has been turned upside down. You don't know who you are anymore. How can you expect to make big decisions? Most newly widowed persons say they can't even make little ones.

And many of these women and men are persons who are used to making major decisions, who are expected to in their careers.

They're persons who were the decision makers in the family.

It shakes people up, not being able to make up their minds about anything after the death. But that's the way it is. It's like this for everyone, no matter how independent and strong you have always been.

And it passes. Slowly, as you recover, you're again able to know what you want.

There ARE Exceptions to the Rule, "Wait"

For some persons, there isn't a choice. They're forced to make a physical move before a year is completed. I'm thinking of the woman I met who had to move into a less expensive apartment because her husband had left no insurance and she had never worked. She couldn't afford to wait.

And there was the woman whose mother became very ill, and it was only five months after she was widowed when she had to give up her apartment to move into her mother's house and become her nurse. (Her parent couldn't afford live-in, paid help or institutionalization, and the newly widowed daughter is a practical nurse.)

The other situation I remember was a man who had been in the middle of selling their house when his wife suffered a fatal accident. The closing date had been set. They had already bought a new home. He felt he had no choice but to go on with what had been their plans.

Generally, though, one can afford to wait a year.

Resisting Pressure

Expect some pressure, during that first year of your bereavement, from well-meaning family and friends, maybe even neighbors.

There's the concerned parent who urges, "Honey, you need to get out of these suburbs and move into one of those apartment houses for singles. You have no children, you're only in your twenties. That's where you belong."

Me, a single? you think. I'm not a single. I'm a wife. (You feel married for a very long time after the death.)

An older man who's a neighbor peers up at your roof, taps

your pipes in the cellar, and turns on your faucets. He says, "This house is ready to go. You can't fix things, you're only a woman. Repairs cost an arm and a leg. Better sell."

A friend exclaims, "Why do you want to stay in this barn? Your heating bill will be enormous. Your income is lower now that you're widowed. Sell!"

"Move closer to us," your sister pleads. "We worry about you being isolated out there. It was all right before, but now you're alone. Suppose someone breaks in? Give up the house."

If you find it hard to say no, you're going to feel especially pressured because you don't want to say yes. So you hedge and give excuses and then you feel angry when they persist. Here's an effective way to say no and say it comfortably:

"I know you're concerned about me, and I really appreciate your concern, but it's too soon for me to make any major decisions about my life. I'm going to wait at least one year before I decide what to do."

If your family and friends keep pushing, repeat what you've said. You are acknowledging their concern and caring, and you are telling them thanks but no thanks, maybe later (and maybe not).

Real estate agents might converge on you.

Some can be very persistent. *And* persuasive.

Well, this is their business, this is how they make their living, so they persist. That doesn't mean you have to say yes. It doesn't mean you need to talk to them for an hour on the phone. (You don't need that aggravation right now.) Say the same thing to them, or just say, "I'll call you if and when I'm ready."

Don't Be Impulsive

Many newly widowed persons become impulsive. It's a tiny voice inside of them urgently whispering, "There's only today. Do it right now. There's only the moment, that's all you can count on, you found that out the hard way. Do everything you always wanted to *right now.*"

You're also not thinking straight. You're so upset that you can't remember what you did ten minutes or ten days ago and what you're supposed to do next. So you do things impulsively.

That's why some men and women wildly spend money those first months. They buy things they don't need or even want. It's a spree. Furniture. A new car. A new wardrobe.

This impulsiveness will pass, but meanwhile you could say yes to the first real-estate salesperson who approaches you (and if she's a personal friend it's even easier to say yes). That first snowstorm, after your husband dies, can mean you literally throw down the snow shovel (you never had to shovel snow before) and say, "I can't do it! I'm selling the house!" (It doesn't occur to you that you can hire someone to get rid of the snow. You're too upset.)

Tell a very good friend, "Stop me when I'm acting impulsively. I don't always know I'm acting this way. Be firm and stop me."

Remember how you had to help your two-year-old when he couldn't stop himself from acting out inappropriate behavior? Well, you need that kind of help right now, until your world isn't so crazy anymore.

The Stress of Moving

Moving is physically exhausting and emotionally stressful, even under normal circumstances. That's another reason for waiting until a year is completed before you decide where to live.

If you have children, their lives have already been disrupted. They don't need the extra stress of moving, leaving their friends in the neighborhood, getting used to the new neighborhood, making new friends, and enrolling in new schools.

Your home may have bad memories. Perhaps you took care of your terminally ill spouse in the bedroom and he died in that room. One woman said her husband was bedridden in that house for ten years. A man said, "My wife killed herself in this house. I can't wait to move." You may want to run. If it's too hard to stay you may have to move. But if you can, stay put the first twelve months.

You Have Already-Established Supports Where You Are

A good reason for staying put, that first year, is your neighborhood support system.

If you have lived there for a little while, you've probably struck up a relationship with at least one person. If you've lived there longer, chances are you've made some good friends. They're no longer just neighbors, they're friends.

You need them. A woman said, "After my husband died, my next-door neighbor visited me every day. She'd sit with me and hold my hand while I cried. I'll never forget her."

A man said, "My neighbors had me over to dinner every week after the death. It went on for almost a year. I not only had cooked meals, I also had company. I think they had it all planned. I think they would decide, ahead of time, who would have me on Saturday and who would invite me on Monday and who would have me on Tuesday and who would have me on Thursday. Only neighbors who are good friends would do that.''

One woman reported that her neighbors took her children to their house to eat, to play, even to sleep over. This gave her a respite from child care when she needed to cry and grieve.

Another woman said she was inert after the funeral. For weeks, she couldn't move. She'd sit in one spot on the sofa all day. She lives in a trailer park, and her neighbors came in to do the dishes, scrub the floor, and drop off groceries.

I must tell you about a twenty-four-year-old widow I met. She said, ''My husband and I are from Vermont. We moved here to San Diego completely alone, with no family. He died three months after our move. A couple of days after the funeral, there was a knock at my door. It was my neighbor from next door, a girl about my age. She's also married. She said, 'I know you're new in town and you probably don't know anyone yet. From this moment on, you're to consider me and my husband your family! You'll hear from me every day. I'll knock to see how you're doing. We want you to have Christmas dinner with us next week, we don't want you to be alone. You hear?' ''

Isn't that a great story?

It's not only neighbors who provide support, it's the institutions in your neighborhood that you always used and counted on. You know the tellers in the bank, especially the one who always talks to you about her dog. Your church or synagogue is in your neighborhood, you go to services every week. That woman behind the desk at the nearby library, the one who saves you the latest mysteries, always has a smile and a friendly word. These institutions, the people in these institutions, make a big difference in your life right now. They help you feel like you're still a somebody, that you're *not* a nothing or a nobody since your spouse died.

And there are the neighborhood stores where you always shop. A man said, "When my wife was so sick, the pharmacist became almost like a good friend. He didn't only fill my wife's prescriptions, he was concerned about how she was doing. He was concerned about how *I* was doing. I'd hate to go to another pharmacist, I'd feel like I was losing someone very special."

People report that shopkeepers always asked about their ill spouse. That they expressed sorrow after the death. A woman said, "The first time I went back to the fruit and vegetable store after the death, the man who owns the store came over to me with a fruit basket, decorated with a ribbon and bow. 'Here,' he said, 'this is for you.' There were tears in his eyes."

"When I shop at the supermarket in my neighborhood, I bump into neighbors," a man said, "and they always stop and talk. That's important to me. The clerks all know me."

Perhaps your doctor and dentist have their offices in the neighborhood. That's comforting, isn't it?

And the feeling of continuity you get from being in the same neighborhood is a very good feeling. A woman said, "We're a neighborhood where people are really close. We have community barbecues. Someone's always having a pool party. This was very important to me and my children after the death, to still feel part of the neighborhood."

Support: use all of the neighborhood support you can get.

What Next?

Every man and woman who's been widowed *eventually* has to decide what to do about housing, even if that decision means staying put.

It's now over a year. You're not as confused (although

you still have some trouble making up your mind and sticking to those decisions). You could stay where you are, but you know there are other options.

How can you make a logical, intelligent decision?

Well, where you live should depend on whether or not you have children, and on your income; also on your psychological, social, and work needs, and the state of the housing market in your area.

First, a financial fact: your housing expense should not use up more than 30 percent of your monthly budget.

If You Have Children

Children need as much continuity in their lives as possible after the death.

If your children have been living in the same place since they were very small—the house you own—see if you can stay where you are. Their closest friends live in the immediate neighborhood. They are known by the teachers at their schools. Their home is part of their environment; it's part of their identity.

And even children who are three and four years of age have made their home a part of their identity. Moving to a new street and a new house or apartment means feeling displaced.

Can you afford to keep the house? If you find it's a struggle, consider taking in a person your age, or renting a room to a medical student, nurse, or secretary. (You can give them kitchen privileges.) You might even consider renting out an entire floor, as an apartment. This means going to the expense of having a kitchen installed, and you have to see if your local zoning laws permit it, but it can mean enough extra income to pay for your monthly mortgage payments and repairs on the house.

(I wouldn't worry about not having a separate entrance.

You can always screen off the staircase for privacy and there are always people who don't mind not having a private entrance.)

Can your basement be converted into an apartment?

Lease space on a monthly, not yearly, basis. It gives you an out if the new tenant turns out to be irresponsible or unbearable.

If, instead, you decide to share your house, and you have children, consider a roommate who also has children. This gives you someone with whom you can share baby-sitting, and it gives your child company. Put an ad in the paper. Screen applicants carefully. Narrow them down to persons who share your values and your lifestyle. (Don't be afraid to ask direct questions when you're interviewing prospective roommates.) Give the children time to play together before you make up your mind and observe the way they get along. Observe the way the parent handles her child: is she authoritarian? Or too permissive? Will that get in the way? Is she nervous, does she yell at her child? (That's important; you don't want the tension level in your home raised.)

Be sure you choose tenants or housemates or roomers who have regular incomes (so their rent is paid on time).

This is not the time to take in a frail elderly person, where a social service agency pays you to provide room and board and take care of them. (You may have heard of this as a way to make extra money.) You don't have the patience or the energy for this right now. You're using all your energy in grieving and child care. And frail elderly persons usually need a great deal of attention.

Sharing space might worry you: will you be able to retain your privacy? Will you get along, all of you?

Safeguard your need for privacy by making certain areas off limits. For instance, use the back bedroom, the small one, just for yourself as a sitting room. (It can double as your sewing or guest room.) Tell your prospective housemate, "Sorry, this is a space I am not sharing."

You don't have to eat every meal together. You don't even have to eat most meals together. Divide the refrigerator shelves and decide when each of you will use the kitchen for cooking. Make mutual decisions about cleanup after dinner (what your standards will be) and the cleaning of shared space throughout the house. You may decide to share expenses for a once-a-week cleaning person.

Before your new housemate moves in, mutually decide how you'll protect each other's privacy if either of you has guests. (You're going to have to discuss how you both feel about sleepover lovers; if there are any differences on this, better find out before you finalize your plans!)

Make it clear you're trying this on a six-month basis. That way, if it doesn't work out for either of you, you'll part with a minimum of ill will. Or, at the end of the six months (if it does work out) you can renegotiate any terms.

Not only can sharing your house allow you to keep your home, but it is a way of keeping your sanity during your grieving. If the person turns out to be compatible, it can mean someone with whom to talk and laugh, someone who will relieve your loneliness.

Other reasons for keeping your home and not selling: your mortgage payments may be much smaller than rent would be for a decent apartment in a good neighborhood; or you bought your home at a lower interest rate than can be negotiated these days and you may not be able to afford to buy another house at a higher interest rate. (At least, another comparable house.)

But you may decide you have to sell your home. It could be for income reasons, or reasons that have to do with your psychological well-being.

Because of a lowered income, you may need to go into cheaper housing. Moving from your big house to a row house means less expensive maintenance. Moving from your house into an apartment means a predictable expense, especially if the rent includes heat and electricity; it means no unexpected large bills for a new roof or furnace!

Your psychological well-being? Well, if your teenager is leaving for college in a few months and you're the only single woman on the block, you may not want to rattle around in that house with no other single persons around to ask in for coffee. You may feel like a sore thumb, being the only single woman on the block. You may resent the fact that every other woman has her husband.

Or you may live in an affluent neighborhood where everyone belongs to a country club and goes to Europe on vacation. When your husband was alive and an executive for a corporation you lived like that, too. Now, it's over. You can't keep up with the Joneses, you don't want to try, and you feel left out.

Or you have a live-in lover; you and your children are comfortable with this arrangement but the neighbors are disapproving.

Other reasons for moving? You feel overwhelmed every time your cellar floods (your husband used to take care of that emergency). Or you live too far from your place of employment. When your wife was alive it didn't matter how far away your office was: you left early in the morning while she gave the kids breakfast, and when you got home at night, the children had already eaten. Now, you are responsible for child care. You have to be at home until the school bus comes to the door. This makes you late for work. The babysitter isn't a good cook (and you don't want to change babysitters); the kids have to wait until you get home before they have their supper, and you don't get home until seven at night.

List the pros and cons of keeping your home. List the pros and cons of selling. Which list is longer?

What to Look for in an Apartment

If you're thinking of moving into an apartment, and you have children at home, be sure you choose a place where the schools are of high quality. (If you stay in the neighborhood where you've been, you won't have to worry about changing schools.)

With preschoolers, you want an apartment that has playground areas on the grounds, and where there are other preschoolers with whom your children can play.

Consider moving into a garden apartment, on the first floor. You can watch your baby from your kitchen window while you cook, and if she cries you can be outside in a few seconds. If you're living on the eleventh floor of a high rise with no balcony, the only time you can take her outside is when *you* go out and stay with her.

It's also good to live in an apartment that is near a hospital.

If your children go to Sunday School or you go to religious services every week, choose an apartment near that house of worship.

And if you count on your mother to baby-sit frequently, find a place that is near her house.

If you have teenagers, choose an area that has good public transportation: you don't always want to be their chauffeur, now that you're the only one chauffeuring.

And pick a place that is near a shopping center. This way, you won't have to always drive your teenagers to the store. (A seventeen-year-old can get pretty frantic when she needs something *right now* for her Saturday night date.)

Being a single parent means you have to find ways in which to conserve time and energy. *Where* you live has a lot to do with that.

If you don't have children, you have more flexibility. You can easily live in the suburbs or the city.

185

You'll be in the company of more singles if you live in the city. Young singles, particularly, like living within walking distance of museums, libraries, the harbor, restaurants, and cafés. They live in condos and apartments, co-ops and renovated old houses.

Consider living in a mid or high rise, rather than in an apartment that is located in a private home. It means there are electronic devices for security. There are elevators. There might be underground parking, so you don't have to scramble for parking on the street. There might be a doorman. You are less apt to experience a break-in on the eighth floor of a high rise than the first floor of an apartment in a private home.

Particularly, it's an easy way to meet other single persons: in the laundry room, the lobby, in the elevator, and by the mailboxes.

Living in an apartment complex that's rented exclusively to singles means no children's voices heard under your bedroom window on Saturday morning when you're trying to sleep. It's also a good place (obviously!) to meet other singles.

See if you can get a short-term lease, no matter what kind of an apartment you've chosen. Now that you're trying to build a second life, you want the freedom to move, if you choose. You can't predict what you'll be doing one year from now, can you? You might be working in England. You might be remarrying. And be sure your lease states you can sublet, in case you need to move even sooner.

If You're Buying a House or Apartment

Some widowed persons never had an opportunity to build equity, and now they want to, so they consider moving from an apartment into a house, or buying a condominium.

Unless you are willing and able to renovate an old house by yourself, forget buying that Victorian pile, or that eighteenth-century, narrow row house that's coming apart. When your spouse was alive it was different.

If you aren't willing or able to take care of outside maintenance by yourself consider buying a condominium. Depending where you live, you may be able to purchase a relatively inexpensive studio (one room, kitchen, and bath). You may prefer a larger space. (It can even be a town house or ranch house.)

You will be building equity without the physical responsibility of maintenance. You *are* charged with a monthly maintenance fee that takes care of that expense. (Altogether, you pay a down payment, monthly mortgage payments, and your monthly maintenance fee. The monthly maintenance fee can go up.)

Some condos are luxurious: Jacuzzis, wet bars, health clubs, saunas, pools, marbled lobbies, doormen, a concierge, and a tennis court. Others are without frills.

See if you can rent with an option to buy. This way, you'll have plenty of opportunity to see how the condominium association works. (Every condominium has an association made up of owners, and there is a board within the association.) For instance, a particular association may vote to purchase expensive lobby furniture that you think is not needed. Can you afford to live there? (This increases your monthly maintenance fee.) Another association may vote to contract for extensive landscaping, when you feel the existing grounds look just fine. If your income is somewhat limited, you want to choose a condominium where the association votes to use your money conservatively.

Also, be sure of any restrictions by management before

you buy. Will they allow children under twelve to use the swimming pool? Will they allow you to walk your dog on a leash through the lobby? (Don't take *anything* for granted: ask!)

You may not be purchasing a condo; instead, you may be looking for a house that's in the same block as your parents' home. You'll have built-in baby-sitters and company when you're feeling lonely.

Do your parents live in a neighborhood that's rapidly deteriorating? That means any property in that area will depreciate in value; it also means that once you move in, you might have a hard time selling the house later.

Are there other children on the block?

How about the neighborhood schools? Are they good?

As you can see, you have many options. (I haven't even mentioned cooperative housing, where you buy shares of the housing and you have a vote as to how the housing is operated.) It's a question of what your changed needs indicate.

Some people think about leaving town and starting over. One woman said, "My husband and I moved here with our baby after my husband graduated from dental school. He got his internship in this city. Well, he died a year after we moved. Now I'm returning to Seattle. Both of our families are there. I want my baby to grow up knowing her grandparents, and all of my friends are in Seattle."

This is probably a good move for her. What she's going to do is smart: first, she'll rent a small house near her parent's home in Seattle, while she sublets her apartment in this city. She'll give it a trial run for a summer. If she finds living back home is a good idea, she'll then give up her apartment and make the move final.

Making the Move Easier for Yourself

This is possibly the first move you're making alone, without your spouse. I hope you'll start packing early, giving yourself enough time to take breaks. Even if you're moving out of a small apartment, it's strenuous. Don't give in to compulsiveness and get everything packed in three days: you'll pay through emotional and physical exhaustion. (If you're working full time, spend no more than one hour an evening packing, and start several months before the moving date.)

Be ruthless. Get rid of things you no longer want or need. A garage or sidewalk sale can take care of that. Or give some furniture to charitable organizations: not only do they pick up, you are allowed tax deductions. (Ask about this when you talk to your accountant.)

Use good friends to help you pack and move. That's what good friends are for.

Making the Move Easier for Your Children

It may be tempting to farm out the kids during the move, to send them to their grandparents' home for the week, or ship them to summer camp. *This is not the time for a separation.* Separation has taken place in their lives in the worst way. They have lost a parent, and now they need to be with you.

Instead, hire a baby-sitter to stay with them while you're moving. The baby-sitter can distract them through games and walks so you can direct the moving men without your son or daughter tugging at your skirt. Or ask your mother to come to you: she can see that they eat and get dressed, and she can take them for ice cream while you're sealing the last boxes.

This move means a move away from the home they had with their deceased parent. The swing under the tree—it has

189

memories. Your child is leaving the bedroom where his daddy read to him every night. Expect your child to be tense on moving day. Temper tantrums. Resistance. Or maybe he'll be hyperactive. Take time out for hugs and kisses.

After the Move

On other moves, before your spouse died, there was an air of anticipation. You looked around, each of you, and felt excitement after the movers left. It was your future home. But now you're alone. It feels desolate and lonely, even with your kids.

Forget the unpacking, the first night. Get out of the new place and go for pizza (a place that is filled with people), or go to your parents' house for dinner. You don't need the stillness of the house or apartment hitting you in the face.

When you do begin unpacking, do it slowly. A little at a time. Purchase a few things that make it your place, not a replica of your married home.

Establish relationships with people in the neighborhood and store owners as soon as you can. A smile and a hello will do it. Take the initiative.

Join the neighborhood association. You'll immediately get to know most of your neighbors, and you'll be part of the process in making it a good neighborhood in which to live.

You may never have taken the initiative before. This time, though, your needs are different. You want to integrate yourself into the neighborhood as soon as possible; as a widowed person you need to build new supports.

Secure Your New Residence—Or Your Old One

This part is especially for widows: as a woman who's alone, you're very aware of physical safety (and you should be). Invest in a good burglar alarm system that is connected to the police station. Grill your basement and first floor windows and doors. A dog is protection. Even if your dog is small, his bark might be big. Ask a locksmith to inspect your locks. Are they adequate? If they're not, ask him to change them. Buy electric timers, so your lights automatically turn on when it gets dark, even when you're not home.

(Of course you'll adapt these suggestions to your own living circumstances: you don't need a burglar alarm system if you're moving to a high-rise apartment house, but you might want one if you're staying in your big house.)

Moving is a Way of Saying Good-bye

This move—it's a way of saying good-bye. You're saying good-bye to your marriage. You're saying another mournful good-bye to your spouse. (You say good-bye many times after the death.)

You're also saying good-bye to a part of yourself, a part of your history as a person.

It's a sad time. It's normal that you feel sad.

Expect to feel intensified grief after the move. A *temporary* setback.

I hope, though, that you also feel you are saying hello. Hello to a new start! Hello to a second life! "Hello!"

14. From Homemaker To Paid Worker

I asked twenty-five younger women who had been widowed, "Who has to go back to work, or who has to go to work for the first time?"

Nineteen shot up their hands. We discussed the reasons.

"I have investments but I don't want to touch the principal," one said. "I have too many expensive years of child rearing ahead of me. The principal is my security blanket. On the other hand, I really can't live on the interest."

"All I have are my social security checks for the kids and my Mother's Benefit checks. I thought I could struggle along on that but I can't," a woman who looked around thirty ruefully said.

A wide-eyed woman said in a rush, "We had no savings! We had only been married two years, my husband was going to law school and our parents were supporting us. I was going to graduate school, getting my Master's degree, so of course I have to go to work!"

And another woman said, "All we had was term life insurance. I'm investing it. I'm going to have to get a job right away. I have two kids."

Money looms as a large problem for most widows, especially those who have small children.

Social Security Benefits

The people who tell you that you can't live on social security benefits—they're right. If you try, it's a very tight and scary squeeze. (Social security benefits were never meant for anything but a supplementary income.)

Every widow receives a lump sum death benefit, which is a fixed $255. But how do you bury a husband on that small amount of money? Most widowed persons dip into savings to pay for a funeral and (if they haven't done it already) to buy a plot.

It's the upcoming years of child care that are frightening, because you know they're going to be expensive years. You will receive modest social security checks on a monthly basis for the children until they're no longer full-time students. However, the checks stop when they are eighteen. (If they cease being students by the age of sixteen, the checks stop then.)

And you, as their caretaker, receive Mother's Benefit monthly checks from the Social Security Administration until your children stop receiving *their* monies.

At the time of this writing, you will get your Mother's Benefit checks, *in full,* if your earn no more than $5,400 for the year. Once you earn more than that amount, your Mother's Benefit checks are reduced.

However, you need to make a social security claim in order to receive any benefits. Call your local social security office and report the death and make an appointment. You'll need to take the following documentation:

- the death certificate
- your husband's social security card
- your social security card
- your birth certificate
- your marriage certificate
- your children's birth certificates

Women who don't have any children and are under the age of sixty are not eligible for any social security benefits as a widow. Many of these women need to return to work, if they aren't working already.

The Women Who Are Already Working

Women who were working before the death report they find work helpful; it's not only the money, it's the psychological benefits.

Even though they have difficulty concentrating on the job and their bosses may become impatient, the job provides a place where they feel visible. It's a place where their skills are valued, and that means a lot at a time when they don't feel they have any value.

Working provides important sociability. One expects to share morning coffee and lunch with certain co-workers. Work forces new widows to leave their home five mornings a week; if they didn't have a job, they might huddle under the blankets, sinking into more depression.

At a time in their lives when they've lost a sense of time, it gives structure to their lives: they know they have to be at their desk at 8:30 A.M., five days a week.

Work forces them to shower, wear clean clothes, and put on makeup when they'd rather stay in a fetal position on the bed in a nightgown all day.

This is good!

If You've Been Home

But it's different for the woman who has never worked, or the woman who hasn't worked in several years. It's also different for the woman who worked alongside her husband in the family business, where she was really her own boss.

These women are suddenly being thrust into a tough work

world where employers know they can be demanding because there are so many job seekers out there; where co-
workers and colleagues are anxious about their piece of pie in
a bad economy, so they're not always sharing.

Many of these women find their skills are no longer mar-
ketable because of changing technology, and they quickly
have to learn new skills (such as learning how to operate a
computer).

And it's still a fact that women earn only 59 percent of
what men are paid for the same job. (That is, for many jobs.)

You Do Have Some Control

Now that you know that it is a tough work world out there,
it's nice to also know you have some control. You can learn
to look for a job in ways that pay off; you can be selective
about your setting; and you can protect yourself on the job.
(In other words, you don't have to look vulnerable because
you're grieving. It's a good idea not to appear vulnerable.)

You can also find cheap places where you can get special
training for the new technology.

And you can gear yourself to look for alternative positions,
just in case they're no longer hiring teachers or nurses or social workers in your area.

Entering and Re-entering the Job World

The first thing you have to do, if you must return to work or
go to work for the first time, is identify what you're able to do
for a paycheck and learn job-seeking skills.

If you do need special training in order to stay in your field
of work, call your local board of adult education and ask if
courses are offered in those areas; if they are, there is no fee
or a low fee. Community colleges also provide job training at
moderate cost.

If you have no work experience, or do not want to go back to the same kind of work you have been doing, get all the support you can to identify your work skills effectively, conduct your job search, write a résumé, and present yourself at the job interview. An excellent resource book is *What Color Is Your Parachute?* by Richard Nelson Bolles. This paperback is substantially revised each year, and it's a practical manual for job hunters and career changers.

Resource centers for women are located throughout the country, where you can get job-seeking help. Many are found on college campuses. Some are located in Y.W.C.A.s. Others are located in state government offices.

If you are over thirty-five, you're eligible for services from a government-funded Displaced Homemaker Center. Their staff will help you every step of the way from assertiveness-training workshops to showing you how to write a thank you letter after coming home from a job interview.

Displaced Homemaker Centers have been established to provide job-finding services specifically for persons over the age of thirty-five who have been suddenly left alone through separation, divorce, or death. A requirement is that they had been full-time homemakers before the loss of a spouse.

If you want more information, write or call:

Displaced Homemakers Network
1010 Vermont Avenue, Suite 817 NW
Washington, D.C. 20005
Ph: (202) 628-6767

Some women must work out of their home, because of the expenses of transportation, baby-sitters, or because they do not want to leave small children with strangers. Approximately 5 million persons work out of their homes, and most of them are women. If you're in this position, read *Women Working Home: The Homebound Business Guide and Directory,* by Marion Behr and Wendy Lazar.

To order this paperback, write:

Women Working Home, Inc.
325 Pierson Avenue
Edison, New Jersey 08837

If you do work from home, make sure you spend at least part of each day outside of your apartment or house. It's very easy to feel housebound, lonely, and depressed, seeing no other adults throughout the day. Even if it's a visit to a neighbor, or a trip to the shopping center, get out of the house.

And if you do work from home, beware of those advertisements in the classified section of newspapers, where you're told you can make good money addressing envelopes. Most of the time, it's a racket.

Whether you plan to work outside or inside your home, go about your job seeking thoroughly and methodically; use the resources I've talked about, and any you hear about on your own.

Use Personal Contacts

Ask friends and family and acquaintances if they know of any jobs in your field.

This is using personal contacts.

If you know someone who owns a business where you may be hired, don't be afraid to call and ask for an appointment. Say, "I'm exploring the job market and I'd like to come in and talk."

Keep your ears open for any openings. One woman said, "I was in my pediatrician's office with my little girl, and I heard the receptionist tell someone she was leaving because her husband was being transferred to another city. Right away, when I took my daughter into this office, I said, 'I hear your receptionist is leaving. I have all the office skills, and I'd love to work for you! Can I set up an appointment to discuss this?' ''

(She got the job.)

Part or Full Time?

If you can afford it, start part time. It's less stress.

But try to find a part-time job where you get a good benefit package. Benefit packages are very important when you're a single parent!

Example: if your package includes dental benefits, it can mean you'll spend $100 out-of-pocket instead of $500 for two root canals. It can mean braces for your children's teeth without going into debt.

One woman told me, ''I discovered, at the job interview, that if I work twenty hours instead of fifteen, I'll be eligible for a full medical coverage package, so of course I'm putting in twenty hours.''

Ask about the benefit package on that interview. It is appropriate behavior.

Working part time can mean you're home when the kids leave for school, and when they return home.

Be Selective About Your Setting

I spoke to a recently widowed woman whose husband had been a pharmaceutical salesman.

''My husband knew several physicians,'' she said, ''and I'm going to ask them about jobs in hospitals. I'm a good secretary.''

I asked, ''Have you visited a hospital since your husband died?'' (He had suffered from cancer and had been in and out of the hospital for treatment before his death.)

''Nooo,'' she answered, looking as though she was wondering why I asked that question.

198

I said, "Why don't you give it a trial run? Visit a hospital. Walk through patient floors. See how you feel afterward. If you feel fine, go ahead with your plan. If you feel upset or anxious afterward, realize that being in a hospital again reactivated your depression and anxiety, and it's not worth it—returning to that setting so soon. You can always work in a hospital after your grieving is over."

There was a silence.

"Why don't you think of getting a job in a pediatrician's office or a dental office?" I asked. "That's nonthreatening."

Slowly, she nodded.

Another woman told me, "I'm so grateful to the hospice program at the hospital. The staff cared so much. They made sure I wasn't alone when my husband died at home. They kept in touch after his death. I want to get a job at that hospice, I want to give back what I got."

I advised her, too, to wait. She can always work or volunteer for hospice, once her grieving is finished.

"This is a vulnerable time," I said. "Don't put yourself in a setting where you'll feel even more vulnerable."

Also, avoid taking a job where you'll be isolated in a room by yourself. Newly widowed persons need *not* to be alone. They need to be around other persons, at least a part of each day.

A woman said, "I'm a bookkeeper, and they put me in this tiny office with no window, and I was all by myself. I felt more alone than I did when I was home! I found myself feeling depressed. I cried a lot."

"What did you finally do?" I asked.

"I quit!" she replied. "Now I work in a library; they're teaching me to catalog. At least there are people always around."

Good for her, she made a change.

*　　　*　　　*

199

Being selective about your setting also means determining the pace of the work place.

Look for a place where the pace isn't frantic. You don't need more tension in your life right now.

How can you tell, ahead of time, about the pace of a place?

Do you know anyone who works there? Ask these questions.

- Is your work load realistic? Can you get everything done without constantly rushing?
- Do you get regular breaks? (A morning and afternoon coffee break.)
- How long is your lunch break? (A half hour is not long enough!)

If you don't know anyone who works there, look around carefully as you're waiting to be interviewed. Observe the workers.

- Are they grimly rushing around, not smiling?
- Are none of them relating to each other?
- Is there a tense, hushed atmosphere?

Of course employers have a right to want maximum production. A job isn't a Tupperware party. But you need a work place where people don't act like robots; where it's all right to get up and stretch; where you're allowed to drink coffee while you're working; where you don't have to gulp down your lunchtime sandwich in twenty minutes.

You need a relaxed work place while you're under so much stress. Be selective: look for it.

If you have children, avoid taking a job where there's a swing shift, or where you have to put in frequent overtime. This is too hard on the children right now.

Certainly, avoid working night shift: your kids need *you* beside them when they awaken from nightmares (and bereaved children have bad nights, as bereaved adults do). No matter how competent the baby-sitter, she can't give the nighttime nurturing that you can, when bad dreams awaken a disturbed child.

You can control the setting in which you work—at least to some degree.

If Concentrating on the Job Is a Problem

Many widows report they have difficulty concentrating on the job. Their mind drifts. They can't remember if they've finished a task or even started it. They can't find papers. They don't remember what the boss told them to do or how to do it.

Here are some self-management tricks to help you function better on the job, even though you are having trouble concentrating:

1. Each morning when you get to work, *immediately* make a list of what you have to do at work that day. Put the list in a conspicuous place.
2. As you complete each task, *immediately* cross that item off your daily list.
3. Every morning, consult the list from the previous day. Is every item crossed off? If not, complete the tasks that still have to be done.
4. Keep your desk organized; this will organize your thoughts. Specifically, keep two trays on your desk—one for unfinished work (labeled) and one for finished work (labeled). There should be nothing else on your desk, besides your telephone and your daily list, writing pad and pen.

5. Take advantage of all breaks, even if you are behind in your work. This will clear your head and calm you.
6. On your breaks, get out of the building, if possible. A brisk walk around the block or a stroll on the grounds will refresh you. If you work in a dangerous neighborhood, at least get out of your office and venture into the cafeteria or the hallways.
7. When you have a conference with your boss, always carry a note pad and a pen: take notes of all instructions. Never leave what you hear to chance. Also, put the current date at the top of the paper, so you know what you've heard and when.

Try these suggestions. You'll find they really work.

Relating to Your Employer

If you sense your boss is feeling impatient with your inability to concentrate, don't wait for him to say something. Say it first. Tell him you realize you're having a problem concentrating and immediately tell him the steps (mentioned above) that you're taking to improve your performance.

Taking the initiative in speaking to him first will give you a feeling of control over your life. Your explanation will reassure him that you are trying, that you do care about the job.

Inability to concentrate after the death is normal. It is a part of the grieving, but it does pass, I promise you.

Controlling Your Expressions of Grief on the Job

The work place is one place where you can't allow the full expression of your distressed feelings. But these are ways of coping:

- If you awaken feeling shaky and teary, wear dark glasses throughout that work day. No one will know when tears well.
- If you have an uncontrollable need to cry hard, escape to the ladies' room. Cry as quietly as possible behind the closed stall door. Put on your dark glasses before emerging. And if you can, use a ladies' room on another floor, in another department where no one knows you. That way, you'll feel less exposed and vulnerable.
- Be selective as to whom you confide your bad feelings: be wary of the office gossip, and the boss's secretary. You don't want your feelings of distress to be reported to your employer.
- If you do find one nurturing person who is truly concerned about you, be sure you only talk about your feelings on her breaks and her lunch hour; you don't want to be accused of distracting her from her work.
- If you awaken feeling upset, try to phone an early morning friend to talk about your feelings before you go to work: that will allow you "crying time," and calm you *before* you leave the house.

Use all of these techniques. Not only will they help you function on the job, they'll help you stay on the job. You won't have to leave work in the middle of the day, make your boss wonder if you can handle the work, or take extra days off.

Meanwhile, use your family and close friends for support; these are persons to whom you *can* express your distressed feelings.

Your Feelings Around Coupled Co-Workers

You can choose your friends but not your co-workers.

There are the co-workers who rush from work to a singles

bar, and when they come to work the next morning they're rattling on and on about who they met and what they did. You unexpectedly feel envy. "Me?" you tell yourself. "Me *envious?*" How awful, you shiver, when you identify that feeling: you hate people who are envious. Read this sentence twice, aloud: *All widowed persons feel envy and it's normal.*

Envy is a natural reaction to loss.

You're still a nice person. You haven't changed. As you recover from your grief, and as you rebuild a new life, you will no longer feel envy when you're around couples and when women talk about the men in their lives. You'll have your own new life.

Your own new persons.

If not a new man, new friends.

What you envy is someone special to be with, to do things together.

That's it: together. That's the key word. You no longer have someone very special with whom to do things together, someone who loves you, and this is one of the biggest things you envy.

And it's understandable.

One way to avoid or handle that envious feeling at work is to remove yourself physically from the cluster of people who are talking about the great time they had the night before. Tune them out, once you remove yourself. Get involved with other people.

You can't avoid the office parties for newly engaged co-workers or the baby showers for co-workers before they take their maternity leave. It hurts, attending these parties, because they're celebrating what *was* in your life, but what never can be anymore. At least not with your husband.

Protect yourself by not lingering after the gifts have been opened. Quietly slip away. Don't return to your desk, that's too conspicuous; instead, go to the ladies' room to kill some time until everyone goes back to work.

If it's past closing time, quietly go home. Protect your frail feelings.

You might feel envious, hearing the older women talk about children and grandchildren and where they're going on vacation with their sixty-year-old husbands. You feel so cheated. Here are these women, in their fifties and sixties, and their husbands are alive and well. They've had their husbands for twenty, thirty, and forty years. You've had yours for two, five, ten, or fifteen years. Of course you're envious. Life isn't fair.

Try changing the subject when it gets too much for you. Talk about a movie you saw on TV, or what's going on in the world. If that doesn't distract them, excuse yourself and say, "Excuse me, I have to get back to work." (It's not that easy, if you're in the middle of eating lunch together in the cafeteria, but you can always say, "Excuse me, I have to make an important phone call.")

No, you can't choose your co-workers. But you will get to the point where their references to lovers and husbands and children won't bother you. You'll get to that point when you've successfully built a new life.

You're Restless, You're Itchy

In doing research for this chapter, I was told by many women that they took a job and then quit; they just couldn't stay put.

"I'm restless!"

"I'm irritable all the time. I can't stand going to that same place every day."

A solution, for the time being, is a temporary agency—an agency where you're hired as a temp, and you're sent into offices where the regular workers are on vacation or out sick.

This way, you're not committed to one boss and one place at a time in your life when you can't make a commitment.

It also offers respites from working; there will be days when you won't be called at all.

This Is a Time of Transition

That first year after the death is not the ideal time to start a new demanding career. Work should be looked at, during this vulnerable time, as a means to an end: a way to get a paycheck, a job during a transition time.

(If you're *already* in a career, that's very different.)

If you have never worked, or you're returning to work for the first time in years, be kind to yourself. Put your toe in the water, don't plunge in. There will be plenty of time for plunging later, after you've finished your deep grieving.

15. Unexpected Questions, Upsetting Remarks

Friends, acquaintances, and family who know all the social skills and the more esoteric ones, too—how to give a party, what gifts to buy for whom, how to make small talk, and how to make stained-glass windows—don't know what to say to the newly widowed woman and man. They never learned. It's a skill that none of our institutions of higher learning teach. There are no syndicated columns in newspapers called, "How to Talk to the Newly Widowed Person." There are no how-to books on the subject. So people often say inappropriate things. They make comments that hurt, or remarks that stun with the invasion of privacy. They ask questions that cruelly probe.

It's because people just don't know what to say. Did you know what to say to the newly widowed person before your spouse died?

Meanwhile, it might help if you better understand the real reasons behind some of these questions and remarks, if you have some stock answers ready to tide you over your shock or your hurt.

Here are twenty-six typical questions and comments heard by younger widowed women and men:

1. "YOU'RE LUCKY YOU DIDN'T HAVE CHILDREN!"
That's luck?

You're so sorry you didn't have children. If you would have had a child, you would have had a tangible reminder of your marriage. Perhaps the child would have looked like your spouse.

(At least this is the way many widowed persons feel.)

What's behind the tactless remark? It most likely is a projection. The person who made the remark—is she a parent? It's a lot of responsibility, being a parent. The person who made the remark no doubt feels the strong responsibility of having children. Knowing the demands this role makes, she made this statement with goodwill. The unsaid part of the statement is, "Thank goodness, you don't have to take care of a sick child by yourself in the middle of the night, or support three children all by yourself. At least you won't have that."

I would like to believe the person who said this to you did mean well. I really think this is the case.

And an appropriate response is merely to smile and then change the subject.

2. *"IT'S TIME TO PULL YOURSELF TOGETHER!"*

This is usually said around four months after the death, when you're beginning to feel worse than before. The shock has worn off, the reality of the death has hit, and you're beginning to realize, "He is gone forever!"

But the person who made that remark doesn't understand the *process* of grieving. She doesn't realize that the fourth or sixth month of your bereavement is very hard. The person who said that might love you: I imagine it was a close relative or friend, who is very concerned about you.

The remark was made out of frustration: this person wants to help you feel better and doesn't know how.

If it is a close family member or friend, someone you care about, try a little educating. Give a gift of a book on the process of grief (perhaps this book). Ask her to read it. Tell her it will help her understand why you still feel so bad.

I think that person will appreciate your response and will

read the book. In turn, it will help her really understand what you're going through.

If the remark was made by a person who recently suffered her own profound loss, you might want to ask yourself if she's worked through it yet. If she suffered a miscarriage, are people saying to her, "It's time to pull yourself together!" If they are, she's possibly angry about it, and she can't contain all the anger so she's letting some of it spill over to you. But you know what loss is, so you can forgive her.

An appropriate response is to say, "We both know getting over loss takes a long, long time."

3. *"You're young, you'll be married before you know it."*

Unless you're ready to think about marriage, that really hurts. You feel the memory of your deceased spouse is being betrayed. You feel misunderstood (don't they realize marriage is the furthest thing from your mind?). You might be enraged. How dare they assume anything like this? Or that you even fantasize about it? (And, if you do, it's *your* business.)

But the person didn't mean to hurt you. The person who made that remark really thought you wanted to hear it. The unspoken part of the message is, "You're desirable." Of course, it could have been said by an embittered older widow who sees no chance ahead for herself in terms of building a new relationship: envy could have inspired the remark. But whether it was said in goodwill or envy, the appropriate response is to change the subject.

4. *"You should be grateful it was a quick death and that he didn't suffer."*

Oh?

Does a quick death make your grief easier? Of course not.

And, right now, you feel you have nothing to feel grateful about.

The speaker usually means well, she is trying to help. She does think it was much better that it was a quick death. She may have nursed a terminally ill spouse for months and can imagine this as the only terrible death.

Perhaps she's being literal: he didn't suffer, she is saying, there was no time to suffer. Be glad for him.

An appropriate response? The same as with the other remarks. Merely nod and change the subject quickly.

5. *"YOUR CHILD IS AN INFANT. THANK GOODNESS, SHE'S TOO YOUNG TO REMEMBER HER FATHER. SHE'LL HAVE AN EASY TIME ACCEPTING A NEW DADDY."*

But you want her to remember her father, and you are very upset because she won't. Objectively, you know the speaker is correct: she won't remember him and she may have an easy time accepting a new daddy (there won't be any comparisons), but it hurts you that she never knew him. You think: how insensitive this person is to say this!

The person making this remark is trying to reassure you. Perhaps you can just smile and talk about something else.

6. *"YOU'RE A MAN, WOMEN WILL BE CHASING YOU AND YOU'LL BE MARRIED BEFORE YOU KNOW IT!"*

This is a hurting remark because it totally disregards your grief. What do people think, that men don't grieve? Why can't you be given the same right to your feelings as a widow?

The myth that every widower is chased by hordes of women is true for some men, but it doesn't mean you're ready or willing to be chased. Or it doesn't mean that taking a woman out means you're finished grieving.

Women usually make this remark. It comes from the hurt of knowing widows have a harder time reestablishing a social life with persons of the opposite sex: that there are more women out there than men.

Realize this remark comes from hurt and be generous: acknowledge women have a harder time than men when it comes to dating and mating and then say, "But this is not what I need to hear right now. I'd much rather hear you say, 'I'm so sorry about the death of your wife.' "

The person will probably get flustered and say, "Of course I'm sorry!" and then leave you alone.

7. *"WHAT DO YOU MEAN YOU'VE LOST YOUR FAITH? YOU CAN'T LOSE YOUR FAITH!"*

Friends, family, and even some clergy persons might have this reaction when you tell them you've lost your faith. They don't realize it's very painful and frightening to you to have lost your faith. That if you had had a choice, you would not have lost faith. But you didn't have a choice. It happened.

Realize the shock they feel is real. It's too bad they're focusing on their shock and not your terror. Questions of faith—everyone has to find their own answers. Perhaps it would be good for you to talk about this with a pastoral counselor. You might also want to read Viktor Frankl's *Man's Search for Meaning.*

He's a psychiatrist/philosopher, a survivor of concentration camps, who explores the question of faith and despair in an existential context. Meanwhile, you'll have a difficult time explaining your feelings to the persons who are making these shocked remarks. Don't even try. Just say, "I know it's hard to understand. I don't understand it myself."

8. *"YOU SHOULD GO BACK TO SCHOOL, NOW THAT YOU'RE ALONE."*

You're going to hear many "shoulds" and "oughts," because you are younger. People assume younger widows and widowers need to be told what to do.

Acknowledge their statement by saying just what they've said: "You think I should go back to school?" They nod, yes. Then you nod. Then change the subject, but go home and think about it: they may be correct.

However, I know you're tired of being told what to do and how to do it. At some point you may have to say, "I know you want the best for me, but I will have to make up my own mind about the future. Thank you, anyway."

9. *"You would make your mother very happy by having her move into your home. After all, you're both widowed now."*

Guilt, guilt. If that's what you're feeling after hearing that remark, it's irrational guilt. Push it away. Take a hard look at the relationship you have with your mother: would it work, living together? If the answer is no, don't consider doing it. Just because someone tells you to do it, that doesn't mean you should do it.

Besides, your mother may want intimacy at a distance, as you do.

You can pleasantly smile at the person who made this remark and say, "I know you think I should do this, but I will have to decide for myself." If arguments follow, disregard them. Refuse to participate in a debate over the issue by not answering the arguments. Change the subject.

10. *"You look GOOD!"*

It almost sounds like an accusation, doesn't it? You wonder—are you supposed to look terrible? Should you be walking around with no makeup, and with your hair uncombed? You hate that remark!

What's really happening is that the person making the remarks wants you to feel better so she doesn't have to deal with your grief (she can't). If you look better, it must mean you feel better. So she says, "You look GOOD!"

Or perhaps you do look good. You may be one of those persons who always leaves the house with your hair and makeup and clothes looking terrific, no matter how you feel; it is a matter of pride and habit. So now you continue your good grooming, and it doesn't reflect how you feel. Your response? Just smile and say, "Thank you."

11. "YOU'RE DATING WITHOUT HAVING WAITED A YEAR!"

This accusing remark may come from traditional persons who *are* horrified when the bereaved picks up his life before a year is completed. Or it could come from the family of the spouse who died. They feel betrayed; they feel the memory of their loved one is being betrayed and forgotten.

You may want to reply, "My wife would have wanted me to continue living. She loved me, and this is the way she would have wanted it."

12. "COME ON OVER WHENEVER YOU WANT TO. I'D LOVE TO SEE YOU."

This vague kind of invitation is so frustrating. You wonder how much the person really wants you to visit; if the invitation was sincere, wouldn't it have been couched in more definite terms?

If it's coming from someone you're not interested in, merely reply, "Thank you," and forget it. If it's an invitation from someone you really like, be honest. Say, "I would enjoy visiting, but can't you make it a more specific invitation? If you tell me when, I can make plans."

13. "YOU SHOULDN'T REHASH THE DETAILS OF THE DEATH LIKE YOU'RE DOING. IT'S NOT GOOD FOR YOU, REPEATING IT OVER AND OVER."

Translation: "I can't take hearing it again and again. It upsets me!"

Well, not everyone is emotionally strong. This person obviously isn't, at least not around the issue of death.

Perhaps you can join a widowed persons support group, where you are actually encouraged to repeat your story again and again. (Repeating it is your way of learning to believe the death.)

Look in the back of this book. There is a directory of widowed persons support groups.

14. "NOW YOUR SON WILL BE THE MAN OF THE HOUSE!"

"Oh, no he won't!" you can say. "He won't because I won't let him. It's too much responsibility for a teenage boy."

"And," you can add, "I prefer it if you don't say this in front of him."

Psychologically astute friends and family realize this is not an appropriate role for boy children. It's being said out of well-meaning ignorance. You are doing the person a service by explaining this is not an appropriate role. (You're doing your son a service, too.)

15. "YOU SHOULD TAKE YOUR DAUGHTER OUT OF COLLEGE TO COME HOME AND TAKE CARE OF THE HOUSE, NOW THAT YOUR WIFE DIED."

Should you? No.

Bereaved children should be strongly encouraged to continue their normal lives, without disruption. If you're having a great deal of difficulty taking care of the house or your life, try other options. Hire a housekeeper if you can afford it, or reorganize your time so you let go of tasks that really don't need doing. Learn to cook with a simple cookbook, or bring in carry-out. But don't urge your child to move back home.

The person making this statement may be an older and traditional person, who grew up learning that daughters should come home and stay with widowed fathers. Realize this is her philosophy: it doesn't mean she is correct.

16. *"I hope he left you well off!"*

Now this is a person who is *intruding*. Your financial status is your own business, and it can be actually dangerous sharing the information with others; you don't know who will tell whom.

How can you reply? Some people vaguely say, "I'll eat."

Others say, "I can only sleep in one bed at a time and eat one meal at a time."

These are ways of answering that are effectively evasive.

Don't feel guilty about being evasive. The person who said this should feel guilty about making such a personal remark.

17. *"You have to lose weight, now that you're widowed. No man will be interested in you, being so heavy."*

Your self-esteem is low, now; so low that you don't need anyone telling you that you look fat. When and if you become ready to lose weight, you want to do it under a physician's supervision, and slowly.

Why do people say things like this? Because they *are* concerned about you, or because they feel bad about themselves and aren't doing anything about it. Hence, they're angry at themselves and allowing the anger to spill over.

If it's a person who does care about you, and you know the statement was made out of concern, say, "I know you care, and I thank you." If it's a person who you suspect is getting rid of some hostility through baiting you, simply ignore the statement and change the subject. (Also, stay out of that person's way as much as possible.)

215

18. "HE GAVE YOU SUCH A HARD TIME WHILE YOU WERE MARRIED, YOU'RE WELL RID OF HIM!"

Maybe he was a difficult husband, but it's none of this person's business. You owe no explanations or apologies!

Persons who were in bad marriages may grieve just as hard, after the death, as persons who were in good relationships. They may suffer from prolonged grieving. There was no time to make things better, or to make the marriage finally work, so there's the grief of unfinished business as well as the grief from the loss.

And bad marriages often had some good things going: many women in these marriages report they had a great sex life together, or men report their wives were excellent mothers.

How do you answer persons who make statements like this? You don't. Instead, you change the subject.

19. "YOU SHOULD SEND THE CHILDREN TO OVERNIGHT CAMP. THAT WILL GET THEIR MINDS OFF THE DEATH."

People who make suggestions like this usually mean well. They just don't realize that children should not be separated from their surviving parent right after the death. In fact, children shouldn't be separated for even a short period until at least a year after their loss. (And then a careful evaluation should be made: is your child feeling strong enough to be separated? What does your *child* want?)

Sometimes the surviving parent will go along with a suggestion like this because she badly needs a respite from child care; it's draining, during this time of deep grief. The solution is to attempt to get this respite without your child leaving home. (A specific solution is offering free room and board to a college student, in return for baby-sitting.)

20. "LET ME KNOW IF YOU NEED ANYTHING!"

There's that vagueness again. Of course you're not going to call for help, because the offer wasn't concrete; the person

216

didn't offer anything in particular, so you wonder how sincere she was.

Friends and family and neighbors need to be concrete: baby-sitting offers; or invitations for dinner at a particular time; an offer to chauffeur the woman who doesn't know how to drive, so she can visit her social security office and file for a claim. These concrete suggestions will be appreciated and heeded.

21. *"WHAT MADE YOUR WIFE DO SOMETHING LIKE THAT, KILL HERSELF?"*

Suicide survivors should protect themselves, if possible, by having other family members answer the phone and screen the calls in the weeks or months following the death. Questions like this, prying questions, are inappropriate and hurting.

If there is no person who can screen calls, invest in an answering machine. That way, during your time of very deep distress, you can answer your calls selectively.

But not all the questions come on the phone. Sometimes the tactless questions come from neighbors and acquaintances you meet in the food market or on the street. If you wish, you have a perfect right to say, "I really don't feel up to discussing it." Then change the subject.

22. *"I HATE TO BE THE ONE TO TELL YOU THIS, BUT THE NEIGHBORS ARE TALKING, BECAUSE YOU BRING THAT WOMAN IN YOUR HOUSE FOR THE WEEKEND, AND YOUR WIFE JUST DIED LAST YEAR!"*

If she hated to tell you, why did she? However, what she is saying is that you live in a neighborhood where this is taboo, and this is what is important.

The question to ask yourself is:

"Is this fair to my kids? They have to live in the neighborhood, too, and they're only in their teens."

217

If you have any uneasy feeling it is unfair to your children, see the woman in *her* home.

23. *"When are you selling the house?"*

One widow, when she was asked that question, indignantly replied, "Why should people assume all widows want to sell their house?"

They do assume that, don't they?

You can be evasive with your answers. Say, "I don't know!" or "Who knows?" or "I'll let you know when *I* know!"

There's a "should" implied in the question, of course. And only you can determine when and if you will ever sell your house.

23. *"Do you think you'll get married again?"*

People who wouldn't think of opening other persons' mail ask that question; it doesn't occur to them that it's a private question.

You can be vague and answer, "I haven't thought about it," or you can say more directly, "Why are you asking?"

One widower eyed the person and, in a shocked voice said, "I can't believe you asked me that." It put the interrogator on the defensive.

However, if you're attempting to rebuild your life and you are looking for a mate, ask, "Do you know anyone I'd like to meet?" (Maybe she does!)

24. *"You should get a job, it'll take you out of the house."*

If you're already looking for work, you can ask, "Do you know of any job that's available?" (Use *all* personal contacts.) But if you are sick and tired of the "shoulds," and you're not job seeking, you can say, "I know you want the

218

best for me, and that may be a good suggestion. I'll think about it at some time in the future.''

You will feel pressured by the shoulds and oughts only if you feel manipulated and pushed by the persons who are telling you what to do. Once you realize you are an autonomous person, *not* bound to do what people want you to do, you are more able to shrug off those shoulds and oughts.

25. *"WHY ARE YOU INSISTING HE WAS A GOOD MAN AND IT WAS A GOOD MARRIAGE? YOU KNOW IT WAS TERRIBLE!"*

Well, maybe you are putting a halo around the marriage and around your husband. If you are, it's because you need to do this in order to validate the years you spent in the marriage. And if that's what you're doing, it's your business.

When you're ready to stop, you will.

Meanwhile, an appropriate response to this person is, ''I guess I have to grieve in my own way, which might not be the way you'd like to see me feel and behave. But this is the way I have to grieve.''

26. *"CRY! YOU MUST CRY, IT'LL MAKE YOU FEEL BETTER!"*

You would if you could, wouldn't you? But apparently you can't. Maybe it's because you were brought up to have a stiff upper lip. Perhaps its because you are afraid you will lose control completely, once you allow yourself to cry, and you're afraid of losing control. Or you might not cry in front of others; you're a private person.

You can smile and say, ''Sorry, I can't cry on demand.''

These are *some* of the questions and remarks people who have been widowed frequently hear. I'm sure you can add some of your own. When you do find yourself getting irritable over the inappropriateness of the questions or the tactlessness of the remarks, ask yourself if you always knew what to say to widowed persons before your spouse died. Many people say inappropriate things simply because they don't know what to say.

Remember that the next time you're stunned by the rudeness of the question or the implications of the remark. It will help.

16. Combating Depression

There are no shortcuts in grieving. There's no absolute, set time frame. You can at different times expect to feel:

- numb
- shock
- disbelief
- anger
- hopeless
- envy
- helpless
- hurt
- guilt
- empty
- anxiety
- symptoms of physical illness
- vague aches and pains
- long-lasting fatigue
- depression

Normal vs. Intense Depression

There's the normal depression that is an inevitable part of grief—deep sadness, and a heavy feeling. You cry often and unexpectedly. Sometimes you think, ''What's the use, life isn't worth living.'' There's a feeling of emptiness. (Did you know the word *widow* in Sanskrit means *empty*?)

221

That's normal depression. There is also intense depression, where you'll want some professional help. How will you know if you're suffering from intense depression?

Ask yourself:

1. "Am I functioning?"
2. "Am I fantasizing about physically hurting myself or anyone else?"
3. "Is it so hard to talk that I've stopped talking?"

Functioning—that means you take care of your children even though you feel resentful about having all of this responsibility and don't know if you're up to it; you go to work every day even though you're having trouble concentrating; you keep your home and your clothes clean, even though you don't care; you spend time with friends or family even though you're distracted when you're with them.

(There are different levels of functioning. I don't expect you to be performing at your usual level.)

I hope you'll go for help if you're spending much of your time curled up in bed or on the sofa. Seek help if you're drinking more than usual. If you feel you've lost hope (and I know that's a terrible feeling), please go for professional help. If you feel worthless now that your spouse has died, you will benefit by professional counseling.

I'm *not* worried if you're frequently crying. Crying is an expression of your pain, and crying heals. There's no such thing as "crying too much," no matter what your family says. Crying will not make you sick. When you are ready to stop crying (and that day will come), you will.

For *intense* depression, you'll want to seek help.

If you feel as depressed three years after the death as you did during the first year of your bereavement, get help.

Persons who have a history of depression—who suffered from bouts of depression before their spouse became ill or died—may continue to feel depressed for years after the death.

Intense depression often occurs if you had strong mixed feelings toward your husband or wife; if you had a love/hate relationship, or if you bit your tongue and took abuse.

If you did hurting things during your marriage and never had a chance to say you're sorry, you might suffer from intense depression.

Anger Turned Inward

Some mental health practitioners believe depression is anger turned inward.

An example is Scott. He was very angry at his wife for abandoning him through death and leaving him alone with three small children. He then felt guilty because he was so angry. ("How can I be angry at such a loving wife who never wanted to die?") Scott's subconscious mind decided, "I have to punish myself for being angry at her. How will I do that? I'll make myself sick." Since he couldn't really make himself sick, he made himself *feel* sick. Every day, he suffered from vague aches and pains. To punish himself further, he self-diagnosed; he decided he had cancer. (His wife had died from cancer.) Now he was anxious as well as depressed. Frantic, feeling he was on the brink of death, he went to his internist. The test results were negative. Knowing Scott was newly widowed and being thorough and perceptive, his physician referred him to a psychologist, who helped Scott look at his anger.

Sherry also turned her anger inward and punished herself. She became accident-prone after the death. Her husband had babied her through the eleven years of their childless marriage. She was his child. He paid all the bills, made all the decisions, chauffeured her everywhere, and they even had a baby-talk code. Sherry was furious after he died. The little girl in her was enraged that she now had to learn how to pay her own bills; that she had to learn how to drive; that she no longer had a daddy. At first she openly expressed her rage. Then she noticed that people were uncomfortable with this—they began to avoid her. So she stopped talking about her anger and turned it inward. Sherry suffered two kitchen knife lacerations that needed suturing. She fractured her leg from a fall. She broke her wrist. All of this happened within a year after the death. She's now seeing a psychiatrist, who's helping her look at the marriage relationship *and* her dependence.

Feelings of Unworthiness

Depression often reflects feelings of worthlessness. It's the same phenomenon. You're angry at your husband or wife for leaving you and you then feel angry at yourself. You punish yourself by deciding you're no good. Being no good, you treat yourself badly. You may not bathe as often, or you may wear soiled clothes. You may drink too much, or you may not eat properly.

You turn your back on anyone who reaches out to you: after all, you decide, if I'm worth nothing, no one can possibly like me. Or, you decide, anyone who likes me can't be worth much either; if they were valuable, they would choose valuable friends. Knowing no one likes you or wants to be with you, you turn away in shame. You reject others before you can be rejected. You don't answer your phone. You don't return calls. You refuse social invitations. You might even stop talking.

Inside, we all have a little child. Your little child cries silently. Your throat feels constricted, because you're holding in your tears and they need to come out. You might need to cry so badly that you have a difficult time eating; when you swallow, your muscles are so tight you feel you're going to choke.

Make Yourself Cry

Try to make yourself cry; it's therapeutic. When I talk to someone who hasn't cried since the death, I suggest they deliberately think sad thoughts. (''Who will take care of me if I get sick?'') That they play a song on the stereo that has mournful lyrics. That they watch a sad movie.

If you were part of a culture where crying was discouraged, you might have a hard time crying.

Men often have difficulty crying. They've been taught it's unmanly.

If control is very important to you. you might be afraid to cry; you're afraid you'll lose control once you start.

(It happens the other way around: when you allow yourself to cry, the feeling of relief is so great afterward that you feel more in control.)

You might not want to cry in front of certain friends who become uncomfortable with open signs of grieving.

One woman said, ''I give myself crying times. I cry when I'm alone in the car, driving. I even have rules. I don't cry in heavy traffic, I don't want to have an accident and I don't want someone in the car next to me to see me sobbing. Instead, I drive out to the country and I cry while I'm driving on empty roads. I do this at least a couple times a week. You should hear me sob in the car.''

A man said, ''My crying time is on Sunday afternoons when I visit the cemetery by myself, without the kids. When I'm all cried out, I go home, and this holds me over 'til next Sunday. Oh, I cry in bed at night almost every night, but then I have to be quiet. The children are in the next bedroom.''

Talking Is Therapy

Talking about your feelings alleviates depression.

Loretta's husband had died at the age of thirty-one. She's twenty-eight. When I first met her, she told me she had lost twelve pounds since the death because she can't eat. She showed me a wedding picture. It was hard to believe the woman in the photograph was the same person. Holding on to her husband's arm, she was radiantly smiling. No hollows under her eyes. No haunted look.

"How did he die?" I asked.

(I already knew, it was on her file card, but I wanted *her* to tell me. Depressed persons need to talk.)

There were pauses between sentences. She sighed a lot. Her voice was so low I had to lean forward to hear. She never looked at me as she told the story of how he had fallen off the ladder, how they had rushed him to the emergency room, and how he had been put in intensive care. Her voice was a monotone.

Once she forgot what she had just said. She then had a painful searching look on her face.

She repeated the story several times.

Finally, she seemed to wind down. Silence.

"How are you feeling?" I softly asked.

With a desperate gleam in her eyes, she said, "Like I'm in a life-size glass of water looking out through the glass at people."

Loretta was telling me she felt separated from the world and other persons. A symptom of intense depression.

She went for professional counseling, and the psychiatrist prescribed an antidepressant. She also joined Recovery, a nationwide group for anyone suffering from depression or anxiety. (Look in your phone book for a Recovery group. There's a donation and no fee.) Group participants felt empathy. Loretta found it a safe place in which to cry and talk.

The group leader was trained and knew how to draw Loretta out. Recovery was an adjunct to the professional help her psychiatrist gave her, and since there were meetings available every day and every evening, she could go whenever she felt a need. (Emotions Anonymous is another well-known nationwide support group. See the listing in the back of the book.)

Nine months later, Loretta again visited me. This time her hair was carefully combed and she was wearing makeup. She had gained a few pounds. She talked without hesitation. She *looked* at me when she spoke.

She said, "I found I needed to talk about my feelings even more than my thoughts, although I talk about both."

These are reasons why talking in a support group helps:

- It raises your self-esteem because people *listen*.
- It validates your past life as a married person because people are genuinely interested in hearing about your marriage.

By identifying your feelings aloud, you are more in touch with the way you really feel.

Talking to a professional helper is beneficial:

- You're given feedback, which further validates your feelings and experiences.
- You learn about the grief process, and this helps you know you're normal in your reactions.

(But use a professional helper who *talks*, who doesn't just sit there and murmur "hmmmm.")

Friends and family are sometimes supportive listeners. A widower couldn't remember the sound of his wife's voice and he panicked. A friend, who had also been widowed, reassured him. "It's okay," he said. "I've gone through that. The sound will come back."

*   *   *

Stay away from persons who scold. You don't need to hear, "You're dwelling on the past!" and "You had such a good life you should be grateful."

Choose listeners who aren't judgmental. Who won't tell others what you say. Who don't interrupt with *their* story every few minutes. Who don't get itchy and need to jump up and do things while you're talking.

Sometimes a caring friend or relative becomes physically and emotionally tired from listening. It does not mean she doesn't care or is tired of you. It does mean every person has a point when she needs a respite from the intensity of good listening.

Broaden your base of good listeners, so you don't feel rejected. All the more reason for joining a group!

Touching Helps

When you've been deprived of being touched, it can make you depressed.

"You won't believe it," one woman said to another, "and I'm not being funny, but I'm so desperate to be touched that I hugged my landlord yesterday, and he's seventy and very formal and I hardly know him."

"Better than hugging your best friend's husband," the other woman laughed.

Nothing was "ha-ha" about that conversation, though. Not really. Each of these young widows was reflecting on how important it is to be touched and to touch, and how being deprived can drive one to inappropriate behavior.

(The woman who hugged her landlord had a broken toilet, and the landlord came over to fix it. Impulsively, she hugged him before he left. Before her husband died, she would never have done that.)

Other women report they are touching their friends' husbands and lovers, and they can't seem to stop themselves. They flick the imaginary piece of dandruff off a jacket. They touch an arm while they're talking. They grab and hug when arriving and leaving. Their welcoming kisses are too ardent. "I see my girl friend eyeing me," one woman said, "and she has been cold lately. But I can't help it!"

Try to help it. You need your women friends now. And you want to respect their couple relationships, don't you? (You wanted yours respected.)

Persons who enjoyed an active sex life particularly miss being touched. And that doesn't mean only lovemaking. It's being petted and fondled.

(Your child's hug is wonderful, but it's not the same.)

"After my husband had surgery, six weeks before he died, I needed to lie down beside him in the hospital bed, just to feel the warmth of his familiar body," a woman said. "We held hands. It was so good."

Some persons seek touching through sexual encounters. This works for them; they're pragmatic. Others report they feel objectified afterward. Used. Just a body. After they leave the bedroom they feel angry at themselves and the other person.

Others rush into a relationship, mainly because they miss being touched. They overlook many things in the relationship they don't like in order to have again a physical relationship.

Everyone finds different answers for themselves. One widow in her twenties bought a cuddly little puppy. "He sleeps with me," she said, "and he's lovable. Of course, he can't make up for the loss or give me the kind of satisfaction a human being can, but *he's a living thing.*"

Laugh Therapy

Norman Cousins, the literary figure, made laugh therapy real to many people. In his talks and books, he describes how he laughed his way to good health. During two life-threatening illnesses, he combated depression through laughing. Watching funny films, he belly-laughed through pain and fear.

"I watch this show on Saturday nights," a man said, "and it's sick funny, it's so irreverent. But I love sick funny. And I laugh! No matter how down I've been that evening, I end up laughing and feeling a little better." Another man said, "I've asked the librarian to put away funny books for me. That's all I read these days, funny books. And it helps."

Try it. It costs nothing—you just switch on the tube or go to the library.

Sleep Disorders

Most persons who are depressed suffer from sleep disorders.

You either have difficulty falling asleep, or you awaken in the middle of the night and have trouble going back to sleep.

Compensate by catching a catnap after work, or, if you're home during the day, a daytime nap. If you feel disoriented after you awaken and you hate the feeling, don't do it. Rest, instead, with a book or a magazine. Or lie in bed and listen to soothing music.

L-Tryptophane, an amino acid, aids sleep, and some physicians recommend taking it before you go to bed. It's not a chemically based sleeping medication. Buy it in drugstores or health food stores. (First, however, check with your physician to see how he feels about it.)

Drink warm milk before retiring.

A glass of wine helps many people sleep.

Soak leisurely in a warm tub before you go to bed.

If you awaken in the middle of the night, turn on your bedside radio and listen to music or an all-night talk show.

"If I lie down in bed while I watch TV," a woman said, "it's like a sleeping pill. If I sit up, it isn't. Who knows why? I don't, and I don't care. The important thing is, I instantly fall asleep if I'm watching television while I'm lying down."

Avoid eating late at night; digesting your food can keep you restless all night. Don't drink a lot of fluid before you go to bed.

Don't be afraid of losing sleep. Your body will compensate through catnaps, dozing, or a heavy sleep one night after five sleepless nights.

Eating Disorders

You've lost your appetite, which is a common symptom of normal grief.

Try eating six small meals a day instead of three large ones. Soft foods are sometimes easier to get down—yogurt, soup, custards. Liquid meals are even easier for occasional lunches or dinners: milk shakes, juices, and mixtures of everything and anything mixed in your blender.

Meanwhile, take a daily multivitamin and mineral supplement.

The thing that helps the most is eating with other people. Their appetite stimulates yours. You feel more up, being with people, and that increases your desire to eat.

Most widows say, "I don't feel like cooking, now that I'm alone." Make arrangements to meet friends at restaurants. Accept all dinner invitations to friends' homes. That's where you can eat all the foods that are good for you—the vegetables you're no longer cooking, the homemade soups, the salads you're too impatient to make. In your own home, when you are alone, you can nibble. Fruit. Nuts. Sandwiches. I'm being practical. We don't have to dwell on eating properly, during a time of grief, as long as we eat.

(And if you have children, clean their plates.)

If you're worried about having lost too much weight, see your physician. If he says you're all right, believe it.

Running Therapy

Running gets rid of depression. If you're fit, and your physician gives you the go-ahead, start out with a walk-jog program and work up to a program where you can run comfortably for a fairly extended period of time. (This could be thirty minutes to an hour.)

Running not only keeps you physically fit, it gives you a feeling of competence and control (which you don't have now, since the death).

People report they solve problems while they're running. They make decisions during their running.

There's no competition with other people in running, and that's a good kind of exercise, because you do not need to be competitive at this stressful time of your life. (It's bad enough if you have to be competitive on your job. Why make life harder with competitive sports? Wait until you're feeling better.)

If you do start running, run regularly, or it will have no effect on your depression. Run every day.

"Morning Depression"

Are you awakening with depression and it simmers down later in the day? Try this:

- Get out of bed the minute you awaken and take a shower. The needlelike sting of the shower is stimulating; it alleviates depression.

232

- After your shower, do exercises to "up" music.
- Get dressed right away, even if you don't work outside of your home. (Don't sit around in your robe.)
- Get out of the house immediately after breakfast.

Leaving the house can mean going to work, or it can mean taking a brisk walk. It can mean bicycling, or jogging. With a small child in tow, it has to mean a leisurely stroll. Closing the front door behind you and walking into the air means you're saying, "I'm part of the world!" You're affirming your aliveness.

(Persons who suffer from morning depression need to move their muscles, and that's what you are doing as you get out of bed, shower, do your exercises, and take your walk.)

"Nighttime Depression"

If your bad time is nighttime, try to talk to persons who care about you. This can mean knocking at a neighbor's door to ask if she'd like a game of Scrabble. It might mean calling your parents and inviting yourself to dinner. It could mean asking a good friend to visit for coffee and cake.

If you can't be with anyone, use your telephone. The point is *talking*—whether it's in person or on the phone. Talk to someone in your support group. Call your sister. Telephone a friend who's also a night person—who doesn't go to sleep before 1:00 A.M.

Bad and Good Ways People Try to Help Themselves Feel Better

Self-help is constructive. But some persons self-destruct.

Excessive drinking is self-destructive. Needing to drink, even if you think you're not drinking too much, is a danger signal. (Did you know alcohol is a depressant? That there are

172 secondary diseases that go with alcoholism?) If you suspect you're chemically addicted to liquor, wine, or even beer, seriously consider attending an Alcoholics Anonymous meeting. Skid row it's not—most meetings are filled with middle-class persons who are high achievers.

Can medication alleviate depression?

Fifty-four percent of the medications used by widowed persons are antidepressants, hypnotics (sleeping medication), sedatives (tranquilizers), and analgesics (pain killers). This high figure tells us that many widows and widowers are in emotional or physical pain—or both. Antidepressants are used less frequently than tranquilizers after a death, but tricyclic antidepressants and monoamine oxidase inhibitors have been shown to be particularly effective for symptoms of clinical depression. They alleviates feelings of hopelessness, insomnia, and bodily complaints. Because the signs of grief are similar to the symptoms of clinical depression, some physicians also prescribe these drugs for bereaved persons. A number of doctors, though, believe drugs mask feelings. They believe one must *feel* in order to heal. Other physicians prefer psychological help to drugs. All responsible physicians are concerned with the potential problems of addiction, drug overdose, and the risks of impaired motor coordination. They'll want to carefully monitor the person taking medication.

The Institute of Medicine in Washington, D.C., completed a lengthly study on bereavement, and in their follow-up recommendations, they state that persons experiencing "normal grief"—the normal depression that is part of grieving—should not use drugs.

When and if you do take a drug, be sure to ask your pharmacist to give you the printout that is available, so you can read about possible side effects. (And let your physician know if you experience any.) Certain foods, if eaten with cer-

tain drugs, can cause a reaction. (*The People's Pharmacy*, a paperback by Joe Graedon, is an excellent resource for food
and drug interactions.)

Depression. I don't have to tell you how bad it feels. You
already know. But you will get through this. You are *not* having a breakdown, not with the normal depression of grief.
Your feelings are not a sign of weakness. It is what you need
to go through in order to say your mournful good-bye.

17. Fighting Anxiety

Drs. Thomas H. Holmes and Richard H. Rahe, who were well-known psychiatrists at the University of Washington Medical School, devised a scale of life events, ranking them by the degree of anxiety they produce. This social readjustment scale, used throughout the world, showed that out of forty-three life events, *the death of a spouse ranks the highest in stress*.

Losing a spouse to death is more stressful, their study showed, than illness, a jail term, or even divorce.

Is it any wonder you're feeling anxious?

Low-Level Anxiety

These are some typical symptoms of low-level anxiety:

- vague feelings of uneasiness
- hives or rashes
- headaches
- diarrhea, stomach pain, or nausea
- inability to make up your mind or stick to a decision
- restlessness
- giddiness or dizziness
- "jelly legs" (feelings of weakness in your legs)
- a feeling of constriction in your chest
- a fear of leaving the house, or other phobias
- muscular aches and pains

Acute Anxiety Attacks

An acute anxiety attack is different. It's sharper in intensity, and it hits suddenly.

Your stomach may feel like you're going down too fast in an elevator—that lurching sensation. Or you feel like you're a rubber band being stretched too far. You can't sit still. You need to pace, you're so agitated. You want to scream. Your mind is racing. You feel a sense of impending doom.

PANIC.

It can be frightening to have an acute anxiety attack, especially if it is your first one. But if you panic over the attack itself, you'll feel more uncomfortable.

Acute anxiety attacks feel life-threatening but they're not. You are not in danger. The attack will pass.

(Read this, again and again, during an attack.)

Separation Anxiety

Death is the total and final separation. That fact is hard to take so you alternate between believing and denying it happened. You swing back and forth. One minute the reality hits, and then a sight, a sound, or even an odor lures you into momentarily believing life is what it used to be—your spouse is still alive.

This inner struggle *not* to believe is physically exhausting. It's a reason you're always fatigued.

After you do begin believing the death more than before, you feel anxious. "Why me?" you exclaim. "How could God allow such a young man to die?" you rant. You torture yourself by asking, "Why did she have to suffer so much?"

Not finding absolute answers raises your anxiety. You also feel depressed. Your world has turned upside down. No one and nothing has prepared you for this final separation, even if there was a terminal illness and you grieved before the death. You no longer trust the idea of permanence.

There are no guarantees in life, and life feels fraught with danger.

Now you're more conscious of your mortality. You leap to dire conclusions when you have an ache or pain. When your children are ill, you panic.

Searching for answers and comfort, you may visit your rabbi, priest, or minister. You ask the same questions, "How could God allow such a young person to die?" Many clergy persons are comforting. Some are still painfully struggling for their own answers.

You go to your physician for reassurance. "I'm anxious, I'm depressed!" you say. Few medical doctors have the time to spend with bereaved persons—it takes a lot of time to listen—so they prescribe tranquilizers or antidepressants for normal bereavement symptoms. Some concerned physicians refer patients to bereavement counselors, widowed persons support groups, social workers, psychologists, or psychiatrists, instead of writing a prescription (or as an adjunct to it).

Everything triggers your anxiety: a slamming door, a television show that is filled with violence, or a sudden sharp noise.

A woman said, "Even laughing makes me anxious. I feel guilty afterward because it means I've forgotten my husband's death."

But you're not having a breakdown. You're going through the normal anxiety that is part of grief.

Compounded Anxiety After the Death

None of us lives in a vacuum. While you're grieving, you're trying to make a living and bring up your kids. Attempting to make a home, you're also trying to relate to other people. Life goes on, even though you might not care about living anymore.

So you're now dealing with compounded anxiety. Compounded anxiety? Facing your children's bewilderment over the death. Taking care of all the bills when you never paid bills before. Worrying about money. Trying to find the courage to sleep in the house alone. Attempting to deal with your teenager's anger. Loneliness. Shopping for a new car for the first time in your life. Wondering if any woman will ever want you or your kids. Loneliness.

"I don't know if I can make it," you think, but you can and you will. You have more inner strength than you realize.

Special Concerns of Newly Widowed Younger Women

A group of widows in their twenties, thirties, and early forties were talking about their concerns.

"I'm worried sick about money," one of them said. The others nodded.

Most woman feel financially insecure after the death, *even if they aren't*. Some of them will have enough money, but they never controlled the family finances or were even aware of how much came in, so they feel afraid. Many of them *will* have real difficulty. A salary is gone. And there are unique problems that face the younger widow. Some couples didn't have enough time to build equity—their careers were just getting started. Some husbands never got around to purchasing insurance: they were taking time for granted. A woman said her husband had been too sick to work before he died; he hadn't worked for over a year. "Our savings are down to almost nothing," she said, "and I can't go to a grown child for financial help, like an older widow might be able to do." Another woman broke in, "I need to work, I'm having such a money problem, but my job skills are rusty. I haven't worked for ten years.'' Someone said, ''I need to work, but I don't want to leave my two-year-old. I'm looking for work I can do at home, and that pays next to nothing.'' A well-dressed woman who had been quiet until now, said in a squeezed voice, ''My husband was out of work for two months before he died. His corporation had laid off some of the executives. We had put all of his money into looking good—you have to do that when you're trying to climb in management. We bought a house we couldn't afford. We joined an expensive club. We bought expensive cars. You see this designer suit? That's all I have, what's on my back. That's all that's paid for.'' The others were silent.

''And who would hire me? I'm forty-two!'' another woman exclaimed.

Here was another concern voiced by one of the women: ''I worry about bringing up a son all by myself!''

Our daughters are our mirror images. We know their worries, we've been where they are. Our sons? Even though we love them, they are the ''other.'' We're startled by their tears. We're awed by their aggression. We're overwhelmed by their silences after the death.

Feeling this barrier, many women use brothers and fathers as surrogate fathers for their sons. Others have discovered the services of the nationwide Big Brothers Association. Located in many cities, this organization provides well-trained male volunteers who act as parent substitutes. These caring men establish ongoing relationships with their ''little brothers.'' They take them fishing. They spend Saturday afternoons at the library with them. They take them to ball games. The sponsors of local Big Brothers Associations are religious and secular, so take your pick. They carefully screen every Big Brother applicant and do a thorough matching process. (Sometimes the organization is called a Big Brother League.) Find your local group in your phone book.

Many issues had been aired, as these women talked. And it seemed to be money and kids that were the most worrisome—besides loneliness.

Issues That Concern the Newly Widowed Younger Man

Widowers also worry. One man said, "I feel overwhelmed by everything. I'm trying to do everything at one time. I'm working at a demanding job. I'm learning how to cook. I have to take care of the kids. I'm trying to keep the house halfway clean. How did my wife ever do it? And she also worked full time."

(With older widowers, child care is not even an issue. Their grown children are worried about them. If these men are already retired, cooking and cleaning can be done at their leisure.)

I told this man who felt overwhelmed, "You don't have to do things exactly as your wife did them." He looked uncertain. "I want to give the kids a sense of continuity," he said. "But it's not so important that they have a hot cooked meal every night," I said. "If popping a frozen dinner in the oven means more time to take them bowling or hold them when they're crying, you already know what's more important." He still looked uncertain. I said, "The continuity can be in other areas. Continue the bedtime stories. Keep up the trips to the zoo and the museum. Continue going with your son to Little League. But cooking? Free yourself from cooking every night so you can really *be* with them." I said, "Who looks for dust behind your bed? Instead of being crazy clean, spend that time playing with them."

One widower said, "I'm slowly building new family rituals and customs by changing things to meet my needs. The kids now know they're going to have pizza on Monday nights because daddy has a rough time at work on Mondays and he's too tired to cook. They know we eat late on Tuesday nights because that's the evening I *do* cook. I start cooking after I have a drink—that's around six-thirty—and I cook for at least two nights. Then, on Friday nights we have frozen fish sticks. Saturdays and Sundays, we make do with anything in the house or we go out to eat.''

''Sure,'' he said, ''it's very different than when my wife was living. She never had frozen fish sticks. But it's the only way I can do it, and it's working.''

There's a Big Sisters Association for men who need mother surrogates for their daughters. It's the equivalent of Big Brothers Association, and it's also nationwide. If you want further information about either group, write or call:

Big Brother/Big Sister
230 North 13th Street
Philadelphia, Pennsylvania 19107
Ph: (215) 567-2748

Here's another expressed concern of younger widowers: ''I need a woman to come into my life and organize me and it.''

If someone means any woman, it's because you feel you're falling apart and you've swallowed the myth that a female can put you back together again. But not every woman is willing or able to be a repair person, especially at this time in our history when most younger women are busy building their own careers. In fact, many of them are single parenting *and* building careers—just as you are.

If you were in a role-defined marriage where your wife was a full-time homemaker, centering her life around you and your kids, it might be very hard for you to imagine organizing your own life. For starters, to feel more whole, join a health club for regular exercise—you'll feel more in control of your body and self. Buy a simple cookbook if you haven't learned how to cook. Ask female friends and family members for tips on food shopping and housekeeping. If you can afford it, hire a part-time housekeeper to keep your home environment in order. You *can* be your own repair person.

Self-Sabotage

Are you constantly saying "If only" and "I should have?"
    It goes like this:
    "If only I had paid more attention when he complained of that pain."
    "I should have gotten her to another doctor!"
    "If only I would have expressed my love more often."
    "I shouldn't have run around."
    Well, maybe you should have and maybe you shouldn't. Now make a list of all the good and caring things you *did* do. Hang the list on your bedroom wall (a private place) and add to the list as you think of other loving things you did. When you're feeling guilty (anxious), read your list aloud.

Events That Trigger Anxiety

Expect to feel anxious before and during certain events: the anniversary of the death, your wedding anniversary, his or her birthday, the date you first got involved, and all the holidays. Expect to feel anxious if you need to plan your daughter's wedding all by yourself, or if your parent dies and you're alone in planning the funeral arrangements. There's no doubt you'll feel anxious those first days of spring; that season means hope, life, and beginnings. If you have to go into the hospital, and your spouse has died, you feel very anxious.
    Try to be with persons who care about you on those days.

Let them know ahead of time that you'll need them, so they can plan their schedule. Have backups in mind if they're not available. Use all the support you can get.

"Free-Floating Anxiety"

Peter, aged thirty-three, had been widowed three years. He seemed to have made an adjustment. He now refers to himself as a widower, indicating he's accepted the reality of the death. He dates. He has had a couple of relationships. One evening, when he was playing bridge with friends, he suddenly felt weak, trembly, and unaccountably afraid. Not wanting his friends to know anything was wrong, he excused himself and went into the bathroom. Peering into the mirror, he saw how terrified he looked. Ah—Peter remembered that look from another time: those months following the death. He also remembered the weak, trembly and afraid feelings that had accompanied the look. "The doctor told you this is anxiety, chum," he told himself silently. He splashed cold water on his face and took a few deep breaths. Then he made himself rejoin his friends and continue the game. He did feel a little better.

Later, when he was back in his apartment, he lay in bed, hands clasped behind his head, and stared at the ceiling. What had brought it on? He had thought he was doing so well. It had been three years! He searched for reasons. He couldn't think of any.

Peter had experienced "free-floating anxiety," a condition where one cannot identify any particular reason for the discomfort. The reason is deep in the unconscious. It could have been a song on the car radio that triggered, unknown to him, memories of the first time he had met his wife. Peter can stop worrying. "Free-floating anxiety" happens to everyone. The next morning when he got up, he did remember that his psychiatrist had once explained this phenomenon to him. This made him feel better. He dressed and went to work. (He also remembered his psychiatrist telling him the anxiety passes, like all anxiety.)

"Displaced Anxiety"

Audrey couldn't acknowledge the anxiety she felt over the death of her husband. She grew up learning that one must "get through" death without falling apart. (Her mother had smiled her way through the death of *her* husband, never acknowledging the pain, even to herself.) But Audrey did feel enormous anxiety, and she displaced it. Not giving herself permission to say, "Yes, I feel anxious because he died," she told herself, "I am anxious because the decorator chose the wrong color for the rug and the new furniture hasn't been delivered yet."

(In her world, it's acceptable to get worked up over late furniture deliveries and mistakes made by decorators.)

Will she ever acknowledge that the anxiety is due to her grief? Possibly not, because she's been programmed so well.

Some persons anxiously focus on things other than the death because *they're trying to buy time.* They're not ready to face the fact of their loss. Displacement of anxiety, for them, is a good defense mechanism; it's a way of coping until they are ready.

How Some Widowed Persons Handle Their Anxiety

Here are some statements made at a support group for younger women.

Ann said, "I consciously use a technique I learned from a counselor in graduate school—I was going through a rough time then. I stage a dialogue with myself when I'm anxious. As soon as I get very nervous I ask myself, 'What is bothering you?' If I can identify the cause of my anxiety, I then ask myself, 'Is there anything I can do about it?' If the answer is yes, I figure out what to do and I do it. Sometimes the answer is no. Then I try to distance myself from my nervousness. I float with the bad feelings.''

"Float?'' a woman asked.

"I ride with my feelings, I let my feelings happen. First, I tell myself, 'This anxiety won't kill me. It will pass,' and then I ignore feeling bad.''

"How do you ignore those feelings?'' the woman asked skeptically.

"I distract myself. I lie on my sofa and listen to a jazz record—it makes me high, it really does. It's distracting.''

Other persons in the group talked about how they handled their bad feelings.

"I deliberately stay away from people who are anxious when I'm anxious,'' a woman said.

"I seek out loving people!'' another woman said.

Some women talked about moving their muscles when they feel anxious.

"I was so nervous and anxious after the death that I felt I couldn't get out of bed,'' Merideth said. "When I got out of bed, my legs felt as though they were made of jelly, they were so weak. My psychologist said, 'Force yourself to walk. It will help.' So I forced myself to get out of bed every morning and move my legs. It showed me I had more control over my life than I thought. I felt more in control.''

Linda confirmed the value of making one's muscles move:

"After my husband died, I became so anxious I couldn't even leave the house. I was afraid to,'' she said. "A friend who had gone through this told me to command my muscles to move. My first goal was getting to the mailbox at the end of my walk. 'Move!' I commanded my legs. I timidly took a couple of baby steps. With each step I'd say aloud, 'Good!' But when I opened the front door, I went into a real panic. I was tempted to turn around and run up to my bedroom.

'Go!' I sternly commanded myself. 'Walk!' I literally commanded myself to make it to the mailbox. And when I got there I was wiped out but I was triumphant.''

"Now," she said, "I make it a point to go to the mailbox every day. My next step is going to the market. How did I get here today? A good friend took me, and I held on to her all the way. It's all in my head, I know it, this fear of leaving my house, and I *will* get over it.''

Anxiety. It shows in so many different forms.

What You Say and How You Say It Helps

We can reinforce bad *and* good feelings by what we say and how we say it. Regina told me, "After my husband passed on, when people would ask me how I was I'd tell them the truth, and in great detail. In other words, I'd tell them how terrible I felt. Then I heard someone ask another widow how *she* was, and she answered very differently: she said, 'I will be all right!' I asked her why she had answered like that. 'I'm making a commitment to myself with that answer,' she said. 'I'm promising myself that I *will* be all right.' Now I do the same thing, I say the same thing, and it does work. I feel hopeful with that answer.''

Hope is a great need in all of us. Losing hope is a terrible feeling. Reinforce your feelings of hope by what you say and how you say it.

For Acute Anxiety Attacks: The Paper Bag Technique

Here's a nonchemical solution for acute anxiety attacks that costs less than a penny.

Always keep a small paper bag in your purse or your briefcase or in your pocket. When you feel the onset of an anxiety attack:

1. Go into a room where you'll be alone. (If you're at work, and you don't have your own office, go into the ladies' or men's room.)
2. Hold the opening of the bag over your nose and mouth. No, you won't suffocate.
3. With the bag covering this part of your face, breathe with your mouth closed for five to fifteen minutes. (Take normal, not deep breaths.)
4. Remove the bag. If you're still very anxious, repeat the same procedure. (You can repeat it several times.)

This paper bag technique works because you breathe incorrectly during an anxiety attack; breathing incorrectly can make your feet or your fingers tingle, it can make you dizzy, it can even give you a constricted feeling in your chest. Add those physical symptoms to the anxiety, and you're *more* anxious. Breathing into the paper bag stabilizes your breathing. It brings it back to normal. You then feel calmer. *Many hospitals throughout the country use the paper bag technique.*

An Exercise to Help You Relax

This should be done every day, in order for it to work:

1. Each morning, before starting your day, sit on your bedroom floor, leaning against the edge of your bed. Wear loosely fitting clothes.
2. Close your eyes.
3. Deliberately and slowly let go of each of your muscles, from your toes to the top of your head. Do one part of your body at a time. Pretend each muscle is a piece of limp liver, as you let go.
4. Then, with your eyes still closed and all your muscles relaxed, inhale through your nose and as you exhale, say "Aaaaah" aloud.
5. Repeat this procedure for five minutes. (After two

weeks of doing this every day, increase the time to fifteen minutes.)

6. When you're finished, sit quietly for a minute with your eyes still closed. Open your eyes. Sit still for another minute. Slowly rise. Start your day.

If you have to go to work in the morning, get up a half hour earlier in order to do the exercise. If you can't bear the idea of getting up so early, do it at night before you go to bed. If you have small children, you can do it while they're napping.

Medication and Drugs

If you do take tranquilizers or antidepressants, do not mix alcohol with your medication. It can kill. Do not even drink a glass of wine while you're taking Valium, Ativan, Librium, Miltown, Equanil, Clinopin, Dalmane, Doriden, Haldol, Serax, or Tranxene. (If you're taking a medication I haven't mentioned, ask the pharmacist if you can drink.) Do not use medication that's been in your medicine chest for years. When in doubt, tell the pharmacist the date on the label, to see if it's still effective or whether there's danger in taking it.

Anxiety. Caffeine heightens it. Stay away from APC's and No-Doze, as well as colas and caffeinated coffee and teas. (Herbal teas have no caffeine.)

The Pattern of Bereavement Anxiety

Your anxiety probably comes and goes. You feel better for a few weeks and then wham! an acute anxiety attack when you least expect it. Some persons suffer a persistent low-level anxiety but they never experience an acute anxiety attack.

I'd worry about you if you never felt anxiety. I'd wonder:

why are you masking (hiding) your fears? You've suffered such a great loss that it's inevitable you feel some anxiety.

This can go on for a long time.

It's normal.

You'll have bad days and better days.

Remember, recovery from grief is a zigzag process. Allowing yourself to feel means allowing yourself to heal.

18. Calling "Help!"

It takes a very strong person to call for help. You're admitting to yourself that you need help and, even though you might be afraid, you are venturing into unknown territory with a professional helper you don't know.

It means telling your story again, and you're so tired of even thinking about it. You are so tired of your preoccupation with yourself. You don't know if you can be helped, or if that person is the right person.

If you're deeply depressed, it means making yourself get out of the house every week to go to your appointment, and that isn't easy when you find it hard to get out of bed or move from the sofa or leave the house.

It takes a strong person to call for help, so be proud of yourself if you're thinking about doing it.

How to Choose a Professional Helper

To whom should you turn? You can choose a clergy person, a social worker, a counselor, a bereavement counselor, a psychologist, or a psychiatrist.

If you do decide to talk to a clergy person, pick someone who has had special training in *pastoral counseling.* (You can inquire about this, over the telephone, before making an appointment.)

Social workers are often as effective as psychologists or psychiatrists, and *psychiatric social workers* are especially trained to work with depression and long-lasting guilt feelings after a death.

Clinical counselors (not school counselors!) have been trained to work with grieving persons. They have taken courses in death and dying, as well as the techniques of counseling.

Bereavement counselors are a newly emerging group, and they know a great deal about the grieving process. Most of them work in hospices and hospitals and do group work rather than one-to-one counseling. If you're interested in participating in a grief group, call your local hospitals and see if there are bereavement counselors on the staff.

Psychologists have Ph.D's. You want a *clinical psychologist.*

Psychiatrists specialize in the diagnosis and treatment of all emotional and mental problems, including grief symptoms that do not resolve themselves. They are medical doctors, with at least three years of residency training in psychiatry beyond medical school and their internship. Some are certified by the American Board of Psychiatry and Neurology, which means they have passed rigorous written and oral tests, indicating a sound knowledge base.

Fees vary. If a professional helper works in an institutional setting rather than a private practice, this means there is usually a sliding fee, where you pay according to your income. Psychologists and psychiatrists in private practice charge the most; the fee for a session of one hour could be as much as seventy to ninety dollars (although some practitioners lower fees for persons who cannot afford that). Your medical insurance will generally pay for fifty to eighty percent.

If your income is very low you may be eligible for medical assistance from the state. (This is medical insurance coverage.) Call your city or state social services office to ask how to apply. If you're eligible, you'll receive your medical assistance card; you present this instead of money. (It is up to the discretion of the person in private practice whether or not to accept the medical assistance card. Many do, some don't.)

Psychiatrists can prescribe medication, such as tranquilizers or antidepressants. Other kinds of professional helpers can't, they're not medical doctors, but they usually can provide a backup person who can, or they might suggest you obtain your prescriptions from your own family physician.

Different professional helpers use different methods of treatment. Some focus on your childhood. Others urge you to look at the here-and-now in your life. Some do both. There are practitioners who seldom speak, they mainly listen. Others give a great deal of verbal feedback. (I have a bias. I prefer helpers to listen *and* give coping strategies.)

Should you go to a man or woman? Whoever is the most nurturing (this is very important while you're in grief) and whoever most understands what grieving is all about.

Women should choose helpers who understand how the special problems of women can be affected and shaped by the broad institutions in our society. The family, for instance. (A feminist therapist is sensitive to this.) If your parents brought you up never to show anger because they felt women should be "ladies"—always charming and pleasing—you need a helper who appreciates how much this may influence your present behavior and feelings. (If you're now suffering from depression, this helper, knowing your background, considers the possibility you're masking your anger over the death, even to yourself; that acknowledging the anger would make you feel very guilty—women are supposed to *smile*. Helping you link your behavior and feelings to the way you were brought up, the helper can then work with you to change your feelings and your behavior, to *show* your anger.)

I know a woman who was taught by her family that a female's main task in life is to be a caretaker to others. (Her particular church also fostered that expectation in women.) After her husband's death she delayed her grieving, pushed it to the back burner, to take care of her dying father and console her newly divorced sister. After her father died and her sister began dating, she was unexpectedly hit with her grief over her own loss, and this was six months after her husband's death. Her depression terrified her. She had thought she was doing so well! She began seeing a psychologist who helped her understand how central caretaking had been to her life and to her feeling of being a valuable person. He also helped her realize how her family and her church had shaped her self-image and expectations. Looking at herself with this newly acquired historical perspective gave her the necessary emotional distance to see that she had to be "intelligently selfish" (her psychologist's term) and put herself first, because no one else would. The last time I talked to her, her minister had asked her to join a sharing-and-caring group in the church, where members visit sick persons. No thanks, she had said. I'm going to join an exercise class and I'm going on a trip with a college alumni group instead. Good for her. *This* is what she needs now.

Consider an initial consultation before you make a final decision as to whom you'll go for help.

Use the fifty minutes to ask important questions: "How many of your patients (or clients) are newly widowed?" and "How many of them are in my age range?" Ask, "What do you see as the main problems of the *younger* widow?" and "How do you differentiate between normal grieving and prolonged grief?" (Prolonged grief goes on and on without seeming to be resolved.) Ask, "How will you be treating me? What are your methods?" Ask about fees.

You'll discover in that initial consultation how you feel with this helper, and that should be a determining factor as to whether you make a second appointment. (Don't look for results in that consultation, it's not realistic; instead, focus on whether or not you like the person and his answers.)

When Your Child Needs Professional Help

Children of any age sometimes need professional help in order to begin or successfully complete their grieving.

Child therapists or family therapists are appropriate choices. A child therapist employs not only talk therapy for children who can hold conversations (they're old enough), but also play therapy for these kids and very young children. The children interact with dolls and toys in the therapist's office, or draw pictures, and this shows the therapist how they're feeling about themselves, their family, the deceased parent, and the death. A family therapist sees the surviving parent along with the child, and sometimes siblings as well. This gives the family therapist insight; it helps him or her to understand how a parent's behavior is affecting the child, and what the relationship is between the siblings.

Groups especially for children who have lost a parent to death are sprouting throughout the country. (There aren't enough of them, but we're seeing a beginning.)

Troubled teens often send parents signals that say, "I need help!" Here are some of these signals:

- Abuse of alcohol
- Use of drugs or drug dealing
- Social withdrawal from friends
- Sudden and frequent spurts of intense anger
- Sexual promiscuity
- Shoplifting, stealing, or vandalism
- Eating disorders (refusing to eat or eating large amounts of food and then vomiting after the meal)

Get immediate help if your teenager tries to hurt himself or others physically. If he *talks* about hurting himself, take his statements seriously: get immediate help.

The runaway teenager also needs immediate help.

Unresolved phobias indicate a need for help.

255

Very young children also show parents when they need special help. Here are some signs:

- Excessive clinging to the parent
- Problems with speech (if a child isn't talking so she can be understood by the age of three, or if she starts stammering, she needs help)
- Constant hitting or biting

Children of school age whose grades dip and stay low after the death should get professional help. If your child is sure it's his fault that his parent died, get him help. Children who constantly get into fights with schoolmates or friends definitely need help.

How can you get your resistant child to *accept* help?

The resistance is due to fear. Kids are very afraid of appearing different or abnormal. They tell themselves, "People will think I'm nuts if they find out I'm going to a shrink."

They're afraid of the unknown, as we all are. The professional helper is unknown to them, and so is the professional setting as well as what's going to occur in this setting.

They're afraid of crying in front of strangers.

To help your child dispel his fears, emphasize the payoff, which is feeling better. A guidance counselor told a troubled, bereaved teenager, "You can either continue to feel this lousy or you can begin feeling better. Going to a psychologist will help you feel better. That's the bottom line. Do you want to feel better?"

Ask your child to go for help *once*. That means he'll agree to go for a consultation. You can say, "I know you don't want to go and I know you might feel uncomfortable once you're there, but I want you to go *once*. If you like the counselor, I want you to try it a second time. Isn't that fair?"

256

(Using this approach, you are acknowledging his feelings and you are giving him options. You're also taking a step at a time.)

If *you're* going for help and your child sees you're feeling better, it gives him hope about going himself.

Some parents report that they've gotten other adults to intervene, when they can't get their child to go to a professional helper.

You have to choose an adult your child likes and trusts. One widow chose a young priest her son admires. Another woman chose the school guidance counselor, who had previously helped her daughter in an academic context. A young widower chose his sister-in-law, because his teenage daughter looks at her as her "glamorous aunt" and likes being with her. A widow chose the family doctor because he was so familiar to her son. And one woman chose her son's "big brother" from the Big Brothers Association.

If you do ask someone to intervene, tell that person what the problem is, so he can carefully approach your child, persuading him to go for counseling with words and phrases that will be effective; so he can be nonthreatening in his approach.

Studies of adults with different kinds of mental disorders (especially depression) often reveal childhood bereavement that wasn't resolved. By taking active steps to get your needy child help now, you may be preventing problems that could crop up in his twenties, thirties, or later.

Reasons Widows and Widowers Go for Help

Successful recovery, after the death, means getting used to your loss rather than getting over it. It means eventually accepting the death and feeling hope about your future.

This is never an easy road. For some persons, it's a very difficult road. It's so difficult that I often hear these remarks:

"All I want to do is die."

"After she died, I started to drink. I drink a lot, I know, but it drowns my sadness."

"I beat my son and I really hate myself afterward, but I can't seem to stop myself since my wife died."

"I'm too depressed to be with people. I don't answer the phone most of the time. I cross the street when I see someone I know."

"I got on a merry-go-round after my husband died. I started going to bars every night and picking up men. I still do. What do I accomplish by this behavior? It helps the loneliness. I get worried about catching herpes, though. And I don't like myself the next morning."

"It's been four years and I haven't touched his clothes. They're still in the closets. His hairbrush and combs are still in the same place on the dresser. I'll never touch anything. In fact, I don't let anyone sit on his recliner."

"I go to the grave every day. Yes, I know it's been three years, but I still go every day. I read every religious book to get an answer to why it happened. I go to church all the time to get an answer. I'm consumed with that question."

"I'm very bitter! Why did it have to happen to me? I've driven away all my friends, I'm so bitter. But that's the way I feel."

"Why should I try to build a new life? I don't want to. There's nothing left for me out there. My life is over."

"My son has become the man of the house. That's what I call him, my little man. He's taken over, even though he's only fourteen. He does everything now. And he won't let me be alone, isn't that wonderful?"

"I live on tranquilizers. If I didn't have my medication, I don't know how I'd get through each day. He's been gone four years and every day is hell."

*   *   *

These are very uncomfortable feelings I'm hearing in these remarks. These men and women are in a great deal of emotional pain. Their pain affects the well-being of their children.

That's one measure of whether you need professional help, the amount of pain you are feeling. Another measure is how long this pain has persisted. And another measure is whether you're physically or emotionally abusing your children.

By the third year of your bereavement, you can expect (in normal grieving) to have more days that are better. There are setbacks, but this is an easier year than the first and second year after the death. If life is as hard this third year, be good to yourself and make an appointment for help.

Society Doesn't Make Recovery Easier

In our society, there aren't too many supports that help bereaved persons. Most widows and widowers are directly and indirectly urged to rush through their distress. We are taught that we should give up ties to the dead as soon as possible. But that's unrealistic. No one feels better in six months. (And yet, family and friends often expect this!)

Contrast this expectation with grief and mourning in other cultures. Some traditional Puerto Rican widows are *expected* to express their anguish though displays of seizurelike behavior. Some Southeast Asian-American bereaved persons wail in public. Instead of valuing emotionality in our society, we stifle it. We're afraid of it. But it's the display of your deep pain, after the death, that will allow you to heal and get on with your life.

A therapist's office—that's a *safe* place where you can express the full range of your distressed feelings. It's also an educational setting where you can learn what grief work is all about. It's a place where you can begin feeling better.

Where you can begin *doing* better.

Guilt Feelings—Getting Help

Guilt feelings that don't go away are a good reason to go for help.

It's very normal to feel some guilt after the death. If nothing else, everyone feels "survivor's guilt"—the guilt that comes with knowing you lived while he died.

Survivor's guilt eventually eases and then disappears.

And there is "earned guilt" as well as "learned guilt."

Earned guilt is felt because you did do something that deeply hurt your spouse. It is based on reality. A man had an affair with his secretary and was blatantly obvious about it. His wife was very hurt; she confronted him and even though he promised to terminate the relationship, he didn't. After his wife died of cancer, he felt torn with earned guilt.

Learned guilt is when you act and feel guilty because you've learned, through your childhood, that guilt is good. Your mother might have always scolded, "You should be ashamed!" or "You should suffer like I do when you have children!" There are some parents who say, "You're killing me!" If this was your experience, remember your immediate reaction of guilt? The pangs of remorse you felt? Several people have told me that their mothers, recognizing the guilt, would then say with triumph, "Good! You're feeling guilty!" Through the following years and decades, you automatically felt reactions of guilt with other persons. You learned that guilt is expected. You internalized that expectation, accepted it yourself. (Besides, it's more acceptable, in our society, to feel guilt instead of acting out anger, even though anger might be the appropriate reaction.)

If you're suffering from guilt feelings to the point where you feel worthless, seek help. A nonjudgmental caring professional helper can facilitate your moving toward self-acceptance.

Excessive Anger—Using Help

Anger is also part of normal grief. Usually, it crops up at different times during your bereavement. One woman said she became very angry at her mother-in-law for outliving her son.

"I knew it was irrational," she told me, "but that's the way I felt. So I avoided her until I felt better. It took about nine months."

Excessive anger needs special attention. Here are some signs:

- You fantasize you're hurting yourself. (Go for immediate help.)
- You imagine hurting someone else. (Go for immediate help.)
- You're physically beating your kids. (Please go for help!)
- You're emotionally beating your children. (You may be calling them "dumb" or "ugly" or you're yelling at them all the time.)
- You're compulsively saying hurtful things to your family and friends.
- Even though you've been widowed over a year, you have little or no control: you act out tremendous rage without being able to stop yourself.
- People are always disappointing you and you're bitter.

Going for help will give you needed relief from your anger.

Feeling You Can No Longer Take Care of Your Children

Life becomes so overwhelming for some widowed persons that they feel they can no longer take care of their children. One woman told me, "Everything had mounted up, and I was in bad shape. Several months after my husband died, I awakened one morning and I *knew* I could no longer take care of my kids. This scared me, so I immediately called a psychiatrist and made an appointment for that day." She added, "It wasn't a matter of choice. I *couldn't* take care of them."

(She's fine today. After a few months of medication and counseling, she was again able to assume the role of mother. Meanwhile, before that recovery occurred, her psychiatrist contacted her local social service agency for child care, and her sister also helped with the children.)

It's hard enough to take care of children during normal grieving; you're drained from your own grief and you're short on energy and patience. If your feelings get out of hand, you may feel you can no longer cope. It *isn't* a matter of choice. This is a time when it's appropriate to call for professional help. (And use all the help you can get from your family and friends.)

Bodily Symptoms—Seeking Help

If you have many more aches and pains than before your spouse's death, it's probably due to the fact that you're turning the pain of your loss into bodily pain. (And I assume you've already been checked by your physician and you've been told you're all right.)

Menstrual irregularities, following the death, are not unusual.

You might experience digestive difficulties or migraine headaches.

You may be sure you're going to die at the same age your parent died. (Magical thinking.)

If your spouse died of cancer, you may be absolutely sure you are also going to die of cancer. (More magical thinking.)

It's when your somatic symptoms take over your life and consume you that you want to go for professional counseling. Don't feel ashamed. Many younger widows and widowers suffer from somatic distress. It seems to be more common with younger survivors of death.

(And ask that your internist send a complete medical report to your psychologist or psychiatrist.)

Get Help for Your Feeling of Emptiness

If you are feeling empty, go for help. I know you're feeling apathetic, you don't care what happens to you when you're feeling empty, but go for help. Make an appointment and don't break it.

Going for help means your hopelessness will be turned into hopefulness.

How Can a Professional Helper Be Helpful?

"What's the difference between going for professional help and talking to a good friend?" a woman asked.

"I have to pay him money," she continued, "and my friend's advice is free!"

Good caring friends are very important in your life, and their friendship and caring is free. If you are suffering from normal grief you may not need professional counseling; good friends may be enough. It's when your feelings of distress become unbearable that you want to seek help.

Here are some differences:

- Professional helpers listen more selectively and they're able to interpret your silences and the emphasis you put on certain words.
- They watch your body language and they can see how you're feeling by your gestures and movements.
- They're trained to understand depression and anxiety, as well as the manifestations of grief.
- They know how to treat your distressed feelings.

Despite the fact that different professional helpers use different techniques, the good ones are nonjudgmental; they have that in common.

They show unconditional support.

Friends often find it difficult to be nonjudgmental. This makes you hold back certain information when you're asking them for help. With an effective professional helper, you're more open because you know that no matter what you say, it will not get back to any of your friends and you will be fully accepted.

The more open you are, the more relief you feel from venting your feelings. The more open you are, the closer you get to your deepest feelings. The closer you get to your deepest feelings, the more you're able to do with those feelings, with your therapist's help and support.

As you do more about your bad feelings, you begin feeling more in control of yourself and your life.

That's good, isn't it? But be realistic: no counselor, social worker, clergy person, psychologist, or psychiatrist can really help you in one session. Give him and yourself the time you both need and see him on a regular basis.

It takes a strong person to call for help—and you did it.

19. The Road to Recovery

"The grieving process is a waiting game of survival, second by second, and I am the only player. I was shocked the following morning after his death to see and hear that life continued; the flowers blooming, the river running, strangers laughing. And there I was, stuck in hysteria. How dare you all go on living without Robert? I was now faced with the most crucial and painful reality of loving—death—quickly and harshly devastating all that I had believed in for thirty-six years of my life. Each person is unique, each relationship is unique; therefore the grieving process and the recovery will be just as unique. We must be allowed to proceed with this in our own way and our own time."

Elaine Briggs-Cox,
Orleans, Massachusetts

Elaine sent this to me in 1985. It was part of a sharing she was doing with me of her thoughts and feelings since her husband had died. Writing was a way of struggling through her grief and coming to terms with the death; it was a way of moving toward recovery. I saw it as a wonderfully creative way of healing herself in (as she would say) her own time.

Time. It takes a long time to heal. I use the word *heal* or *recover*. I don't mean recovery from an illness. I'm speaking of recovery from the impact of your loss.

Even after recovery, life will never be exactly the same

again, but life will go on. It may even become very good. There will be the emergence of a new identity. During the time of your grieving, there are the seeds of this. The seeds are reflected in the bereaved person's wishes: "I think when I feel better I'll get my Master's degree," and "I'd like to get married again someday."

When a woman does return to school, this is taking an active step toward establishing a new identity; it is no longer merely a wish. When a man announces his forthcoming marriage, he is turning his wish into his new identity.

(Persons who always wait for things to happen rather than make things happen may find it takes longer to establish a new identity.)

As you recover, there is the reality of the present as well as new hope for your future. Before, you lived in the past. Although you may still search for your lost spouse at springtime, when life and renewal are in the air, your searching is no longer a major preoccupation. Anniversaries and holidays still give you sad feelings, but the sadness is softer.

As you move into new roles, your helplessness turns into hopefulness. "After a couple of years, I moved to San Francisco and opened a yarn shop," a woman said. "I had always wanted to own a yarn shop but I was too busy being a wife and mother. Now that he's died, and my kids have left home to go to college, I have the time. It feels good. I feel like a new person, different than when I was grieving hard." She *is* a new person.

In our society, it is expected that women have a sense of separateness before they marry. It is also expected that they give this up when they put on their wedding ring. Now that you're widowed, you must again seek that separate identity, but this time it'll be different. By now, you've lived and learned more. It doesn't have to be a lonely sense of separateness, it can be a strong, good one. A woman I know, a painter, told me, "He died three years ago and I refer to myself as Jane Howell, instead of Mrs. Leon Howell. I am the painter, Jane Howell, and that made it easier to see myself as a separate person, no longer his wife.''

Your new sense of identity may depend on the work you do, the relationship you've recently established, your political involvement, the child you've now adopted as a single parent, going back to school, opening a business, losing twenty pounds, becoming a very young grandparent, or making a switch in careers. Learning to live alone—*that* can redefine your identity.

While you were in deep grief, you may have joined organizations that gave you comfort: a widowed persons support group where you saw your major identity as a widow or widower. Now you're ready to move on, as a woman or man who has traveled the long road from spouse to widowed person to person. Leaving the group is legitimate. You don't want to become a ''professional widow'' (or widower), stuck in a role you've outlived.

Or you might have chosen a certain kind of volunteer or paid work that you identified with as a widowed person. Perhaps you volunteered in a hospice program or maybe you deliberately sought work in a doctor's office. A woman told me, ''I've applied for a transfer at work. Now that I'm recovering from my grief and trying to build a new life, I want to turn to life instead of clinging to death. I don't want to be a floor nurse anymore, I'm asking to be a nursing instructor.''

You may be at the point in your recovery where you're even looking at your grief period as a time of growth. I remember these remarks:

''I've now changed my priorities in life. Accumulating material things isn't as important as it used to be. Being loved is more important than anything else in life—and loving another!''

"I can now understand the pain of others. I'm no longer uncomfortable when someone cries."

"After my husband died, I felt terrible because I hadn't expressed my love for him often enough. Now, I make it a point to tell important persons in my life how much I love them. I tell them often and I show my affection."

Hope returns during recovery. Your renewed hope is partly based on the realities of being younger. You are probably in good health. You have energy and mobility. (Your energy level was depleted during your hard grieving and it returns to a higher level as you recover.) Your earning power will no doubt increase, where the older widowed person may be on a fixed income. Because you *are* younger, society considers you sexual and desirable so it'll be easier to find a relationship.

Hope is never thought about until we lose it. Doesn't it feel like a gift, feeling it again?

Your sense of humor returns during recovery. You're smiling and laughing more now (without the guilt you previously felt).

You're now more aware of how you look to others. You look forward to events. Your anger is not as intense. You're less scared of the future.

You've learned how strong you are to have been able to endure the pain of your loss. You feel you again have some control over yourself and your life, even though you now realize you'll never have complete control—no one does. (That was a bitter lesson to learn, wasn't it?) If you're looking forward to another significant relationship or you're already in one, you're showing courage. You're displaying a love of life. In your own way you are saying, "I know that loss is an inevitable part of life, I've learned that the hard way. Nevertheless, I'm still willing to go through it because I refuse to stop living."

Life will never be the same again; it must be different, but it can be very good. It can be as good as before. However, you don't—you can't—return to being the same person you were before the death.

First you had to make your own kind of sense out of your loss and then, emotionally, you had to accept the fact it happened. That took a long time. You may still be grappling with those tasks while you're recovering. But you're no longer suffering an oppressive, continuing awareness of the death. You have times of relief. Sunsets and rainbows again have the capacity to give you deep pleasure. You're now *hearing* when someone speaks. After the death, it hurts to load your shopping cart for only one; today, you can do it without thinking. You may even be able to take a lover into your bed without guilt, because it's no longer your married bed, it's merely your bed.

You are finally attempting to build a second life. You grieved in your own way and in your own time, and this is as it has to be. You may have limited the time and energy you gave to remembering, keeping busy, busy, busy. That was the only way you could get through it. You may have clung to your married past for a very long time. That was the only way you could survive. Or you may have moved toward your new identity fast. There is no right or wrong way, as long as you allowed yourself to grieve.

Here are three persons who are recovering:

Carol

It was a lived-in room, that living room in New York where Carol typed, listened to Bessie Smith, curled up in the chair and read Cynthia Ozick, and sat on the floor discussing radical feminism. I was the one sitting on the floor with her now. She got up to take the potato pancakes out of the oven. I looked around. A red velvet sofa, obviously old, and an equally old dog snoring in his sleep, burrowed in the corner of that worn sofa. A couple of comfortable chairs that I wouldn't be able to remember the next day when I tried to describe them for this book. An earth-colored Mexican rug bought in Oaxaca, where Carol had done much of her research on the manuscript about Indian culture. Handwoven wall hangings bought in the *zocola* in Oaxaca. The black pottery of that region. Books strewn on the floor. We ate the potato pancakes from paper plates and Carol said, ''We had led separate and together lives, Jonathan and I. He was an anthropologist—we had met in Mexico—and I write, as you know. We had decided not to have children, so we could center on our work and each other. We did that for seven wonderful, crazy, marvelous years.'' She looked away, a fleeting pain in her eyes. I put my plate down. She glanced at the two pancakes, intact on the plate. ''What?'' she laughed. ''You don't love frozen potato pancakes? My *bubbe* would have been horrified if you didn't like her potato latkes. She had a wonderful recipe. She was from Russia.'' She kicked off her sandals and tucked her legs under her. ''She was widowed when she was twenty-eight, almost my age. Now I wonder how she made it, with five children. I thought I couldn't make it with *no* kids.''

We listened to some Ella Fitzgerald, turned low, on the stereo. ''This year is much better, though,'' Carol said. ''I can write again, after two years. Do you know that for two whole years, I couldn't finish a chapter? It's good I was still getting royalties from my other books. It was good my dad sent money.''

''Tell me, what else is different now?'' I asked.

''I can concentrate and that's what I'm elated about.

That's all I can think about. I can *write*." And then, face-
tiously, "I don't get tears on the pages anymore."

"Are you seeing any men?"

She fingered the silver bracelets on her arm. "Here and
there. One or two. I had an affair going for a while. He was a
writer, too. But he was into structure and neatness and he
couldn't stand my doggy hairs and the crumbs on the rug."
She picked up my potato pancake and ate it. "Someone will
come along. I'm not worried."

"So you're not intent on getting married again or having
a serious relationship?"

"Hey now!" she said. "I didn't say I don't want a relationship. But it has to be a good one. I have plenty to do until
the right guy comes along."

"Such as?"

She stared at me in astonishment. "My writing!"

Carol, after grieving for a long time, has reinvested herself
in her work, and she's fortunate that her work is also her pas-
sion. She is open to meeting someone, but she's not feeling
desperate about it. Her writing will keep her from feeling
desperate.

There is a gestalt to her life; all of her close friends are
writers or artists. No jarring contradictions or conflicting
messages about lifestyle preferences or values. And being
only thirty makes it easier: that's a good age for new beginnings. I have good vibes about Carol's recovery, and where
it's going.

Wendy

Wendy was eating dinner at the dining-room table with
her husband when he suddenly slumped over and died.
When I first met her, she was waiting for the autopsy report,
which she had requested. She was obsessed with that report,

what it would say. The doctor, she said, thought he had a heart attack but he wasn't absolutely sure. "I thought doctors always know those things!" she wailed. She added, after a few seconds' silence, "In a way, I hate getting the report, though."

Just before he died, only a few minutes before, they had been planning their annual vacation in Bermuda. Paul had been remembering other times in Bermuda, with Wendy and the kids, and with his grandmother when he was little. Then he dropped dead.

During our first meeting she sat upright, her hands folded, her face tight, as she talked about their life together in Boston. "We met in dancing class. Our whole crowd went to the same dancing classes, our parents had gone to those classes when they were small. Then Paul went away to prep school and Princeton. I went off to Smith. We weren't involved until after we graduated, when we met again at a friend's house."

"Bells?"

"Loud bells. We had a big wedding, we bought this house, we had our first child, and life was perfect. We had our second child. Paul worked for his father and grandfather, and we were considered the perfect family."

Her mind seemed to be someplace else as she stared at the ticking mantel clock. I asked, "What did you do all those years, besides be a homemaker and a mother and a wife?"

"Oh, I volunteered. I served on committees. I was always on several boards. I was active in my garden club."

Then she said in a low voice, "I hate seeing that autopsy report. But I have to see it."

The next time I saw Wendy, it was five months after the death. She had taken in her mother-in-law, who was a widow. Her two children, teenagers, were at summer camp. She didn't sit still, as she had during our first meeting, when

I had felt that sitting so still was her way of holding herself together. Today, she frantically ran from the telephone (it rang several times) to the second floor, where her mother-in-law was calling her (she was bedridden) to the kitchen where she prepared a tea tray, to the wing chair near the fireplace where she perched on the edge, balancing her cup and plate. She wore a denim wraparound skirt and a shirt with tiny sailboats printed on it. Her face was as pinched as the first time. "I'm constantly running," she said, "I can't seem to sit still. Sometimes I think I'm manic." I looked at the piano, the portraits of great-grandparents, and the other accumulations of a seventeen-year-old marriage. "Are you still active on your committees and boards?" I asked. "More than ever," she said. "I can't seem to slow down. I think I'm manic," she said again. "Do you think I'm hyper or manic or something? I think I should see a psychiatrist. My mind never stops racing, I think I'm going crazy." Suddenly she got up and paced up and down. "I'm so agitated all the time," she said, and she looked at me helplessly.

Wendy finally did go to a psychiatrist. He put her on medication and saw her weekly for a year.

The next (and last) time I saw Wendy, we met near her home. I was attending a conference in Boston and had called her. Lovely! she had exclaimed, and she gave me directions to the restaurant. I got there first, and I sat watching the women in their tweed suits eating their salads. I looked up. I couldn't believe this was the same woman. She was smiling and the pinched look was gone. Dropping in the chair, she wordlessly held out her hand, displaying a small diamond. "You're getting married!" I said. "I certainly am," she answered, beaming. She told me about her new life: it was a man in their circle, she said. A man she and her husband had known for years and years. His wife had died from cancer two years ago, a lovely woman who was in Wendy's garden club, who had also grown up in Boston. His children were around the ages of her children. In fact, their children had gone to school together.

She dug in her purse and brought out a snapshot. "Here," she said, handing it to me. At first I was startled. He looked like her husband! Later, I thought about that. Many widowed persons unconsciously choose persons who look like their first spouse. They are seeking a continuity in their lives, of course. Some are doing more—they're attempting to retrieve the deceased person. This is fraught with potential problems: keen disappointment when the new spouse doesn't act and react like the deceased. The more Wendy and I talked over lunch, the more I realized it was continuity she sought: she was well aware of the two men's differences.

She told me her mother-in-law is now in a nursing home. She no longer recognizes Wendy or the children. Her teenagers seem happy over the forthcoming marriage. Well, the younger one is happy. The older one—she has high hopes he'll come around. "We're not pushing," she said confidently, stirring her tea. I asked her what kind of a life she thinks she'll have after she's married. Will it be very different? She stopped stirring and looked at me, wide-eyed. "Oh, no," she said. "It'll be pretty much the same as it always was, even when I was married before. I'll still be active in my garden club. Chad—that's his name—belongs to the same clubs Paul did. We have the same friends. Nothing will really change."

Wendy is a holding-on person. She's not a risker. One reason she needed professional help during her deep grieving is that she *is* a holding-on person. She desperately clung to everything and everyone who was familiar during her long years of marriage. The house, her mother-in-law, her committees, her boards. Clutching so hard was exhausting. She became more desperate: she rushed faster from one meeting to another: she joined *another* committee; she arranged the institutionalization of her mother-in-law all by herself. She needed permission to slow down. The psychiatrist helped. She needed a strong familiar symbol—a person—to hold her up and then, later, to keep her going. Chad, her future husband, filled those roles perfectly.

I can picture Wendy's life five years from now. She and Chad will be seated at the dining-room table, talking about their annual trip to Bermuda. He will then pat his lips with the cloth napkin, rise, walk to the other end of the table where he will kiss his wife good-bye and tell her to have a good day. (He always says this.) As he leaves the room to go to the office, Wendy looks through the French doors into the garden where she had planted the perennials twenty-two years ago, and she feels secure and content.

Richard

Richard is an appliance salesman. He and his wife, Gloria, had been married for enough years to have had two girls, now eight and ten years of age. They were meeting monthly payments on a small house in Miami. Their lives were satisfying to both of them: once a week bowling with a league, occasional weekends at the ocean, and dinner out on Saturday nights. They frequently invited their families and friends over for barbecues. They were deeply involved in their children's dancing lessons and scout activities. They were very active in their church. When Gloria started to complain about pain, they weren't too worried when she made an appointment with the family doctor: sickness, not a part of their lives, was unfamiliar except for colds and the flu. After a series of tests, Richard got a phone call. "Can you come in this afternoon?" the physician asked. Stunned, Richard heard the doctor tell him and Gloria that she was very ill indeed. "Not that there isn't hope. One can always hope for cures," he hastened to say, "but—well, I am sorry to have to say it, but Gloria, you have a rare kind of malignant tumor."

Everything happened so fast that later, Richard would tell people he couldn't remember the few weeks after the death, he had been in such shock. It was good the two families had helped out with the girls.

I met Richard three years later. I was moderating a panel where widows and widowers were telling the audience what it had been like for them. He had sounded so comfortable that I wanted to ask him how he had gotten to this point.

"It was a nightmare the first year, and the second year," he said as we filled our cups from the coffee urn. "Now I think I'm doing okay, at least most of the time."

"What made it better?"

"Time! Friends and family! The church!"

We sipped. "How are your girls doing?" I asked.

"Fine. I'm not saying they don't miss their mother, of course they do, but we're a praying and a talking family. We touch a lot, too. It all helps."

I had to go, people were waiting to take me to my motel, but I asked if we could meet again before I left town and talk some more. He suggested I visit his house the next day.

It was a Sunday afternoon and after Richard ushered me into the living room, I sat down while he answered the phone. The murmur of his voice came from the kitchen, I could smell a cake baking, and a girl's shrill voice was briefly heard from upstairs. The furniture all matched—pseudo-Colonial, sofa and two chairs. Plastic flowers in a bowl on a shiny maple coffee table. A painting of a girl with very large sad eyes on the wall. (I had seen the same painting in a dentist's office.) A small pair of sneakers on the shag rug. I got up to look at photographs on the wall—two girls at various ages, and a pleasant-looking woman smiling out at the camera. Richard returned, apologizing. "I'm president of my singles group," he explained, "and the calls never stop coming. Sorry." We sat down. "We're having a supper tonight, a potluck, and we advertised it," he said. "The response has been terrific, just terrific. Did I say our singles group is sponsored by my church? It's a great group." He leaned back, a sandy-haired man, wearing shorts and a flowered shirt hanging out over the shorts. "What else can I tell you? I'd like to be of help. If I can help other widows and widowers, I'd like to. That's why I agreed to be on the panel."

I asked again: How had he gotten to this point?

He glanced upstairs.

"The children helped. Listen, when you have kids, you have to get yourself together. And my minister helped. He and his wife had lost a child, they know what loss is. The worst part of my grieving was when I lost faith. I don't mind telling you, that was the worst part. When you lose faith, you have *nothing*. The minister helped a lot there."

The phone rang again. Excusing himself, he jumped up. A child's face appeared over the upstairs railing. "Hello!" she called.

"Hello!" I said.

She disappeared.

Richard returned, this time with two plates of cake. "Another call about tonight's supper. Sorry."

As we talked further, over the cake and instant coffee, he said if he wanted to, which he doesn't because of the girls, he could have something to do every night with members of his singles group. "And," he added, "I've met some mighty nice women in my group."

"Do you ever consider remarriage?"

He paused, his fork stilled.

"Sometimes. I guess I will, someday. Maybe when the girls are a little older. Sure, I think that someday I will get married again."

The phone rang again and Richard made a comical, exasperated face as he got up.

Richard has reinvested himself not in one person, as Wendy has, but in many persons. He has made the women and men in his singles group his extended family. The church members, at least many of them, are like family; they include Richard and the girls in holiday dinners and they go out of their way to invite the girls to sleep over if they, too, have children. He didn't talk much about his wife that Sunday. I got the feeling he wasn't avoiding the topic, he just didn't need to. Richard has traveled the road from grief to recovery.

Three very different kinds of persons. But no matter how different the lifestyle, value system, or income, the road to recovery is pretty much the same: a person loses a spouse; a person cannot believe the death; a person is finally hit hard by the loss; a person hurts hard for a very long time; and then, after a person has grieved much of the acute pain out, the recovery begins.

It is while the recovery is taking place that a letting go occurs. A letting go of the deceased. A letting go of the marriage. A letting go of one's past identity as a husband or a wife. It is when one replaces what has been relinquished that recovery is more fully realized.

Where are you now? Are you in your fifth month of your loss, deeply grieving? Are you in your second month of your bereavement, feeling empty and terrified? If you are, it is probably very hard for you to believe you will someday heal, but you will.

Are you in your second year of your grief, worried because you feel worse, not better? Next year will be better, I promise you.

If you're already feeling you're in recovery, I am so glad, so glad.

It has been said that the death of a spouse leads to either a dramatic growth in one's personality or, instead, to a quiet adaptation to a new life. Every person is different. How you will be after you recover, I don't know. But I do know that you will recover.

A woman in a younger widows group said to me, "I don't believe I'll ever feel better. I don't care if I die. I avoid people. I'm angry at life and God and everyone. I don't want to try to get better." (She had been widowed three months.)

The wondrous thing is, despite the fact she cannot believe she'll recover, she will. Despite the fact she doesn't care if she dies, she'll recover. Despite the fact she might not try to recover, she will.

As you will.

You will!

Suggested Readings

Atlas, Stephen L. *Parents Without Partners Sourcebook*.
Running Press, Philadelphia.

Atlas explores single-parent households. Single-parent finances. Helping new relationships work—for you and your children. Remarriages and stepparenting. A valuable book to help you build your second life.

Caine, L. *Lifelines*. Doubleday, New York.

Caine attempts to build a second life, after she's been widowed a while. It is a difficult and challenging task, and she shares its problems and joys. This book, as well as *Widow*, are reading "musts" for every younger widow, no matter how alike or different her background is from Caine's.

Caine, L. *Widow*. William Morrow, New York.

The story of one young widow's attempt at coping. Caine is an urban, urbane, and well-educated woman who worked in the field of publishing when her husband died and she was left a single parent. An account of the times right after the death.

Frankl, Viktor. *Man's Search for Meaning*. Washington
Square Press, New York.

Frankl writes about his concept of an existential vacuum in the process of bereavement. Existential vacuum, as Frankl defines it, is a feeling of meaninglessness that every bereaved person inevitably feels. This book should give every widowed person a better understanding of the grief process.

Grollman, Earl A. *Talking About Death: A Dialogue Between
Parent and Child with Parent's Guide and Recommended Resources*. Beacon
Press, Boston.

Rabbi Grollman provides invaluable help for the surviving parent who feels helpless in attempting to cope with a child's grief. No matter what the age of the child, every widow or widower with children still living at home should read this.

Hewitt, John H. *After Suicide*. The Westminster Press, Philadelphia.

Survivors of suicide can be helped by this book. All of the anguished feelings that the survivor experiences are explored, and how to live with the fact of the suicide is addressed.

Kohn, Jane B., and Kohn, Willard E. *The Widower*. Beacon Press, Boston.

These authors give considerable information about the younger widowed man, and how he feels and grieves. Willard Kohn has been a young widower. He shares his fears, concerns, and hopes. He tells how he built a second life.

Krementz, Jill. *How It Feels When A Parent Dies*. Knopf, New York.

Sensitive portrayals of children whose parent has died . . . children of all ages. Krementz, a gifted photojournalist, shares the child's feelings with you in the child's own words. Each child tells what life is like now.

Stearns, Ann Kaiser. *Living Through Personal Crisis*.
Thomas Moore Press, Chicago.

This is a gentle, informative book about coping with all kinds of losses, and the younger widowed person will find much in it that relates to what she's now feeling. Coping strategies are addressed around different issues that come up during bereavement.

Support Groups and Organizations

WIDOWED PERSONS SERVICE
Sinai Hospital
Greenspring and Belvedere Avenues
Baltimore, Maryland 21215
Ph: (301) 578-5018

Adele Rice Nudel, the author of this book, directs this service. Serving Maryland, it provides support groups for younger and older widowed persons as well as teenage children. Peer counseling over the telephone is also available. This is the first hospital in the country to have implemented a counseling service for widowed persons, a pioneer in the field.

WIDOWED INFORMATION AND CONSULTATION SERVICES (WICS)
Family Services of King County
500 Lowman Building
107 Cherry Street
Seattle, Washington 98104
Ph: (206) 246-6142

This is one of the most comprehensive widowed persons programs in the country. It serves the greater Puget Sound Area of the state of Washington. There are many support groups, including ones for younger widowed persons, and young children.

WIDOWED PERSONS SERVICE
American Association of Retired Persons
1909 K Street, N.W.
Washington, D.C. 20049
Ph: (202) 728-4370

282

This service is non-age related, serving younger as well as older widowed persons. It is a national organization, having over 100 offices in cities throughout the country. For a copy of their directory, with addresses and phone numbers of each of their chapters, call the above number. (Each of their chapters provides support groups.)

THEOS FOUNDATION, INC. (They Help Each Other Spiritually)
Penn Hills Mall Office Building, Suite 410
Pittsburgh, Pennsylvania 15235
Ph: (412) 243-4299

A nationwide organization of support groups for widowed persons. It has a spiritual orientation. Write or call for information as well as educational materials.

SOCIETY OF MILITARY WIDOWS, INC.
5535 Hempstead Way
Springfield, Virginia 22151
Ph: (703) 750-1342

This national organization has offices throughout the country, providing military widows with legislative information and social activities.

NATIONAL ASSOCIATION OF MILITARY WIDOWS
4023 25th Road North
Arlington, Virginia 22207
Ph: (703) 527-4565

Write or call to learn about survivor benefits that are available for many military widows.

SURVIVORS OF SUICIDE
Suicide Prevention Center, Inc.
184 Salem Avenue
Dayton, Ohio 45406
Ph: (513) 223-9096

Write or call for their directory of nationwide support groups for suicide survivors.

FAMILIES OF HOMICIDE VICTIMS PROGRAM
c/o Victim Services Agency
2 Lafayette Street
New York, New York 10007
Ph: (212) 577-7700

This service provides one-to-one counseling for the surviving spouses of murder victims. It also giver peer support and telephone reassurance to other family members.

EMOTIONS ANONYMOUS
P. O. Box 4245
St. Paul, Minnesota 55104
Ph: (612) 647-9712

Worldwide organization with 800 chapters. Self-help groups for persons suffering from depression or anxiety, using the same twelve-step program of Alcoholics Anonymous. Write or call for support group directory.

RECOVERY, INC.
802 N. Dearborn Street
Chicago, Illinois 60610
Ph: (312) 337-5661

Worldwide organization with 1,000 groups. These self-help groups meet during the day and evenings, and they promote good mental health for persons suffering from depression or anxiety. Write or call to get address of the group nearest you, or a copy of their directory.

GROWING THROUGH GRIEF
P.O. Box 269
Arnold, Maryland 21012
Ph: (301) 974-4224

This is an organization that sponsors workshops about grief work and provides support groups for bereaved persons; it maintains a book service and speakers bureau. A spiritual orientation.

Index